Reading Althusser

Reading Althusser

An Essay on Structural Marxism

Steven B. Smith

Cornell University Press

Ithaca and London

First published 1984 by Cornell University Press.
Published in the United Kingdom by
Cornell University Press Ltd., London.

International Standard Book Number 0-8014-1672-8
Library of Congress Catalog Card Number 83-45943

Printed in the United States of America

*Librarians: Library of Congress cataloging information
appears on the last page of the book.*

*The paper in this book is acid-free and meets the guidelines
for permanence and durability of the Committee on Production
Guidelines for Book Longevity of the Council on Library Resources.*

For Susan
with love and affection

Contents

Preface   9

Abbreviations   11

1   Introduction: The Problem of Althusser   15

2   The Humanist Context   29

Marxist Humanism 30
The "Reification" Controversy 39
Kojève and the End of History 46
Sartre's "Recovery of Man" 59

3   The Althusserian Project   71

The Problem of Reading 75
"The Indispensable Theoretical Minimum" 82
One Marx or Two? 92

Contents

4   A System of Epistemological Marxism   101

Practice 104
The Problem of Knowledge 108
Ideology 128

5   Marxism and the Problem of History   141

The Fundamentalist Thesis 142
The Internal Relatedness Thesis 149
The Overdetermination Thesis 157

6   The Structural Science of History   174

Marxism and Structure 179
Theoretical Anti-Humanism 192
Nihilism: The Moral Intention of Structuralism 200

7   Conclusion   212

Bibliography   219

Index   227

Preface

This work was occasioned by the claim of Louis Althusser to provide a "philosophical" reading of Marx. The practical importance of a critical "settling of accounts" with a doctrine that now encompasses the lives of millions of people throughout the world can scarcely be gainsaid. Whether or not such a project is theoretically rewarding will have to be left for each reader to decide.

Althusser himself has been read in two ways. The first is a type of textualist reading that results in exclusive concentration on the Althusserian texts. The second is a form of contextualism that explains the texts simply by referring to the social, economic, or even linguistic circumstances under which they were written. Whereas the one leads to a narrow *explication de texte*, the other focuses exclusively on the inherited values, assumptions, and beliefs of its subject and therefore fails to see what is unique in his writings. My own reading of Althusser attempts to steer a middle course between these approaches. In the first place I take Althusser at his word by viewing him as a Marxist writing from within the Marxist tradition, and I try to determine his individual contribution to that tradition. I also view Althusser's philosophy in relation to the wider crosscurrents of European thought, notably the ideas associated with Freud, Bachelard,

9

Lévi-Strauss, and Foucault which are sometimes categorized under the label of "structuralism." What these writers appear to have in common is a concern with unconscious structures, literally the "non-sense" that silently conditions intentional human thinking. This concern with unstated presuppositions behind the level of conscious human activities leads to comparisons between Althusser and his existential and "humanist" predecessors, such as Lukács, Kojève, and Sartre.

In this book I have concentrated chiefly on Althusser's two major works to date: *For Marx* and *Reading Capital*. I have referred to his subsequent studies only where necessary to elucidate a point. Despite his own professed "self-criticisms," these later works have added little to, and in some places have even obscured, the not-inconsiderable achievements of the earlier studies. About Althusser's various collaborators and acolytes, I say scarcely anything at all. A study of the dissemination of Althusser's ideas and even the creation of an Althusserian "school" not only in France but also in England and in the United States would no doubt make an interesting essay, but it is not one I have chosen to write. Throughout this book I rely on Ben Brewster's translation of the revised 1968 edition of *Lire le Capital*.

I would like to thank those of my teachers at the University of Chicago who worked with me most closely on this project at its earlier stages—Joseph Cropsey, Brian Barry, and Adam Przeworski. In very different ways each gave generously of his time, patience, and critical understanding. I can only hope that they will not regard their efforts as ill spent. Most of all I am grateful to my wife, Susan, for her constant support and encouragement as well as for creating an atmosphere of domestic tranquility in which this book could be completed.

STEVEN B. SMITH

Austin, Texas

Abbreviations

I have used the following abbreviations for translations of the
works of Althusser:

ESC   *Essays in Self-Criticism,* trans. Grahame Lock (London:
New Left Books, 1976).

FM   *For Marx,* trans. Ben Brewster (London: Allen Lane, Penguin Press, 1969).

LP   *Lenin and Philosophy and Other Essays,* trans. Ben Brewster (London: New Left Books, 1971).

PH   *Politics and History,* trans. Ben Brewster (London: New Left Books, 1972).

RC   *Reading Capital,* trans. Ben Brewster (London: New Left Books, 1970).

Reading Althusser

1

Introduction:
The Problem of Althusser

Recently we have been exhorted to "read *Capital*," that is, to read it not through the writings and commentaries of those who have read it for us, but "to read the text itself, complete, four volumes, line by line." And what is more, it is not enough to read it in translation, but one must go to the German original "at least for the fundamental theoretical chapters and all the passages where Marx's key concepts come to the surface." Only thus, so we are told, is it possible to do justice to Marx's magnum opus. In this study I intend to provide a reading of the man who proposes this reading—Louis Althusser.[1]

[1]A few of the more recent studies on Althusser are Raymond Aron, *D'une sainte famille à l'autre: Essais sur les marxismes imaginaires* (Paris: Gallimard, 1970); Alain Badiou, "Le (re)commencement du matérialisme dialectique," *Critique*, 240 (1967); Alex Callinicos, *Althusser's Marxism* (London: Pluto Press, 1976); Jean Conilh, "Lecture de Marx," *Esprit*, 360 (1967); Norman Geras, "Althusserian Marxism: An Exposition and Assessment," *New Left Review*, 71 (1972); André Glucksmann, "Un structuralisme ventriloque," *Les Temps Modernes*, 250 (1967); Saul Karsz, *Théorie et politique: Louis Althusser* (Paris: Fayard, 1974); Leszek Kolakowski, "Althusser's Marx," *Socialist Register*, 1971; Henri Lefebvre, "Les paradoxes d'Althusser," *Au-delà du structuralisme* (Paris: Editions Anthropos, 1971); Jacques Rancière, *La leçon d'Althusser* (Paris: Gallimard, 1974); Adam Schaff, *Structuralism and Marxism* (New York: Pergamon Press, 1978); E. P. Thompson, *The Poverty of Theory and Other Essays* (New York: Monthly Review Press, 1978); J. M. Vincent, ed., *Contre Althusser* (Paris: Union Générale d'Edition, 1974).

15

But is this not a redundant exercise to provide a reading of a reading, a commentary on a commentary? Does it not violate what we have just seen as Althusser's first hermeneutical principle, "to read the text itself"? This process whereby a work of original merit tends to produce a body of interpretive studies which become themselves subject to further interpretation is clearly an instance of what the English philosopher J. L. Austin once described as the Law of Diminishing Fleas. If, then, our reading of Althusser is not to be entirely parasitical, it must aspire to raise some issues of historical and theoretical significance not only for the study of Marxism but for political science generally.

This work grew out of a long-standing interest in Marxism and Marxist thought and particularly out of a dissatisfaction with what one critic has described as the "thinness" of Marx's own account of the human and metaphysical grounds of his teachings. This thinness can no doubt be explained in part by the fact that Marx himself was not a philosopher in the strict sense but a sociologist, economist, and historian interested in the origins and development of mid-nineteenth-century industrial capitalism. Nevertheless, Marx could not and did not disregard philosophical matters altogether, but his own theoretical remarks remained either extremely sketchy or buried within the topical particularity of his empirical studies. This lack of well-thought-out foundations, upon which his theories could be made to stand, was certain to appear to his disciples as a serious lacuna in his work. Althusser's ambitious project seeks to fill the gap.

The very idea of a philosophical inquiry into Marx may strike the reader as comical. After all, Marx taught that we must change the world, not interpret it. Until recently, it could have been plausibly maintained that the development of Marxism, at least as a theory, was all but at an end. For a long time Marxism aspired to turn itself into—and to a large extent succeeded in the undertaking—a closed ideological system with no wish to question its own premises or to communicate with the outside world. But whatever justification this view might have had, it is no longer the case today. Leaving aside the attempt to retain something like the old orthodox façade, there has developed over the past few years an array of Marxisms associated in Germany with Horkheimer, Adorno, Habermas, and the Frankfurt School, in Italy with the work of Gramsci, Della Volpe, and Colletti, in England with E. P. Thompson, Perry Anderson, and the *New Left Review,* and in France with Sartre, Lefebvre, Goldmann, and most recently Althusser and his school. Indeed, what has characterized all of these thinkers has been a concern with cultural and philosophical matters, or to use the Marxist term, ''superstructural'' problems, which until recently would have been unthinkable within the orthodox Marxist framework.

Of course the philosophical dimension of Marxism has not become an issue only recently. Early attempts at a philosophical evaluation came largely out of what the eminent socialist scholar George Lichtheim once called the ''Central European'' strain of Marxism. Thinkers like Lukács, Korsch, and Mehring came to Marxism from a background in German romanticism that made up part of the idealist reaction to late nineteenth-century positivism and evolutionism. These thinkers, along with one notable southern European, Antonio Gramsci, stressed the Hegelian and utopian origins of Marx's writings as well as those of his youthful writings that were available and even called for a ''revolt'' against the deterministic laws of *Capital.* Politically, this group comprised men and women of the extreme left who were able to combine a passionate commitment to social revolution with the readiness for personal sacrifice and self-discipline called for by the communist parties to which they adhered. While prior to 1914 these thinkers could be easily absorbed into the mainstream of Marxist orthodoxy, their position became increasingly untenable after the Bolshevik seizure of power and more so later, with the canonization of ''Leninism'' as the official creed of the Soviet Union to which complete obedience was required. Those with a more independent cast of mind either were driven out of the communist movement altogether or accepted a self-imposed silence on all but the most trivial issues.

The revival of Marxism as a serious intellectual movement

occurred only after World War II. The spirit of the Resistance especially in France brought with it a renewed taste for freedom and debate which had all but withered away during the Stalin era and the rigors of socialist construction in one country. Thinkers such as Sartre, Lefebvre, and Merleau-Ponty, who had absorbed the speculative philosophies of Husserl and Heidegger before the war, found no difficulty in combining it with Marxism afterward. The subsequent collapse of Stalinism as an official ideology, if not as a system of rule, lent further credence to a movement which had come to challenge the received orthodoxy from within. Marx was then presented to an eagerly awaiting public as an existentialist, a phenomenologist, a humanist, and an Enlightenment rationalist, as well as a moralist congenial to the religiously inclined. Sooner or later a reaction was bound to set in. And so it has, under the aegis of Louis Althusser.

Althusser was first introduced to the English-speaking public by a sympathetic reviewer in the London *Times Literary Supplement* of December 1966. Prior to that time he was known only to a select audience in France, as the author of a short study on Montesquieu and the translator of some of Feuerbach's philosophical essays. Beginning in the early sixties, however, he began publishing in journals like *La Pensée, Esprit,* and *La Nouvelle Critique* a series of articles that promised the coming of a major new reading of Marx. These articles were collected in 1965 in a single volume under the title *Pour Marx,* the same year which saw the publication of another work, *Lire le Capital,* based upon materials presented at a seminar at the prestigious Ecole Normale Supérieure, where he was professor of philosophy. Throughout these writings Althusser's aim has been to turn attention away from the "ethical" and "humanistic" works of the young Marx, particularly the *Economic and Philosophical Manuscripts of 1844* with their concern for "alienation," to the more "scientific" and "deterministic" writings of the older Marx, particularly *Capital.* Between these works, Althusser tells us, there is nothing short of a break, a "coupure," which not only separates the young Marx from the older man, but separates the very "object" of *Capital* from that of Marx's predecessors, notably Feuerbach, Hegel, and the classical economists. Just how much of the early writings make their way into the later is not clear, although Althusser seems unwilling to accept anything as being fully "Marxist" written prior to 1845.

The success of Althusserian Marxism has been startling even by French standards. But Althusser's sudden rise to prominence has been clouded with controversy stemming largely from his highhanded treatment of socialist humanism as well as his own declaration that Marxism represents a "theoretical anti-humanism." This in turn gave rise to the belief that Althusser was in fact some kind of party apparatchik whose chief aim was guardianship of communist orthodoxy. Indeed, Althusser's unwillingness publicly to criticize Stalininism, as a system of rule, and his embarrassing silence over the Soviet invasion of Czechoslovakia in 1968 further confirmed this suspicion. Unlike his long-time rival Roger Garaudy, who quit the party in disgust, Althusser refused to air his grievances in public. Since any interpretation of Althusser must at some point come to terms with this charge, let us do so from the start.

The most sustained and eloquent statement of this hostile verdict has come recently from the English Marxist E. P. Thompson in his anti-Althusserian tract *The Poverty of Theory*. Ostensibly defending the historian's craft against Althusser's structural Marxism, Thompson concludes with a scathing political indictment. According to Thompson, Althusser has produced a complete theorization of Stalin as well as of the Stalinist practices embodied in the various Western communist parties: "Althusserianism is Stalinism reduced to the paradigm of theory. It is Stalinism at last, theorized as ideology."[2] Soviet doctrine previously lacked such a justification, although Althusser has presumably now emerged to provide one for it. "It is only in our time that Stalinism has been given its true, rigorous and totally coherent theoretical expression. This is the Althusserian or-

---

[2]*The Poverty of Theory*, p. 182.

rery."[3] As such it is a "straightforward ideological police operation."[4] Since for Thompson, Althusser's anti-historicism and anti-humanism provide a perfect ex post facto rationalization for the deeds of the tyrant, it is necessary to call for an "unrelenting intellectual war" against Althusser and all "such Marxisms."[5]

Thompson's charge raises one of the fundamental "problems of Althusser," namely, his relationship to Stalinism or more generally the relationship of Marxism to tyranny. There are, of course, strong grounds for assuming such a relationship to exist. Because Althusser intervened against "Marxist humanism" or against the Marxism of the New Left, that is, against those who professed to be anti-Stalinist, the obvious charge is that in opposing Stalin's enemies, Althusser must be Stalin's friend. But upon closer examination, this charge turns out to be false or at least not a simple truth. For Marxist humanism or so-called "Western Marxism" cannot be understood as merely anti-Stalinist. In fact many of the proponents of this "humane" and cultured Marxism were all at various points in their careers defenders of Stalin, some up until the very end. Indeed, the moral or "humane" case against Stalinism is not at all self-evident or transparent. From Merleau-Ponty's *Humanism and Terror* to Marcuse's essay "Repressive Tolerance," it is not clear that the case of tyranny is simply dead.

One possible response to Thompson's charge is, then, that in making his case against the humanists, Althusser was attacking the true defenders of Stalin. But this would be disingenuous. Just as anti-Stalinism is scarcely the core of Marxist humanism, neither is philo-Stalinism. If, however, we examine the evidence that Thompson and others have adduced to support their thesis, it turns out to be remarkably flimsy.[6] Nowhere, for instance, does

[3] Page 141.
[4] Page 183.
[5] Page 189.
[6] A more elaborate defense of Althusser against this charge from a Marxist perspective is in Perry Anderson, *Arguments within English Marxism* (London: New Left Books, 1980), esp. ch. 4 entitled "Stalinism."

Thompson examine Althusser's relationship to the French Communist Party (PCF), of which Althusser has been a member since 1948. Nor does Thompson take sufficient account of Althusser's various political utterances. Had he done so, he would have seen that it is precisely the massive edifice of Stalinism with its "contagious and implacable system of government and thought" that Althusser takes himself to be writing against (*FM, 22*).

The fallacy of Thompson's charge rests on the very indiscriminateness with which it is leveled. Nowhere is it ever made clear what is meant by Stalinism or how exactly this applies to the case of Althusser. In a precise historical sense, of course, Stalinism means a system of rigid party dictatorship maintained through the systematic use of terror and dedicated to the forced industrialization of a backward economy and the defense of a privileged bureaucratic substratum against both workers and peasants alike. As an epithet applied to Althusser, Stalinism means nothing more than "dogmatic" or "doctrinaire." For Thompson, Stalinism applies to the "rigorous" and "coherent" character of Althusser's utterances. But if this is the case, then any systematic thinker—Descartes, Spinoza, Kant—could in principle be accused of Stalinism. To accuse Althusser of carrying out an "ideological police operation" is not only to do injustice to his thought, but to trivialize the true horrors of Stalinist rule. Furthermore, if Althusser really is providing a "totally coherent theoretical expression" of Communist Party practice, this contribution must surely have come as a shock to his own party leadership, who regarded the publication of his two main works with extreme skepticism, if not hostility.[7]

Temperamentally, of course, Althusser is a doctrinaire, but of the learned variety. Tolerance is, after all, a moral, not an intellectual virtue. His refusal to compromise has worked two ways. As a defender of what he takes to be "scientific" Marxism, he has castigated as "ideological" everything associated with the

[7]Cf. Waldeck Rochet, "Le marxisme et les chemins de l'avenir," *Cahiers du communisme,* 5–6 (1966).

rhetoric of humanism. But at the same time, his own works are written in a style that could scarcely be to the liking of orthodox communists. Among his own sources we find not only the works of classical Marxism, but those of Spinoza, Kant, Nietzsche, Freud, and Lévi-Strauss as well. Indeed, his own terse and laconic prose in the best French style of Montaigne and Pascal has given rise to the opposite charge of "elitism," that he is writing only for a tiny portion of the Parisian intelligentsia without due consideration for the needs of the workers' movement.

This point has been well expressed by another critic, Raymond Aron, who in an equally fierce anti-Althusserian diatribe castigates both Althusser and Sartre for their extreme esotericism. "After all," he writes, "neither the *Critique of Dialectical Reason* nor *Reading Capital* is designed for the masses; these books do not serve to recruit militants or sympathizers but answer the needs of a small number. In the language of Pareto, they constitute 'derivations' which do not modify 'residues,' they rationalize attitudes or commitments: they do not provoke them."[8]

The linchpin of Thompson's charge is really against Althusser's denial of the role of human agency in history and consequently against the type of philosophical determinism he has embraced. This far more serious charge gets to the heart of Althusser's conception of history as a "process without a subject." Thompson regards this, quite correctly, as an attempt to expel from the Marxian canon the humanist thesis that "we make our own history" for the scientific or structuralist edict that "history makes itself."[9] The true "subjects" of history are no longer individual human actors who form themselves into classes, but the social relations of production which determine the places and functions that they occupy. The larger philosophical difference at issue here turns on the role of conscious human choice, value, and action in history—terms that Thompson subsumes under the

[8]*D'une sainte famille à l'autre*, pp. 8–9.
[9]Page 86.

master category of "agency." In place of the conception of ourselves as "free agents" who pursue our own goals and projects by the light of an independent intellect, Althusser would have us view ourselves as *Träger,* that is, bearers or supports of the relations of production. Thus what is ultimately at stake is the replacement of the doctrine of free action by a type of class determinism which Thompson exhorts us to resist at all costs. "Whatever we conclude in the endlessly receding argument of predetermination and free will," he writes, it remains profoundly important that "we should think ourselves to be 'free' (which Althusser will not allow us to think)."[10]

This is an issue to which I shall return at greater length in Chapter 6; for now suffice it to say that Thompson has isolated the real philosophical problem of Althusserian Marxism. That Althusser does deny that concepts like will, volition, agency, and choice have a place within a Marxist "science of history" is, no doubt, correct. That there is an implicit moral teaching suggested here in the form of a "theoretical anti-humanism" is also true. Indeed, Althusser's attempt to focus attention on the underlying structures of production relations at the expense of concrete individuals who inhabit those structures is but one of a number of sophisticated ways of denying the reality of human freedom. It is also, as theorists like Sartre would no doubt argue, an evasion of moral responsibility as well. But while the philosophical doctrine of determinism and the denial of the possibility of free action is certainly open to criticism, to see in this, as Thompson does, a rationale for the forced liquidation of millions of people is unwarranted in the extreme. Althusser's determinism, we shall see, is derived from that of Spinoza, who found no contradiction in deriving a humane and liberal morality from it. Thus if Thompson insists on calling Althusser a Stalinist simply on the basis of his structuralism, he must be prepared to extend this label to many of the leading figures of contemporary thought who have embraced some type of determinism.

[10]Page 152.

These rather cursory remarks will probably be insufficient to put to rest the suspicion that Althusser is in fact an orthodox Marxist parading in structuralist's clothes. This belief has been expressed humorously and with much aplomb by Fredric Jameson who writes:

> Consider the following comedy of errors: the showman announces a re-invention of the original, Simon-pure, orthodox Marxism from before the Fall. The spectators, enthralled by the exotic machinery he empties out of his suitcase, turn his name into a household word for some unfamiliar country one is not likely to see for one's self. Meanwhile the work advances; a few final flourishes and an embarrassed public finds itself eye to eye with an only too recognizable and banal likeness of Marx on the order of commercial busts of Beethoven. In the rush for the exits, amid shame-faced recrimination, the supreme reproach may be overheard: why he was nothing but an orthodox Marxist in the first place![11]

The assumption here, mistaken in my view, that Althusser is merely an "orthodox Marxist," already presupposes what is still at issue. For what is "orthodox Marxism?" If we define it in some doctrinal sense as the total sum of writings and theories ascribed to Marx or of Marx in conjunction with one or more of his heirs, Marx and Engels, Marxism-Leninism and so on, then this argument requires not only an authoritative body of texts, but an officially approved interpretation of these texts that is considered canonical by its followers. But this definition will immediately raise the question: which texts and which interpretation of them? Is Marxism to be identified with the early Marx of the *1844 Manuscripts,* with his concern for the "self-alienation" of man in modern society? Or is it primarily to be identified with the later Marx of *Capital,* concerned with "the economic law of motion" of capitalist society in which human agents figure only as "personifications" of certain given relations of production?

[11] "The Re-invention of Marx," *Times Literary Supplement,* August 22, 1975.

24

To identify Marxism, then, with a fixed body of doctrine based upon a certain selection of texts already presupposes a prior criteria of selection which the texts themselves do not indicate. Or we may define it, as Lukács argues, by explicit attention to Marx's method.[12] But without further specification about what this consists of, we get no closer to the truth. Any attempt to isolate and identify Marx's method will inevitably run up against the same kinds of interpretive difficulties involved in attempting to define its doctrinal core or content. In neither case will we be able to account for the wide range of Marxisms, all of which can lay claim to derive their inspiration from one common source.

Such reasoning indicates, if only negatively, the type of approach to be adopted in this study. Rather than judging Althusser against a preconceived notion of "true" Marxism—"the original, Simon-pure orthodox Marxism" of Jameson's description—we must try to take Althusser at his word, that he already is a Marxist, writing from within the Marxist tradition. This approach may seem to some to be insufficiently critical, for if we do not have a conception of what Marxism is, how will we be able to identify Althusser as contributing to this tradition? And if we simply take him at his word, how can we be assured that his own self-explanation is adequate? The response to these questions is that in textual interpretation, just as in everyday discourse, it makes sense to assume as a start that what an author (or speaker) says or does is a reliable guide to what he means or intends. The assumption here is that an author has an intention, that he has managed to communicate it, *and* that it is worth recovering. In any case, while Althusser writes from within the Marxist tradition, he does not merely accept the authority of that tradition. Rather he assumes there is something defective about it which

---

[12]Georg Lukács, "What Is Orthodox Marxism?" *History and Class Consciousness: Studies in Marxist Dialectics,* trans. Rodney Livingstone (Cambridge, Mass.: MIT Press, 1971), p. 1: "Orthodox Marxism, therefore, does not imply the uncritical acceptance of the results of Marx's investigations. It is not the 'belief' in this or that thesis, nor the exegesis of a 'sacred' book. On the contrary, orthodoxy refers exclusively to *method.*"

has made his intervention necessary. His manner of reading Marx assumes, therefore, a position of superiority to those who have read Marx before. In taking Althusser at his word, we will be forced to consider whether the claims he makes are justified. In this sense, exposition points toward criticism.

This reasoning may no doubt be rejected as virtually the opposite of Althusser's own hermeneutical prescriptions or his own manner of reading Marx, which begins with an explicit disavowal of authorial intent and assumes that all interpretation must be essentially creative or "productive." To be sure, there is a powerful tradition of critical hermeneutics to support this view stretching from Spinoza's reading of scripture to Heidegger's and Gadamer's claims to provide a textual reading superior to the author's own self-understanding. I will return in Chapter 3 to the problem of reading. Suffice it to note here that any textual reading that claims superiority to the author's own understanding must already encompass what the author's intention is, lest it would have nothing to be superior to.

This general approach enables the various parts of this study to hang together as a whole.

Chapter 2 develops in detail the context or "conjuncture" within which Althusser describes his "intervention." This conjuncture, which was politically dominated by the crisis of postwar Stalinism, was intellectually dominated by the advent of Marxist humanism. Although humanism is admittedly a vague term, within the current debate I have tried to isolate three pertinent dimensions of it. First, there is the emphasis upon alienation or reification discovered by Georg Lukács in his now classic study *History and Class Consciousness;* second, there is the idea of an "end of history" taken from Hegel and developed in France most perspicaciously by Alexandre Kojève in his lectures on Hegel's *Phenomenology of Mind;* and third, there is the attempt to "recover" man within Marxism or to reestablish the ineradicable subjectivity of experience most fully developed in Sartre's "existential Marxism." The humanist context constitutes the necessary point of departure for any analysis of Althusser's work.

Chapter 3 examines a number of the basic concepts of the Althusserian reading of Marx. First we shall look at Althusser's own form of structural hermeneutics or manner of decoding texts. Then we shall take up some of the more important conceptual tools used in his reading of Marx, particularly the concept of the "problematic" and the "epistemological break" taken from, or at any rate similar to, a set of related ideas to be found in non-Marxist philosophy of science, such as Bachelard, Feyerabend, and Kuhn. Next we examine his theory of the two Marxes to see whether the bifurcation which he claims divides the Marxian corpus can be maintained.

Chapter 4 focuses on Althusser's critique of the traditional theory of knowledge. It begins by taking a look at the claim that Marx's philosophy, dialectical materialism, represents a philosophy of science and that all genuine philosophy follows in the wake of revolutions in scientific knowledge. We examine the key Althusserian concept of "practice" and particularly the claim that Marxism contains a theory of "theoretical practice" or a self-referential means of validating itself as a science. We examine also his theory of ideology or non-knowledge and see how this differs from science proper.

Chapter 5 deals with Althusser's solution to the notoriously difficult problem of the relationship between base and superstructure. We begin by examining two alternative interpretations of this relationship, the fundamentalist version, which sees the relationship between the economic base and the ideological superstructure as one of external causal connection, and the internal relatedness version, which regards the various components of the social whole as forming an organic totality held together by bonds of mutual and irreducible interdependence. We then look at Althusser's solution to this problem based upon the concept of "overdetermination," which respects the "relative autonomy" of the superstructure while still trying to retain some notion of determination "in the last instance'' by the base. It is suggested that the concept of overdetermination leads Althusser to embrace a form of pluralist functionalism by no means unfamiliar to those working within the tradition of mainstream social science, but definitely challenging some well-known conceptions of Marxism.

Finally, Chapter 6 deals with Althusser's own ''structuralist'' understanding of historical materialism. We examine first of all his attempted formalization of Marx's achievements in *Capital,* showing this to be closer to a metaphysics of history than to a form of empirical historical inquiry. We then go on to treat his conception of history as a ''process without a subject'' and the implications of this understanding for our traditional conception of history as the arena in which human agents act and reveal themselves in the world through speech and deed. I suggest that Althusserian structuralism, like that of Foucault and Lévi-Strauss, culminates in a type of nihilism in which the very concept of the human, as a term of distinction, disappears altogether in any sense meaningful for either thought or action.

If, after this basic outline of my inquiry, it should still be necessary to ask why Althusser has been chosen as the focal point of this study, it can only be said that, with the possible exception of Habermas, his work remains the most comprehensive reinterpretation of Marx since the early Lukács. But while the works of Habermas and Lukács have been subject to the most exhaustive scrutiny and analysis, those of Althusser (with only a couple of exceptions) have been left to the more or less narrow concerns of partisans. Here, however, is a corpus of work that merits attention, not only for an understanding of Marxism, but for the possible future of social science. If I may borrow a phrase from Tocqueville, in reading Althusser I saw much more than Althusser. I saw the future of the social sciences.

2

The Humanist Context

While intellectual debates need to be examined as ideas in their own right, it is occasionally necessary to remind ourselves that ideas develop within the context of an economic, political, and intellectual environment, that as a general rule provides the framework within which they can be interpreted. I do not mean to suggest that the ideas of a thinker or of a group of thinkers can be equated to the context or that the context ultimately determines what is or can be meant. This is never more true than when we are dealing with political theorists who presuppose an end to be attained pointing beyond existing reality to some possible state of affairs that ideally ought to exist. Whatever is dogmatically asserted, thought never simply mirrors or reproduces an external reality, but rather helps to shape and determine the reality within which that thought develops. There is, we might say, a "dialectical" relationship between thought and reality so that any attempt to attribute primacy to one over the other cannot but raise more problems than it can hope to solve. Nowhere is this more evident than in the study of Marxism, where theory and practice are so intimately related that to abstract the Marxist "vision" from the empirical features of the situation within which that vision is expressed is to misrepresent both.

The aim of this chapter is to develop a sense of the context within which Althusserian Marxism has developed. The context or, as Althusser calls it, the "conjuncture" which gave rise to his own thinking was dominated by two events. On the political side, we see the denunciation of Stalin and the "Cult of Personality" at the Twentieth Congress of the Soviet Communist Party in 1956 and, later, the breach between the Soviet and Chinese Communist Parties (*FM*, 11). On the intellectual side we find the advent of postwar existential Marxism, or Marxist humanism.[1] In opposition to classical or "orthodox" Marxism, which presented itself as a highly combative and militant doctrine based upon an intense opposition to what it regarded as the conflict-ridden and oppressive nature of existing society, Marxist humanism was relatively accommodating and open. Party spokesmen like Roger Garaudy came to extol the virtues of humanism as a bond uniting Communists, Socialists, and Christians in building an "advanced democracy" under the benign rule of de Gaulle's Fifth Republic. Even the Soviet Party was declaring "Everything for Man" as a mass slogan for the era of peaceful coexistence with the West. Marxism was no longer represented as an institutionalized dogma based upon an officially approved interpretation of a set of "canonical" texts, but as a philosophy of history which could incorporate the insights of Aristotle and Thomas, Pascal and Kierkegaard, Husserl and Heidegger. It was into this atmosphere of bouyant optimism created by the advent of Marxist humanism that Althusser's "theoretical anti-humanism" came to intervene.

Marxist Humanism

In the Introduction to *For Marx,* Althusser describes the immediate stimulus for his "intervention" as produced by the crisis

[1] Individual works would be too extensive to cite but the best recent history of this context is Mark Poster, *Existential Marxism in Postwar France: From Sartre to Althusser* (Princeton: Princeton University Press, 1975); also extremely reliable for the postwar intellectual climate is George Lichtheim, *Marxism in Modern France* (New York: Columbia University Press, 1966); David Caute, *Communism and the French Intellectuals, 1914–1960* (New York: Macmillan's, 1964).

of postwar Stalinism. This crisis was itself made possible by the "profound" and "stubborn" slowness of Marxism in making any impact at all upon French political culture. As he puts it: "In this way we came to realize that under the protection of the reigning dogmatism a second, negative, tradition, a French one this time, had prevailed over the first, a second tradition, or rather what, echoing Heine's 'German misery,' we might call, our 'French misery': the stubborn, profound absence of any real *theoretical* culture in the history of the French worker's movement" (*FM*, 23). The reasons he gives for this specifically "French misery" are of both a political and a theoretical nature.

Politically, Marxism was slow in coming to France because there was already an indigenous radical tradition ultimately stemming back to the Jacobinism of the Revolution which found its greatest practitioner in the conspiratorial and insurrectionist politics of Blanqui. This coupled with the anarcho-syndicalism of Proudhon and his followers served to dominate the labor movement in France well into the twentieth century. Together with this, however, we must not forget the profound differences separating the French and German situations during the period of the Second International (1889–1914). Marx and Engels had originally come out of the German democratic movement which had reached its peak in 1848, and it was only natural for them and their followers to identify the new doctrine with Germany. For the French of that period, barely recovering from a humiliating defeat at the hands of their traditional foes in the war of 1870–1871, being a Marxist was by no means regarded as a political asset. Rhetorical appeals to proletarian internationalism notwithstanding—"workers of the world unite, you have nothing to lose but your chains"—the labor movement of these years was still rigorously divided along national lines.

Theoretically, Marxism in France had serious intellectual competitors of a purely homegrown variety. Although Marx and Engels' doctrine of historical materialism had come of age during the politically tumultuous years of the 1840s, by 1867, the year which witnessed the publication of the first volume of *Capital,* they had become sufficiently evolutionist in their thought to allow that the transition to socialism could come about through peaceful means, at least in some of the more developed capitalist countries. In principle this change was but a variant of the same creed taught by French academic sociologists from Auguste Comte to Emile Durkheim. Throughout this period, Marxism was identified by its apologists and critics alike with economics and particularly with a deterministic interpretation of history, a position not incompatible with positivism. Besides, there was also Marx's admitted penchant for baffling his readers with his often farfetched German dialectical vocabulary, a fact which had not gone unobserved by an early French critic who complained in a review for the Comtist journal, *La Philosophie positive,* of Marx's "metaphysical" treatment of political economy.[2] While a partial translation of *Capital* was available from 1875 onward and had won Marx a reputation as a first-rate economist, most Frenchmen remained skeptical of accepting any system of analysis that had not evolved on French soil.

The relative slowness of Marxism in making any theoretical impact in France can perhaps be further explained by the position occupied by French intellectuals throughout the late nineteenth and early twentieth centuries. So successful had been the bourgeois revolutions in France of 1789, 1830, and 1848 in breaking the hold of feudalism and the church that the middle class was able to assimilate the intellectuals and to keep them on its side even after the seizure and consolidation of power. With very few exceptions, Althusser tells us, the French intelligentsia, unlike their German, Russian, Italian, and Polish counterparts, were willing to accept this situation and felt no need to align themselves with the emergent working classes. This was reflected also at the level of the universities, where, due largely to the profoundly "spiritualist" character of French philosophy from

[2]Cited by Marx in the Afterword to the second German edition of *Capital,* trans. Samuel Moore and Edward Aveling (London: Lawrence and Wishart, 1979), 1: 17.

Maine de Biran to Cousin and Bergson, Marx was read (if at all) only from a standpoint of distrust. In the 1960 Preface to the *Critique of Dialectical Reason,* Sartre eloquently recalled his generation's first tentative groping toward Marxism as a "philosophy of the concrete."

> In 1925, when I was twenty years old, there was no chair of Marxism at the University, and Communist students were very careful not to appeal to Marxism or even to mention it in their examinations; had they done so, they would have failed. The horror of dialectic was such that Hegel himself was unknown to us. Of course, they allowed us to read Marx; they even advised us to read him; one had to know him "in order to refute him." But without the Hegelian tradition, without Marxist teachers, without any planned program of study, without the instruments of thought, our generation, like the preceding ones and like that which followed, was wholly ignorant of historical materialism. On the other hand, they taught us Aristotelian and mathematical logic in great detail. . . . We rejected the official idealism in the name of "the tragic sense of life." This Proletariat, far off, invisible, inaccessible, but conscious and acting, furnished the proof—obscurely for most of us—that not *all* conflicts had been resolved. We had been brought up in bourgeois humanism, and this optimistic humanism was shattered when we vaguely perceived around our town the immense crowd of "sub-men conscious of their sub-humanity." But we sensed this shattering in a way that was still idealist and individualist.[3]

The lack of a coherent theoretical tradition was felt even more later, during the era of the Popular Front and the Resistance. While during this period large numbers of scientific, literary, and artistic fellow travelers did flock to the Communist Party, to which they could have made an important contribution, they did not come in their capacity as intellectuals, but as political activists seeking to expiate the sin of not having been born proletarian.

[3]Jean-Paul Sartre, *Search for a Method,* trans. Hazel E. Barnes (New York: Alfred A. Knopf, 1973), pp. 17, 19.

Speaking out of his direct experience of this period, Althusser says:

> So many of the young philosophers who had come of age in the War or just after it were worn out by exhausting political tasks but had taken no time off from them for scientific work! It is also characteristic of our social history that the intellectuals of petty bourgeois origin who came to the Party at that time felt that they had to pay in pure activity, if not in political activism, the imaginary debt they thought they had contracted *by not being proletarians*. . . . *Philosophically* speaking, our generation sacrificed itself and was sacrificed to political and ideological conflict alone, implying that it was sacrificed in its intellectual and scientific work. A number of scientists, occasionally even historians, and even a few rare literary figures came through unscathed or at least only slightly bruised. There was no way out for a philosopher [*FM*, 27].

Only during the 1930s and particularly after 1945 did Marx's work begin to have an intellectual impact on French life. The sudden popularity of Marxism can be explained by the joint struggle of Marxists and non-Marxists against fascism, but it was also due to the rediscovery and transmission of the works of the young Marx during this time. During the nineteenth century, only the *Communist Manifesto, Capital*, and a few of Marx's occasional writings on economic and political themes had been translated into French.[4] In 1927, however, the Molitor translations of his early writings began making their appearance with the publication of Marx's doctoral dissertation on the Democritean and Epicurean philosophies of nature and later of *The Holy Family*. Not until 1937, though, was even a partial translation of his important Paris Manuscripts published, under the title of *Economie politique et philosophie*. This translation was unfortunately based upon Landshut and Mayer's earlier German edition of the work, which was marred by many editorial flaws and inac-

---

[4]On the introduction of Marxist texts into France, see Alexandre Zévaès, *De l'introduction du marxisme en France* (Paris: Rivière, 1947).

curacies. While Marx's *Critique of Hegel's "Philosophy of Right"* had appeared two years earlier in 1935, his famous *Grundrisse,* the unpublished draft copy of *Capital,* did not appear in the original-language version until 1939 and in French until 1967. Finally, it was not until 1962 that Emile Bottigelli's definitive translation of the *Economic and Philosophic Manuscripts* became available to the French public, an occasion that marked what Althusser himself described as a "real event" in the development of Marxist humanism (*FM,* 155).

In Marx's *1844 Manuscripts,* which occupy a well-defined position between his early idealist Jacobin phase and his later materialist communist phase, far and away the most important notion was the concept of "alienation." Indeed, for those repelled by the economic reductionism implied by some of the later Marxist texts, the emphasis upon alienation provided a theretofore neglected insight into the possible moral and psychological dimension of man in modern society. In fact, Marx criticizes thinkers like Proudhon, who, he says, "overcomes economic alienation only within the bounds of economic alienation" without looking beyond the economic domain to the deeper longings of the human soul. Marx in these early writings was clearly looking for a type of revolutionary humanism that would offer the possibility of a fully developed human species, "l'homme total," instead of one-sided economic life developed under capitalism. This rediscovery of the young Marx, with his emphasis upon the alienating aspect of history, came as a liberation from those who knew his works only through the rather wooden sociology of Soviet "diamat." It also provided a means to query whether or not a residual layer of alienation might still continue to exist in those countries that please to call themselves socialist.[5]

In the years immediately following World War II throughout the European continent a tremendous enterprise of criticism and conversion began in which Marxism was interpreted as an ethical

---

[5]Henri Lefebvre, *Dialectical Materialism,* trans. John Sturrock (London: Cape Editions, 1968), pp. 16–17.

system. The origins of this new wave can be traced back to Marx's theory of alienation in the *1844 Manuscripts,* where he first became critically aware of the conditions of human existence under capitalism. According to this argument, alienation became the central concept of Marxism and in turn was seen as a development without rupture from classical German philosophy, particularly from Hegel and Feuerbach. Curiously, the debate over the young Marx was inaugurated not by Marxists themselves but by Catholics and Existentialists, who sought to reconcile Marx with the natural law theories of Aquinas or the religious existentialism of Kierkegaard.[6] This debate caught orthodox communists completely unawares so that with little dissension they too tried to incorporate the young Marx into the Marxian corpus.

The view that the entire Marxian corpus could be understood as a sustained reflection upon the concept of alienation was accepted by nearly all the commentators. For Landshut and Mayer, the original German editors of Marx's early manuscripts, these works represented a ''new gospel.'' It was, for them, ''the revelation of authentic Marxism,'' ''the central work of Marx, the principal nodal point in the development of his thought.''[7] For Roger Garaudy, a longtime PCF member writing in *Cahiers du communisme,* these works ''can be considered as the act of birth of Marxism as for the first time we see converging in the text the 'three sources' of Marxism so clearly described by Lenin: classi-

---

[6]Some of the more important works are Emmanuel Mounier, *Le personalisme* (Paris: Presses Universitaires de France, 1949); Jean Lacroix, *Marxisme, existentialisme, et personalisme* (Paris: Presses Universitaires de France, 1949); Pierre Bigo, *Marxisme et humanisme: Introduction à l'oeuvre économique de Karl Marx* (Paris: Presses Universitaires de France, 1953, 1961). For the Marxist response to the Catholic ''main tendue'' see Roger Garaudy, *L'église, le communisme et les chrétiens* (Paris: Editions sociales, 1949), and *De l'anathème au dialogue,* (Paris: Plon, 1965). Clearly, neither all Catholics nor all Marxists were happy with this rapproachement, as for instance Gaston Fessard, *Par delà le fascisme et le communisme* (Paris: n.d.); George M-M Cottier, *L'athéisme du jeune Marx: Ses origines hégéliennes* (Paris: Librairie philosophique du J. Vrin, 1959).

[7]Karl Marx, *Der historische Materialismus: Die Frühschriften,* Vol. 1, S. Landshut and G. Mayer, eds. (Leipzig: Alfred Kröner, 1932).

cal German philosophy (from Kant to Hegel), English political economy and French socialism."[8] In an early article for *Die Gesellschaft,* Herbert Marcuse stated that these writings put "the entire theory of scientific socialism on a new footing" and represent the philosophical foundations of historical materialism throughout all the stages of Marx's works.[9] For Jean Hyppolite, a Hegelian and professor at the Collège de France, this work represented "one of the most remarkable works of Marx. It perhaps contains the meaning and foundation of his entire philosophy. . . ."[10] And even in such orthodox Marxist periodicals as *Recherches Internationales à la lumiere du marxisme,* entire issues were devoted to discussion of the young Marx and his early writings were described by two Soviet scholars, Wolfgang Jahn and Leonid Pajitnov, as "the birth of scientific socialism" and "the crucial revolutionary turning point in the development of the social sciences."[11]

This reinterpretation of Marx along moral and humanistic lines also entailed a rethinking of his relationship to traditional philosophy and especially to Hegel. Hegel, as Marx himself recognized, was the first to have raised the problem of alienation, in the *Phenomenology of Mind,* although he treated it in his characteristically "abstract" and "idealistic" form. For Hegel alienation was a feature of the mind which it experiences in its development toward a true understanding of itself and its relation to the world, while for Marx it signified a feature of life in modern

---

[8]"A propos des Manuscrits de 1844 et de quelques essais philosophiques," *Cahiers du communisme,* 3 (1963): 108.

[9]"The Foundations of Historical Materialism," *Studies in Critical Philosophy,* trans. Joris de Bres (Boston: Beacon Press, 1973), p. 3.

[10]*Studies in Marx and Hegel,* trans. John O'Neill (London: Heinemann, 1969), p. 128.

[11]Wolfgang Jahn, "Le contenu économique de concept d'aliénation du travail dans les oeuvres de jeunesse de Marx," and Leonid Pajitnov, "Les manuscrits économico-philosophiques de 1844," *Recherches Internationales à la lumière du marxisme,* 19 (1960): 160, 117. All articles in this volume were reviewed extensively in Althusser's essay "On the Young Marx," *FM,* pp. 51–86.

bourgeois society which rested upon a historical separation of producers from the tools of production. While for Hegel alienation signified the sense of "otherness" which exists when the mind confronts an objective reality independent of itself, for Marx this "otherness" referred to only one particular form of reality, capitalism, and not to its objectivity or heterogeneity vis-à-vis consciousness. While the precise filiation between Hegel and Marx was extremely intricate, the "inverted" or materialized Hegelian problematic could be seen as infused throughout Marx's later writings. Indeed, as late as 1867 in the first volume of *Capital,* Marx reintroduced the concept of alienation under the guise of the "fetishism of commodities."[12] By "fetishism" Marx meant a system of production which makes value relations appear in the exchange of commodities, not as relations between their producers, but as relations between material things. This condition Marx hoped to rectify by reuniting the workers with their means of production under socialism. Thus fetishism as an aspect of what in 1844 Marx had called "human self-alienation" served as a reminder, at least to certain critics, that the mature Marx had never completely abandoned his original position.

The advent of Marxist humanism, which gained in popularity from the immediate postwar period to about 1960, can be seen as focused on three central themes: (1) alienation or reification, (2) the end of history, and (3) the recovery of man. These themes, which dominated Marxism after the war, were (with a couple of notable exceptions) scarcely touched upon before it, when Marxism was regarded either as a politico-economic doctrine of capitalism and the class struggle or as a total "world view" embracing both human history and the natural cosmos and conceived along positivist lines. All this changed after 1945, however, with the full-scale assimilation of Hegel and Existentialism. But this assimilation was made possible only by the influence of a number

[12]Pages 72–80.

of key European figures before the war, the most significant of whom were Lukács and Kojève.

The "Reification" Controversy

The controversy over the young Marx, which did not appear in France until after the war, was in fact the continuation of a debate that had been raging throughout central and eastern European intellectual circles for more than twenty years. The origins of this debate can be tentatively dated from the publication of Georg Lukács' classic study *History and Class Consciousness* (1923).[13] A Hungarian and the son of a wealthy Jewish banker, Lukács came to Marxism from a background in Dilthey, Weber, and that unique strand of late German romanticism known as "Lebensphilosophie," which had its counterpart in the vitalism of Bergson. In the history of Western Marxism, Lukács is a towering figure whose central insights will be examined here only as they bear upon the problem of alienation and how this problem came to be refracted through his chief disciple, Lucien Goldmann. Lukács' influence, however, spread well beyond its rather belated reception in France and has been largely responsible for giving rise to the Frankfurt School, whose leading figures—Horkheimer, Adorno, Marcuse, and more recently Habermas—have largely devoted their efforts to developing a "critical theory" of history.

The main thrust of *History and Class Consciousness* was to shift the emphasis away from Marxism as a theory of nature, as this was understood by Engels, to Marxism as a theory of human alienation, a redoubtable accomplishment considering that Marx's early writings on this subject had not yet been discovered. In the Preface to the new 1967 edition of the work, Lukács writes

[13]*History and Class Consciousness: Studies in Marxist Dialectics,* trans. Rodney Livingstone (Cambridge, Mass.: MIT Press, 1971).

that to assess the book's importance "we must consider one problem that surpasses in its importance all questions of detail. This is the question of alienation, which, for the first time since Marx, is treated as central to the revolutionary critique of capitalism and which has its theoretical and methodological roots in the Hegelian dialectic." And shortly thereafter he writes that "the alienation of man is a crucial problem of the age in which we live and is recognised as such by both bourgeois and proletarian thinkers, by commentators on both right and left."[14] As these passages indicate, Lukács claims to have discovered first the concept of alienation in Hegel, in whom he says "we encounter alienation as the fundamental problem of the place of man in the world vis-à-vis the world" adding that "of course, in Hegel, it arises in a purely logical and philosophical form." Yet as he points out in the same Preface (no doubt aimed at appeasing party functionaries), it was the "fundamental and crude error" of *History and Class Consciousness* to have confused alienation, which for Marx signified the specific condition of man under capitalist society, with objectification, the very existence of things or objects in the world.[15] Yet whatever its inadequacies and the "formal" recantations that ensued, both Lukács and his critics were well aware that it was primarily this identification of alienation with objectification which attributed to the enormous popularity of his work of 1923 especially among its youthful readers.

To be more specific, the "error" of the work to which Lukács refers pertains to an elementary conceptual confusion between alienation (*Entfremdung, Entäusserung*) and objectification (*Verdinglichung*). Hegel regarded alienation as an ontological property of things. In other words, alienation consists in the very "otherness" or externality of objects in relationship to us. In Marx's philosophy, by contrast, the two mean something very different. Marx understands objectification as a form of creativity or self-expression. It refers to the externalization of man in nature

[14]Page xxii.
[15]Pages xxiii–xxiv.

and society through work. In creating objects through work, we not only express the powers we already have, but discover new possibilities and capacities. Objectification is, therefore, the natural means by which we express ourselves as well as master the world. Consequently, Marx can say that only what is "objective, observable, visible" is real. And that an individual becomes real only when he objectifies or externalizes himself, thus making him both dependent upon, as well as depended upon, by others. "A being which has no object outside itself is not an objective being. . . . A non-objective being is a *non-being*."[16]

Marx's view is, then, that Hegel confounded objectification, the process whereby we express ourselves in the world, and alienation, the process whereby once we have so expressed ourselves we fail to find ourselves or recognize ourselves in the product of our work. These two processes, which are ontologically distinct, under capitalism, phenomenologically overlap. Under capitalism our work is not a source of aesthetic fulfillment or enjoyment, but is rather "alienated" because we have no control over how our activity and the products created by it are to be used. The object is estranged not, for Marx, by virtue of its "objectivity" or heterogeneity but because it has acquired the sociohistorical character of a commodity. It is alienated precisely because it is the product of wage-labor, that is, because it is produced exclusively for exchange on the marketplace.

Lukács claimed to have seen the error of his ways only after reading the relevant passages from the *Economic and Philosophic Manuscripts,* where Marx made clear the distinction between alienation and objectivity. Indeed, writing a full thirty years after the fact, Lukács could still characterize his first reading of the *Manuscripts* in the Marx-Engels Institute in Moscow thus: "I can still remember even today the overwhelming effect produced in me by Marx's statement that objectivity was the primary material attribute of all things and relations." This recognition of the

---

[16]*Early Writings*, trans. T. B. Bottomore (London: C. A. Watts & Co., 1963), p. 207.

primacy of objectivity means that "objectification is a natural means by which man masters the world and as such it can be either a positive or negative fact" whereas "alienation is a special variant of that activity that becomes operative in definite social conditions." This recognition that objectification is not an evil in itself but the sole means whereby man transforms nature turning it into an expression of his humanity was for Lukács the insight that "completely shattered the theoretical foundations of what had been the particular achievement of *History and Class Consciousness*."[17]

While *History and Class Consciousness* was not translated into French until as late as 1960, various pirated editions had been circulating throughout Europe for years. Under these conditions Lucien Goldmann, a Roumanian by birth, first discovered Lukács and thereafter became his principal link with the French. In his first work, originally a doctoral dissertation for the University of Zurich and later published in France under the title *La communauté humaine et l'univers chez Kant* (1948), Goldmann went so far as to present Lukács in the same company with the great thinkers of the German dialectical tradition from Kant to Marx calling him "the most important philosophical thinker of the twentieth century."[18] Later, however, he would modify this somewhat extravagant assessment, arguing that Lukács was in fact a great "essayist," that is, a precursor, one who announces the forthcoming of a system rather than a systematic thinker in his own right. Throughout his career Goldmann was to present Lukács as the purveyor of a humanistically inclined existential Marxism, whose early work *Soul and Forms* (1910) had set the stage for the later thought of Heidegger and Sartre with its concern over the problem of authenticity and the problem of death.[19]

Goldmann's own work has been largely devoted to developing a sociology of literature, and his most important work *Le dieu*

[17]*History and Class Consciousness*, p. xxxvi.
[18]*Immanuel Kant*, trans. Robert Black (London: New Left Books, 1971), p. 17.
[19]*Recherches dialectiques* (Paris: Gallimard, 1959), pp. 247–59.

42

caché, a study of Pascal and Racine, attempted to apply Lukács' aesthetic theory to the phenomenon of cultural creation generally.[20] Still it is his comments on the alienation or reification debate in his later work *Recherches dialectiques* which concern us here. The concept of reification, which is based upon Marx's fetishism chapter in *Capital,* provided, for Goldmann, the key to understanding the relationship between base and superstructure, showing how production for the market deformed consciousness, reducing it to a mere "reflex" of economic categories. In a series of captivating images he depicts the deterioration of the psychic lives of men living under the reified structures of the capitalist world, in which human relations come increasingly to take on the appearance of relations between things. "In an immediate manner," he says,

> the judge applies the law, the baker makes bread to sell in order to obtain money. For the judge, the accused is only an abstract being; for the baker the buyer is only a sort of automaton who enters his shop, buys his merchandise and puts his money on the counter. And, moreover, for the greatest part of his life and of his person, the baker himself is no more than an automaton who goes through the opposite actions. It is true that these two automata are men who must enter into contact with one another, speak together, and as with the grand intellectual and financial bourgeoisie to entertain social relations, to meet one another at various localities, etc. . . . . But all of this is no longer essential, it is no more than the inevitable façade of a single fundamental fact, an inert thing—the commodity—exchanging itself for another inert thing—money. From one side to the other, the psychic life of man is no more than a prolongation, an accessory to a single active reality: inter things.[21]

Under these conditions even the private, noneconomic life of man becomes perverted and artificial as the following allusion to sexual relations indicates:

[20]*Le dieu caché* (Paris: Gallimard, 1971) is based largely upon Lukács' youthful study *Theorie des Romans* (1916).
[21]*Recherches dialectiques,* p. 83.

It is the psychology of the salesman who professionally praises his merchandise—even if he knows it to be the worst rubbish—who is always amiable with his clientele—even if at bottom he would like to send them all to the devil. The stock phrase, chatter, the conventional lie, political and social demagoguery all become general phenomena overrunning almost the entire existence of the majority of men and even penetrating to the most hidden roots of their personal lives or even their erotic relations. Love also very often comes to transform itself into an exterior and conventional decor of the marriage of convenience—as relations between parents and children, brothers and sisters very often become problems of social rank or heritage.[22]

What is striking here is the way in which Goldmann treats reification as a general feature of daily life, "la vie quotidienne" which would later become so important for Henri Lefebvre.[23] But whereas for Marx, reification is built into the very structure of the capitalist mode of production and as such exists independently of consciousness, for Goldmann, it is much more a problem of human psychology. This emphasis comes out very clearly in a passage immediately following the one cited above where Goldmann speaks of reification as bordering upon a form of pathology. "Implicitly," he says, "[man's] psychic life, his 'personna,' his 'mind' loses all essential contact with reality which appears to it as something strange, as something in the last instance unreal."[24] This reification comes to appear as what in psychological terms is known as schizophrenia, which, according to Goldmann, expresses a "fundamental human reality," which is only "more or less" intensified under capitalist society. For this reason Goldmann came to stress the importance of psychology for Marxism and in particular Piaget's genetic epistemology as a further refinement of the theory of reification.[25]

It is to the lasting credit of Lukács and through him Goldmann

---

[22]Page 84.
[23]Henri Lefebvre, *Critique de la vie quotidienne* (Paris: B. Grasset, 1947).
[24]*Recherches dialectiques*, p. 84.
[25]Pages 118–28.

for having unearthed a whole area of Marx's thought, that is, his theory of alienation and reification, which had previously been consigned to oblivion in the interpretive studies of Engels, Plekhanov, and Lenin. Having said this, however, Goldmann must be accused of merely repeating what according to Lukács was the "fundamental and crude error" underlying his work of 1923, that is, the identification of alienation with objectification, which he noted also was in large part responsible for the book's success. Here one need only think of Sartre and, following another of Lukács' allusions, "the mixture of Marxist and Existentialist ideas" popular "after World War II, especially in France."[26] This comes out clearly in Goldmann's well-known thesis that the roots of *History and Class Consciousness* lie in the Heidelberg School of neo-Kantianism and that it in turn influenced Heidegger's *Being and Time*. The "true" and "false" consciousness discussed by Lukács presumably became the "authentic" and "inauthentic" existence discussed by Heidegger, and Lukács' distinction between "essence" and "phenomenon" became Heidegger's distinction between "ontical" and "ontological."[27]

Whether or not Heidegger's work really was at least in part a polemical response to Lukács' is for our purposes beside the point. The question of who was first or who influenced whom is not particularly interesting. What is interesting though is that for Heidegger and many existential Marxists the critique of society was converted into a general philosophical critique so that alienation, which Marx construed as a purely social and economic problem brought about by class society, was transformed into an eternal "condition humaine." It might be, of course, that the Existentialists had the better argument in following Hegel's view that any objectification always involves a certain alienation, or that the Marxist view is overly sanguine in its belief that alienation can finally be abolished with the abolition of classes. This sanguine view is surely what underlies the young Marx's state-

[26]Lukacs, *History and Class Consciousness*, p. xxii.
[27]Goldmann, *Lukács et Heidegger* (Paris: Denoel/Gonthier, 1973).

ment: "Communism as a fully developed naturalism is humanism and as a fully developed humanism is naturalism. It is the
definitive resolution of the antagonism between man and nature,
and between man and man. It is the true solution of the conflict
between existence and essence, between objectification and self-
affirmation, between freedom and necessity, between individual
and species. It is the solution of the riddle of history and knows
itself to be this solution."[28] Nevertheless, by failing to distinguish adequately between the Marxist theory of alienation as a
societal category, which is fated to disappear along with the
disappearance of class society, and the Existentialist account of it
as inseparable from existence, Goldmann must also stand condemned to the same self-critical severity with which Lukács came
to judge his own early work.

Kojève and the End of History

At the same time that Lukács had returned to Hegel as the
source for Marx's theory alienation, a number of other thinkers
were attempting to rehabilitate systematically Hegel's dialectic
and theory of history. This was no easy task, since French social
theory until very recently was dominated by a form of rationalism
that regarded with great suspicion any form of dialectical logic.
Recalling Kant's strictures against the dialectic in the *Critique of
Pure Reason,* Hegelian metaphysics came to be regarded not only
as nonscientific but as positively retrograde. Indeed, so late was
the acceptance of Hegel that as late as 1930 Alexandre Koyré in
his paper covering the state of Hegelian studies in France could
do little more than apologize for the thinness of this study.[29]
All of this was to change drastically, however, because of the
influence of a Russian emigré, Alexandre Kojève (Kozhev-

---

[28]*Early Writings,* p. 155.
[29]"Rapports sur l'état des études hégéliennes en France," *Etudes d'histoire
de la pensée philosophique* (Paris: Armand Colin, 1961), pp. 205–30.

nikov), whose lectures on Hegel's *Phenomenology of Mind* at the Ecole Pratique des Hautes Etudes between 1933 and 1939 were to captivate an entire generation.[30] Not published until 1947 by his student Raymond Queneau, these lectures attempted to establish for the first time a direct philosophical connection between Hegel and Marx. In fact Kojève's "existential" reading of the *Phenomenology,* which incorporated also certain Heideggerian insights, provided a direct means of access to Marxism for thinkers like Merleau-Ponty and Sartre. Indeed, so profoundly had the philosophical climate changed in just a decade and a half that Maurice Merleau-Ponty writing in 1946 could remark:

> All the great philosophical ideas of the past century—the philosophies of Marx and Nietzsche, phenomenology, German existentialism, and psychoanalysis—had their beginnings in Hegel; it was he who started the attempt to explore the irrational and integrate it into an expanded reason, which remains the task of our century. . . . If we do not despair of a truth above and beyond divergent points of view, if we remain dedicated to a new classicism, an organic civilization, while maintaining the sharpest sense of subjectivity, then no task in the cultural order is more urgent than re-establishing the connection between, on the one hand, the thankless doctrines which try to forget their Hegelian origins and, on the other, that origin itself.[31]

There are several ways in which one could regard Kojève's reading of Hegel as "Marxist." First, he choses to begin his work by quoting Marx's famous dictum from the *1844 Manu-*

[30]Alexandre Kojève, *Introduction to the Reading of Hegel,* Allan Bloom, ed.; trans. James H. Nichols, Jr. (New York: Basic Books, 1969). For other readings of Hegel that pursued essentially the same theme see Jean Hyppolite, *Genèse et structure de la Phénoménologie de Hegel* (Paris: Aubier, 1946); Georg Lukács, *Der junge Hegel: Über die Beziehungen von Dialektik und Ökonomie,* 2 vols. (Frankfurt: Suhrkamp, 1973); for a somewhat less satisfying effort see Roger Garaudy, *Dieu est mort: Etude sur Hegel* (Paris: Presses Universitaires de France, 1962).

[31]*Sense and Non-Sense,* trans. H. and P. Dreyfus (Evanston: Northwestern University Press, 1964), p. 63.

scripts that "Hegel . . . conceives *labour* as the *essence,* the self-confirming essence of man" (Hegel . . . erfasst die *Arbeit* als das *Wesen,* als das sich bewährende Wesen des Menschen). Second, Kojéve sought to direct attention away from the theological and even mystical overtones of Hegel's *Naturphilosophie,* which Kojève regarded as disastrous, to its more radical and revolutionary social theory. Third, Kojève came to regard the famous dialectic of Master and Slave as the real set piece of the *Phenomenology,* the key to Hegel's entire philosophy of history. The sentiment that all history is the history of the struggle between Master and Slave lays, for Kojève, the real basis for Marx's later theory of class struggle, once the transposition from Master to owner of the means of production and Slave to alienated labor is made. Thus in Hegel's social theory we see for the first time that notions like struggle and labor are elevated to the decisive categories of historical transformation. Finally, Kojève rediscovered in Hegel the idea of an end of history, that is, the idea that history has an identifiable end, or *telos,* all its own which is leading us through its own "cunning of reason" to a condition of universal freedom and rationality. This end state, which Marx identified with communism, Kojève describes as the "universal and homogeneous state" whose principles were first enunciated by the French Revolution and the Napoleonic Empire. As a spokesman for this eschatological vision of an end of history, Kojève brought Hegel to the French.

The intention of Kojève's reading of Hegel can be seen as providing an anthropological foundation for history based upon a basic human passion or desire.[32] Desire is what disquiets the mind and moves it to act. The simplest form of desire is simply the desire to satisfy some corporeal need or other, hunger for example. But if man acted only to satisfy his basic biological urges, his existence would never rise above that of the brutes. Obviously, then, the satisfaction of basic animal needs is only a necessary but not a sufficient condition for the fulfillment of a

[32]Kojève, *Introduction to the Reading of Hegel,* pp. 3–7.

civilized form of life. Because man has the capacity to desire not only natural objects, but non-natural objects, or values, he is able to rise above the level of brute nature and create for himself and out of himself a human world, a "second nature" of history. There comes a time, in other words, when man is no longer satisfied in the mere appropriation of external things as the possible objects of desire, and feels that only through association with others can he be fulfilled. When this time comes, man desires some sign of "recognition" for himself as a self-conscious being with worth and dignity in his own right; in Kantian terms what he desires is to be regarded as an "end in himself."

The problem, as Kojève describes it, is that at least at the beginning of history this recognition of worth and dignity was not immediately forthcoming from others. Each person wants to be recognized without in turn having to grant recognition to others, and this one-sided and unequal state of affairs leads men to enter a life and death struggle, not unlike what Hobbes described as a *bellum omnium contra omnes*.[33] From this struggle, in which man's passion for honor and prestige is asserted over his fear and terror at the possibility of violent death, the all-important relationship of Master and Slave arises. This juxtaposition arises because in the struggle one of the parties is unwilling to go all the way and risk his life for the sake of recognition, thereby submitting to the other and granting recognition without requiring it in return. In short, the vanquished person subordinates his own desire for recognition to the stronger desire for self-preservation. Thus in contrast to the standard liberal dogma, which sees the origins of society in a type of consensus brought by men who are all free, equal, and rational, for Kojève society has historically been based upon an inequality between a master class, which was prepared to risk everything for the sake of recognition, and a subordinate class, which accepts slavery as the price for its own

[33]That Hegel's philosophy bears a striking resemblance to Hobbes' has been noted on many occasions. For but one example see Leo Strauss, *The Political Philosophy of Hobbes: Its Basis and Its Genesis*, trans. Elsa M. Sinclair (Chicago: University of Chicago Press, 1966), p. 58.

self-preservation. The Kojèvian reading of Hegel not only points backward to Aristotle; it points forward to Nietzsche.

The dialectic of struggle between Master and Slave provides us with the real motor of historical change. The conceptual basis for this dialectic is the need of one self-conscious mind to be recognized by another, and under the conditions of mastery and slavery this turns out to be logically impossible. The Slave grants recognition to the Master by the very fact that he is forced to work in the Master's service. The Master's enjoyment is based upon his freedom from work. However, the recognition which the Master now receives is not from an equal but from a degraded laborer, who is used merely as an instrument to satisfy his lord's material comforts. The recognition thus granted cannot possibly be satisfying. Furthermore, rather than having attained a level of contemplative autonomy, the master comes to realize his dependence upon the slave to satisfy his desires. He is not as he believed himself to be a "being for himself." He is in fact a being for another.

This change in self-consciousness on the part of the Master finds a corresponding change on the part of the Slave, who through a strange dialectical twist becomes the mover of humanity toward a higher and deeper level of self-awareness. The Slave had initially accepted his position out of fear, but through labor (*Arbeit*) he learns to conquer his fear and develop a sense of his own worth and dignity. Work is, according to Kojève's reading—again relying on certain latent Marxist themes—not the biblical "curse of Adam" but the basis for historical becoming. Through work the Slave transforms nature into something other than it is, that is, he creates a specifically human world of culture (*Bildung*). But this is not all. Through labor the Slave not only humanizes the world around him, he humanizes himself as well. His labor educates him beyond the level of his fear of death and prepares him for freedom, to take his place along with Master. "Work," Kojève says, "is *Bildung* in the double sense of the word: on the one hand, it forms, transforms the World, humanizes it by making it more adapted to Man; on the other, it transforms, forms, educates man, it humanizes him by bringing him into greater conformity with the idea that he has of himself."[34]

By liberating the Slave from the fear that once held him in thrall, work now becomes the key to human emancipation. Kojève writes: "The future and History belong not to the warlike Master, who either dies or preserves himself indefinitely in identity to himself, but to the working Slave. The Slave, in transforming the given World by his work, transcends the given and what is given by that given in himself; hence, he goes beyond himself, and also goes beyond the Master who is tied to the given which, not working, he leaves intact."[35] For Kojève, then, the future of history belongs to the once terrorized Slave who has learned to conquer his fear and demand also to be recognized as a free and equal human being. Universal freedom and equality become the condition of man not at the beginning of history but at its end. This view of history, as being made by the workers and for the workers, Kojève claimed to have discovered in Hegel's *Phenomenology*. The belief that the industrial working class, the modern day "wage slaves" as Marx called them, would inevitably triumph over their capitalist masters was clearly what made this reading of Hegel so appealing, at least to those young Marxists in his audience in search of the metaphysical underpinings of their faith.

If Kojève's reading of Hegel provided a point of access to Marxism for Merleau-Ponty and other Marxist humanists, it remained nonetheless a highly idiosyncratic form of Marxism. As an interpretation it departs from Marxism in its conception of labor, in its conception of class, and in its conception of an "end" of history. Let us examine, then, these three departures.

First, Kojève, following Hegel, regards labor as the power of the "negative." The concept of negativity is related to other concepts like creativity, violence, and freedom. To say that labor is a form of negation implies a kind of opposition or adversary

[34]*Introduction to the Reading of Hegel*, p. 52.
[35]Page 23.

relation. To work or act is to work or act on something or someone. Consequently, it is to bring about a change in that person or
thing, to leave it as something different from what it was before.
Since nothing can happen in the social world without the intervention of some action, it follows that all action must be a negation of what already exists. This negation is described as a form
of freedom or creativity. Thus we read:

> But if Freedom is ontologically Negativity, it is because Freedom
> can be and exist only as negation. Now in order to negate, there
> must be something to negate: an existing given and hence an
> identical given-Being. And that is why man can exist freely—that
> is, humanly—only while living as an animal in a given natural
> World. But he lives humanly in it only to the extent that he
> negates this natural or animal given. . . . Freedom does not con-
> sist in a choice between two givens: it is the negation of the given,
> both of the given which one is oneself (as animal or as "incar-
> nated tradition") and of the given which one is not (the natural
> and social World). . . . The Freedom which is realized and man-
> ifested as dialectical or negating Action is thereby essentially a
> creation. For to negate the given without ending in nothingness is
> to produce something that did not yet exist; now, this is precisely
> what is called "creating."[36]

   This conception of work as pure negativity or freedom can
find no basis in Marxism. In fact in a footnote appended to the
passage cited above, Kojève quotes from Rousseau's *Second Discourse:* [I]t is not so much understanding which constitutes the
distinction of man among the animals as it is his being a free
agent." But this conception of freedom or indeterminacy as the
essence of man is virtually the opposite of Marxism. Marx is
absolutely clear that what distinguishes man from the brutes is
not the quality of agency but his ability to produce. In the *German Ideology* he writes that, "men can be distinguished from
animals by consciousness, by religion or anything else you like.
They themselves begin to distinguish themselves from animals as

[36]Page 222.

soon as they begin to produce their means of subsistence."[37] The act of production—the first authentically "human" act for Marx—in no sense implies a radical negation of what is but the transformation of a determinate raw material using determinate means of production into a socially useful product. Indeed, the identification of the essence of man not with useful labor but with "freedom" or "ontological negativity" is not a Marxist but an Existentialist formulation. Freedom for Kojève becomes, then, a sort of longing for pure nothingness—*Nichtung*—which reaches its height in the nihilistic destruction of things. It should come as no surprise that Kojève regards Hegelianism as the philosophical pendant of Robespierre and the French Revolution for whom the pure act of terror becomes the most dignified form of human activity.[38] While Marx accorded violence an instrumental role in history as a "handmaid" of the new order, he never endowed it with any of these moral or ontological attributes. Taken to its limits, the concept of negativity implies rejection not of one particular historical order of society, but the absolute annihilation of things.

Second, Kojève treats his two major categories of Master and Slave as the outcome of a struggle for recognition. In other words, the fundamental division of society into classes is not the result of material scarcity but is first of all determined by a "non-natural" property, the desire to be recognized or esteemed. Consequently Mastery and Slavery are said to be produced by "absolute liberty" insofar as it departs from purely natural or corporeal desire. Since man is not born either a Master or a Slave but only a free agent, the condition of servitude can only be one entered into by free or voluntary consent, by convention. To suggest that slavery can be deduced or predicted from the past would be to return man to what Hegel called that "animal kingdom of the human spirit." Rather the desire to be recognized is for Kojève

---

[37]*The German Ideology* (Moscow: Progress Publishers, 1976), p. 37.

[38]This terroristic conception of politics reaches its apotheosis in Merleau-Ponty's *Humanism and Terror: Essay on the Communist Problem*, trans. John O'Neill (Boston: Beacon Press, 1969).

the "final cause" of all human action which has its origins in an absolutely undetermined expression of human freedom.

For Marx, however, classes are not the outcome of free choice. It is true that the conception that the major classes of society are self-produced has a certain basis in Marxism. Marx, it is well known, was fond of quoting Vico's dictum that "men make their own history," and at least in his early writings he held the working classes responsible for their own alienation. But Kojève's interpretation of Mastery and Slavery is far too subjectivist and voluntarist for Marxism. The traditional Marxist thesis is that a person's class is defined exclusively by his place within the network of ownership relations. His consciousness, culture, or politics has nothing to do with his class. In fact this definition of class is necessary if one is to salvage anything from the claim that class position strongly influences consciousness, culture, and politics. The need for recognition, far from being a fundamental datum as it is for Kojève, would be for Marx merely epiphenomenal, built upon the real material substructure of society. Thus to see class as the product of our "absolute liberty" is to fail to see that, once established, these classes take on an independence apart from the volition of human agents.

Finally, just as Kojève and Marx differ from one another in their conceptions of human nature and in their derivation of class, so too do they differ in their visions of where history is tending. The end of history as interpreted by Kojève means the generalization of the principles of freedom and the rights of man first articulated during the French Revolution and perfected by the rational state described in Hegel's *Philosophy of Right*. At this point Kojève reminds us that this "Hegelian theme, among many others, was taken up by Marx" at the end of *Capital,* volume three. Here Marx made a distinction between "the realm of necessity" (*Reich der Notwendigkeit*) and "the realm of freedom" (*Reich der Freiheit*). The former consists of "history properly so-called, in which men ('classes') fight among themselves for recognition and fight against Nature by work" while the latter refers to that "beyond" (*jenseits*) in which "men (mutually recognizing one another without reservation) no longer fight, and work as little as possible (Nature having been definitely mastered—that is, harmonized with Man).'' The end of history will mean not only the transition from the realm of necessity to the realm of freedom but will culminate in ''the disappearance of Man,'' not to be sure as a biological phenomenon but ''Man properly so-called—that is, Action negating the given . . . or in general, the Subject opposed to the Object.'' The disappearance of man at the end of history will also mean the disappearance of philosophy because, since ''Man himself no longer changes essentially, there is no longer any reason to change the (true) principles which are at the basis of his understanding of the World and of himself.''[39]

Here too one can only wonder whether Kojève is perhaps taking liberties with the Marxian text. Marx actually says that ''the realm of freedom actually begins only where labour which is determined by necessity and mundane considerations ceases.'' This passage would seem to support Kojève's reading of Marx's famous passage as implying a complete separation of freedom and necessity at the end of history. But shortly after this sentence we read that ''the true realm of freedom'' based upon ''the development of human energy which is an end in itself . . . can blossom forth only with the realm of necessity as its basis.'' In other words, freedom does not consist in transcending necessity but in learning to find one's way about in it. Freedom, to use a phrase from Spinoza, consists in recognizing necessity, not in abolishing it. Our actions, whatever the level of technological achievement and control, remain constrained by certain necessities imposed by the very structure of the natural and social worlds. Thus as opposed to Kojève, for whom the realm of freedom consists in an absolute liberation to engage in ''art, love and play,'' Marx gives a more sober-minded assessment of it as in many ways determined by considerations of necessity. Marx says, therefore, that ''the shortening of the working day is its absolute prerequisite.''[40]

[39]Kojève, *Introduction to the Reading of Hegel*, pp. 158–59.
[40]*Capital*, 3: 820.

Kojève left unclear to what extent he felt that the end of history was already upon us. In his response to Leo Strauss' *On Tyranny,* Kojève spoke of this end of history as a combination or synthesis of the "pagan" or "aristocratic" morality of antiquity and the "bourgeois-Christian" morality of the modern world.[41] From antiquity and in particular from "Socratic-Platonic" philosophy we have inherited the idea of a "universal state or empire." But ancient universalism is distinguished from modern in one decisive respect. It is predicated upon the idea of human inequality; for the ancients, there could be no "mixture" of masters and slaves for these were taken to be two distinct classes, or natures. This pagan morality, which Kojève analyzed at length, was transformed by Christianity, which for the first time in history introduced the concept of the "fundamental equality" of the species. But this equality was as yet only an equality of faith in a single God. It was not yet equality in the human or terrestrial, that is political, sense of the term. It only remained, then, for these two distinct strands of morality to be synthesized by Hegel into the idea of a "politically universal state" that is also at once a "socially homogeneous state or 'classless society.'"[42] The resulting social order pursued by the "greatest statesman" is to be one, then, that provides comprehensive recognition for every human being, a recognition of that person's full dignity and equality—an idea, we must admit, that is not unique with Hegel or Kojève. If men are truly satisfied, then, through recognition of their equality, it follows that the universal and homogeneous state, the classless society, will attain to the true end of history, the final reconciliation of the rational and the real. All that will be necessary, or left to do, will be for the philosopher to describe this happy race in the plenitude of its existence.

Still in all, one might wonder whether this condition of a

[41]Alexandre Kojève, *Tyrannie et sagesse* (Paris: Gallimard, 1954); reprinted as "Tyranny and Wisdom," Leo Strauss, *On Tyranny* (Ithaca: Cornell University Press, 1975).

[42]"Tyranny and Wisdom," p. 183.

homogeneous mankind could prove ultimately satisfying to those living under its dominion. This was the gist of Strauss' rejoinder to Kojève, where he pondered whether the complete satisfaction of every human desire, even if possible, would prove to be a blessing or a curse.

> Now if it were true that in the universal and homogeneous state, no one has any good reason for being dissatisfied with that state, or for negating it, it would not yet follow that everyone will in fact be satisfied with it and never think of actively negating it, for men do not always act reasonably . . . men will have very good reasons for being dissatisfied with the universal and homogeneous state. . . . There are degrees of satisfaction. The satisfaction of the humble citizen, whose human dignity is universally recognized and who enjoys all opportunities that correspond to his humble capacities and achievements, is not comparable to the satisfaction of the Chief of State. Only the Chief of State is *"really* satisfied."[43]

In other words, in the world that Kojève finds fully satisfying or "rational," Strauss sees nothing so much as the world of Nietzsche's "last man" or the one great herd without a shepherd. In such a world modern men would be mere epigones, late arrivals with nothing great left to accomplish:

> The state through which man is said to become reasonably satisfied is, then, the state in which the basis of man's humanity withers away, or in which man loses his humanity. It is the state of Nietzsche's "last man." Kojève in fact confirms the classical view that unlimited technological progress and its accompaniment, which are the indispensable conditions of the universal and homogeneous state, are destructive of humanity. It is perhaps possible to say that the universal and homogeneous state is fated to come. But it is certainly impossible to say that man can reasonably be satisfied with it. If the universal and homogeneous state is the goal of History, History is absolutely "tragic."[44]

[43]"Restatement on Xenophon's 'Hiero,' " *On Tyranny,* p. 222.
[44]Page 223.

But, Kojève kimself had occasion to reconsider the implications of his position. In a lengthy footnote appended to a later edition of his lectures on Hegel, he came to question whether the complete satisfaction of human desire promised at the end of history would mean not the liberation, but the rebarbarization of humanity. If, as Machiavelli had put it, "men's hands and tongue, two most noble instruments for ennobling him, would not have done their work perfectly nor would they have carried the works of men to the height to which they are seen to have been carried, if they had not been driven on by necessity," then there might be reason to think that the complete transcendence of the "realm of necessity" would result in the abolition of man as a term of distinction. We read:

> If one accepts "the *disappearance* of Man at the end of History," if one asserts that "Man remains alive *as animal*," with the specification that "what *disappears* is Man *properly so-called*," one cannot say that "all the rest can be preserved indefinitely: art, love, play, etc." If Man becomes an animal again, his arts, his loves, and his play must also become purely "natural" again. Hence it would have to be admitted that after the end of History, men would construct their edifices and works of art as birds build their nests and spiders spin their webs, would perform musical concerts after the fashion of frogs and cicadas, would play like young animals, and would indulge in love like adult beasts. But one cannot then say that this "makes Man *happy*."[45]

Whatever the enormous differences between them, both Strauss and Kojève regarded this vision of an end of history as profoundly unsettling. Strauss attempted to put an optimistic gloss on it by suggesting that "there is no reason for despair as long as human nature has not been conquered completely . . . as long as sun and man still generate man."[46] The hope of a "nihilistic negation" or a "nihilistic revolution" would remain a permanent human possibility. But this is not the only conclusion to be

[45]Kojève, *Introduction to the Reading of Hegel*, p. 159, note in the second edition.
[46]"Restatement," p. 223.

drawn. The other is that there is no "human nature," that man is defined entirely by his history. And if this is true, then the end of history would surely mean the end of man or at least "Man properly so-called." It was this second possibility that came to be celebrated by those "Parisian Nietzscheans" in the mid-1960s under the banner of "the death of man."[47]

Sartre's "Recovery of Man"

The third component of Marxist humanism centers in the concept of man or the human subject. The idea that man makes history or that we can know history because we have made it is an idea, we have seen, taken seriously by Marxist humanists. Marxism could be seen, then, as a philosophy of history providing a connection between events from human origins through to the end of history and grounded in a phenomenological investigation of the subjective experience of individual agents. The elevation of the subject tó the center of this historical drama was ultimately an attempt to vouchsafe individual liberty and responsibility against both materialist determinism as well as from theological philosophies of the Absolute.

Sartre's effort to theorize the role of the subject in history goes back to his early *Being and Nothingness*. Here Sartre conceived man along largely libertarian and individualist lines as a being "condemned to be free" with no fixed essence or permanent hierarchy of needs. The idea of a permanent human nature could only be regarded as a species of determinism and therefore an affront to human "dignity." Furthermore, it would represent a form of "bad faith" since determinism of whatever kind is ultimately a moral posture and not a particularly attractive one at that. It follows, then, that man alone is responsible for what he is, since to blame someone or something else is to deny our ability to change our circumstances, that is, to deny the possibility of choice, which is the essence of "humanity." The recognition of

[47]Aron, *D'une sainte famille à l'autre*, p. 341.

this freedom or "nothingness" which is at the core of humanity was only compromised for Sartre by the freedom of others. The result was a conception of the "human condition" as one of perpetual conflict and struggle between the solitary ego aware of its freedom and the denseness and opacity of the "other" which constantly threatened it. From this struggle no truce or hope of compromise could be possible. In the Sartrean moral universe the only legitimate position was a type of nihilistic dread or "nausea" in the face of this freedom. The only grounds for perseverence in the face of this despair were not from any reasons but from an ostensible comprehension of the worthlessness of all reasons.[48]

It was not until 1946 under the political tutelage of Merleau-Ponty, then co-editor along with Sartre of the socialist journal *Les Temps Modernes,* that Sartre attempted to bring his "existential phenomenology" in line with Marxism. This ambitious project was undertaken in a series of articles published between 1952 and 1954 entitled *The Communists and the Peace,* where he tried to articulate directly the role the Party and its relation to the proletariat. Sartre's conception was then criticized at length by his erstwhile friend and colleague in a lengthy rejoinder entitled *The Adventures of the Dialectic,* which was, among other things, the first work to use the phrase "Western Marxism" to distinguish the open and accommodating form that Marxism took in the West from the imposition of Leninism as the sole canon of authority on both political and intellectual matters in those countries found east of the Iron Curtain.[49]

[48]See Stanley Rosen, *Nihilism: A Philosophical Essay* (New Haven: Yale University Press, 1969), p. 142.

[49]Maurice Merleau-Ponty, *Adventures of the Dialectic,* trans. Joseph Bien (London: Heinemann, 1974). For the official Marxist response to Merleau-Ponty's work, now largely forgotten, see Jean Kanapa, *Les mésaventures de l'anti-marxisme* (Paris: Editions Sociales, 1956); for a non-Marxist polemic see Raymond Aron, "The Adventures and Misadventures of Dialectics," *Marxism and the Existentialists,* trans. Helen Weaver (New York: Harper and Row, 1969); for a more sympathetic treatment see Barry Cooper, *Merleau-Ponty and Marxism: From Terror to Reform* (Toronto: University of Toronto Press, 1979).

Sartre's attempt to accommodate Marxism took the form of designating the Party as the social agent which best realizes the conditions of human freedom. The Party, for Sartre, was always justified in its actions because it manifested the pure and absolute negation of the bourgeoisie. As opposed to the mechanical solidarity and inertia imposed by everyday life, the Party became the focus of all initiative and creativity. It was the Party that was responsible for organizing the workers from an inchoate mass into a class conscious of itself and organized around a common aim or "project." True politics was, then, a politics of the will, which is then hypostatized into the doings of a single imaginary social actor—the Party. The earlier struggle between the ego and the other merely became metamorphosed into a struggle between the Party and the bourgeoisie, where the one represents the principles of action and creativity and the other the forces of inertia and routinization.

It is not difficult to see how Sartre's hypostatization of the Party failed to move beyond the position articulated in *Being and Nothingness*. According to Merleau-Ponty the basic drawback of Sartre's Marxism is that it remains stuck on a dualistic ontology between the single isolated ego and the external world of brute fact which receives meaning only from and through that ego. "What distinguished Sartre from Marxism, even in this recent period," Merleau-Ponty claimed, "has always been his philosophy of the cogito. . . . Many times in these articles one finds a movement of thought that is Cartesian."[50] Taking the Cartesian "I think" as his point of departure, Sartre finds himself unable to provide a convincing account of historical events except as manifestations of the pure will. The question that befuddled Sartre is how history could have any intelligibility or transparency at all, if it is composed of a plurality of individual agents each with their own "projects" and purposes which continue to clash with and frustrate one another. These difficulties were compounded by his attempt to designate the Party as the social agent whose actions

[50]*Adventures*, pp. 158–59.

most closely approximated this Cartesian consciousness. This for Merleau-Ponty was evidence of Sartre's "ultra Bolshevism." In place of this extreme subjectivism, which Sartre had tried to graft onto orthodox Leninism, Merleau-Ponty called for a system of analysis which could explain the complex "mediations" which link the individual to the total situation in which he finds himself. What was needed was a "dialectical" Marxism which could capture human experience as a dense web of interrelationships without recourse to the dubious dialectic between the free and spontaneous will, one the one hand, set against the dense and recalcitratnt material world, on the other. In any case one could easily show that the Party that Sartre had in mind was not the French Communist Party, which could never have tolerated this eccentric understanding of its own practices, but an idealized party distinct from the sordid world of practical politics with its compromises and "dirty hands."

Sartre's later work the *Critique of Dialectical Reason* can be seen as a sustained effort to carry out the program outlined by Merleau-Ponty of bringing Marxism and phenomenology together. "To reconquer man within Marxism" it became necessary to free the Hegelian-Marxist dialectic from the grip of materialist determinism. By wedding itself to the belief in a dialectic of nature, orthodox Marxism, according to Sartre, had transformed itself into a metaphysical system incapable of grasping the concrete particularities of history and human experience. The concept of "dialectical materialism," which at one time had played a positive role in freeing the proletariat from the hold of religion, now threatened to lead man into the impasse of mechanism by treating him as a passive object ruled by blind forces. Such a system was not only amoral but immoral as it militated against the notions of freedom and responsibility by making men dependent upon the laws of an exterior world. In keeping with his plan to establish a Marxist ethic along humanistic lines, Sartre was led to elaborate a method of dialectical rationality more attuned to what he believed was the immanent logic of human action.

In the Preface to the *Critique,* called simply *Search for a Method,* Sartre spelt out how this recovery of man was to be accomplished. Sartre begins by distinguishing between Marxism and Existentialism. The former, he declares, is the one great philosophy of our time, by which he means a "totalization of contemporary knowledge." Marxism is the third and final of the great philosophical systems of the modern era beginning with Descartes and Locke and extending to Kant and Hegel and will remain "unsurpassed" until the collective praxes that have engendered it have themselves been overcome. By contrast Existentialism is described as only an ideology, an "enclave" living on the margins of knowledge which attempts to "exploit the domain" carved out by the greater system of thought. But for all this, Sartre does not hesitate to criticize Marxism for having become a scholastic system removed from the concrete conditions that brought it into being. This is where Existentialism can have a "humanizing" impact. In an ironical moment, Sartre does not hesitate to play Existentialism's Kierkegaard to Marxism's Hegel.

We see that Kierkegaard is inseparable from Hegel, and that this vehement negation of every system can arise only within a cultural field entirely dominated by Hegelianism. The Dane feels himself hemmed in by concepts, by History, he fights for his life; it is the reaction of Christian romanticism against the rationalist humanization of faith. It would be too easy to reject this work as simply subjectivism; what we ought rather to point out, in placing it back within the framework of its period, is that Kierkegaard has as much right on his side as Hegel has on his. Hegel is right: unlike the Danish ideologist, who obstinately fixed his stand on poor, frozen paradoxes ultimately referring to an empty subjectivity, the philosopher of Jena aims through his concepts at the veritable concrete; for him, mediation is always presented as an enrichment. Kierkegaard is right: grief, need, passion, the pain of men, are brute realities which can be neither surpassed nor changed by knowledge. To be sure, Kierkegaard's religious subjectivism can with good reason be taken as the very peak of idealism; but in relation to Hegel, he marks a progress toward realism, since he insists above all on the *primacy* of the specifically real over thought, that the real cannot be reduced to thought.[51]

The problem that Marxism has failed to take seriously is the irreducible "subjectivity" of the human agent. While Marx himself, according to Sartre, had sought in texts like the *Eighteenth Brumaire of Louis Napoleon* to synthesize subjective intentions and objective results, his epigoni were all too ready to fall back on an abstract schema of categories and concepts to explain particular facts and events. Thus he has no difficulty in ridiculing Lukács—the older Lukács who had long since made his peace with Stalinism—for simply dismissing modern literature as too "subjective" or for treating Valéry simply as a "petit bourgeois intellectual." "Valéry is a petit bourgeois intellectual," Sartre affirms, "But not every petit bourgeois intellectual is Valéry."[52] What makes Valéry (or Flaubert) interesting is not simply how they mirrored or reproduced the conditions of their class, but what they did to rise above them.

Sartre's aim, then, was to establish the value of the dialectic as a "heuristic" device which could help to articulate a new conception of the individual in history. This heuristic would depend upon the use of what he called the "progressive-regressive" method. The method is progressive because it looks to the specific aims, intentions, and projects which human agents form and which give meaning to their actions. It is regressive because it incorporates the material conditions or context within which those objectives are pursued. There must be a continual two-way or dialectical interplay between the men who make history and the given social conditions which to some extent make them. In any case, the emphasis throughout was on the active role of human agents in creating not only history but themselves. This principle of creativity was called by Sartre the "project."

> Only the project, as a mediation between two moments of objectivity, can account for history; that is, for human *creativity*. It is

51*Search for a Method*, pp. 11–12.
52Page 56.

necessary to choose. In effect: either we reduce everything to identity (which amounts to substituting a mechanistic materialism for dialectical materialism)—or we make of dialectic a celestial law which imposes itself on the Universe, a metaphysical force which by itself engenders the historical process (and this is to fall back into Hegelian idealism)—or we restore to the individual man his power to go beyond his situation by means of work and action. This solution alone enables us to base the movement of totalization *upon the real*.[53]

The bulk of the *Critique* consists of a sustained attempt by Sartre to break the grip of his obdurate Cartesianism and to develop a social theory based upon the reciprocity of individuals engaged in collective enterprises. In keeping with his earlier work, Sartre retained the primacy of concepts like conflict and struggle, but now conceived it as struggle against material scarcity. Scarcity now became the fundamental fact of human history which both unites men in their efforts to overcome it and divides them in their competition over limited resources. Under the conditions of scarcity the relationship of man to nature as well as to his fellows has been one of constant violence. Violence is in fact nothing other than "interiorized scarcity." These relationships have been, then, not characterized by a dialectical tension but of implaccable opposition or what Sartre calls "alterity." This relation of alterity gives rise to serialized ensembles in which the individuals who compose them are indifferent or even hostile to the aims of their neighbors. Such series have been the predominant form of social organization throughout history. Indeed, there is a strongly Kantian flavor in Sartre's denunciation of the series as it implies that its members regard others as means to their own private satisfactions and not as ends in themselves.

The only alternative to the series is the "group-in-fusion," examples of which can be found in the moments of "apocalypse" during mass revolutionary upheavals. Fused groups are collectivities organized around a common purpose which has become interiorized as the individual's own. These fused groups

[53]Page 99.

have been relatively infrequent occurences in history, and when they have arisen have been in constant danger of ossification brought about by the demands of specialization and bureaucratic inertia. The only means, then, of preventing this relapse into seriality is through institution of a reign of terror. Terror, as Sartre described it in a passage referring to the events of 1793–1794, is abstract freedom made actual. For Sartre, terror is the only bond of fraternity in a world dominated by scarcity. In the end he advances a terrorist conception of politics as the only alternative to bureaucratic stagnation and control. Marxism is for Sartre ultimately a philosophy of terror culminating in a synthesis of tyranny and wisdom. But terror remains necessary only so long as scarcity prevails as a fact of life. When scarcity is overcome, Marxism itself will disappear, and in its place we will find "a philosophy of liberty." But as of now Sartre is forced to admit, "we possess no means, no intellectual instrument, no concrete experience, which permits us to conceive either that liberty or that philosophy."[54]

Theoretically the *Critique of Dialectical Reason* represented the high-water mark of Marxist humanism. But no more than Kojève's could Sartre's work claim to be authentically Marxist. First, the concept of scarcity around which everything is made to turn is not Marxist at all but owes its origins to classical economic theory, particularly that of Malthus. For Marx, the primitive condition of man was not one of penury but of abundance. The subsequent division of society into classes and the "pauperization" of the workers was not the result of natural scarcity but of the unnatural appropriation of surplus. Thus scarcity is the product of exploitation; it is not a fact of nature.

Second, Sartre's distinction between series and groups obscures what is for Marx the all-important fact of class. For Sartre, the distinction between a series and a group turns not on some observable characteristic but on the degree of internal commit-

[54]Page 34.

66

ment to a common purpose or cause. The example Sartre gives of a series is a number of people waiting in line for a bus. Here every person has the same end but each is profoundly indifferent to the aims of the others. Because of the shortage of seats on the bus, each may even wish that the others were not there. "Hell," one recalls from one of Sartre's earlier works, "is other people." The archetypal example of a group would be a sports team where the aim of each member is intrinsically bound up with the success or failure of the group as a whole. The success of one is identical with the success of all. But here again it is not the degree of commitment to a common purpose but the relationship of control or non-control over the means of production that determines, for Marx, the reality of class. The criteria of class are purely external and in no sense depend upon the consciousness or commitment of any of its members. Third, as we have seen with Kojève, Marx will have nothing to do with anything like Sartre's creative use of terrorism. The true precursor of Sartre was not so much Marx as Sorel, whose belief in the efficacy of violence as a purgative anticipated his own. Curiously Sartre's apologia for "terrorism-fraternity" found its real home not on French soil, but in the underdeveloped countries of the "third world," where terror was recommended as a cure-all for colonial-induced psychopathologies.[55]

The major problem of the *Critique* was, however, that despite (or perhaps because of) its attempt to "reconquer man within Marxism," it remained implicitly within the orbit of Cartesianism. For all of his efforts to do so, Sartre had never really managed to transcend the dualism of subject and object. The result was ultimately a form of solipsism in which the exterior objective world remained the dead "practico-inerte" waiting to receive meaning and be transformed through the creative praxis of the subject. Whatever his intentions, Sartre had failed to penetrate

---

[55]Preface to Franz Fanon's *Wretched of the Earth*, trans. Constance Farrington (New York: Grove Press, 1963).

what Maurice Merleau-Ponty called the "interworld" which stands at the interstices between mind and nature. This charge was made explicit by Claude Lévi-Strauss in a polemic against Sartre's *Critique* in the concluding chapter of *The Savage Mind:* "He who begins by steeping himself in the allegedly self-evident truths of introspection never emerges from them. . . . Sartre in fact becomes the prisoner of his Cogito: Descartes made it possible to attain universality, but conditionally on remaining psychological and individual; by sociologizing the Cogito, Sartre merely exchanges one prison for another."[56]

One way of capturing this interworld might be through the study of symbols or language. Indeed, Merleau-Ponty had regarded the "structural linguistics" of Saussure as providing the conceptual tools necessary for a "new philosophy of history" based upon the theory of the sign.[57] In his *Course on General Linguistics,* Saussure had broken with the historical study of the evolution of language and concentrated instead on linguistic structures or systems. Rather than regarding language as a vehicle for individual self-expression, Saussure held the use of language from the perspective of the speaker as irrelevant to its systematic coherence. While language may be used by individual subjects, it is not created by the subject nor does it depend upon the subject for its meaning. The linguistic structures conceived by Saussure were more like an anonymous background for humanity which made all meaning possible. The claim was that by studying these structures we could have access to the ultimate furniture of the human mind without falling prey to relativism or historicism. There is no doubt that Saussure and, following him, Lévi-Strauss would have agreed with the words of the Oxford logician P. F. Strawson that "there is a massive central core of human thinking which has no history" but that the basic concepts and categories

[56]*The Savage Mind* (Chicago: University of Chicago Press, 1966), p. 249.
[57]*In Praise of Philosophy,* trans. John Wild and James M. Edie (Evanston: Northwestern University Press, 1963), p. 55.

of this thought "are commonplaces of the least refined thinking; yet are the indispensable core of the conceptual equipment of the most sophisticated human beings."[58]

The idea of enlisting some form of structuralism as a way of exorcising Cartesianism found increasingly widespread acceptance from those dissatisfied with the conclusions of Sartre's *Critique*. Sartre had seemed to put too much emphasis upon the creative powers of human praxis, thus leaving the philosophy of history nothing more than so many individual "unit acts." Sartre did not deny, of course, the reality of structure but argued only that it was also the outcome of praxis. "I am in complete agreement," he said in an interview with the *New Left Review*, "that social facts have their own structure and laws that dominate individuals, but I see in this the reply of worked matter to the agents who work it. . . . Structures are created by activity which has no structure, but suffers its results as a structure."[59] But this is just what his critics were attempting to deny: that "being" could be created out of "nothingness."

The aim of Sartre's structuralist critics, then, was to replace man as the unified center of history with the study of structures as the "unconscious foundations" of historical change. Whereas previously the intelligibility of history had been sought through a phenomenological description of states of human consciousness, now it was sought through a decomposition or "deconstruction" of consciousness into certain physico-chemical laws of the brain. While Sartre had tried to recover man within Marxism, structuralists were declaring the "death of man" and the elimination of all intentionality from Marxism. As one recent critic has humorously put it: "With Sartre there is too much history, with Lévi Strauss, Foucault, Althusser and Lacan there is no longer any history; yesterday object and structure were dissolved into

[58]Strawson, *Individuals: An Essay in Descriptive Metaphysics* (London: Methuen, 1959), p. 10.

[59]Sartre, "The Itinerary of a Thought," *Between Existentialism and Marxism*, trans. John Matthews (London: New Left Books, 1974), p. 55.

69

the subject; today subject and consciousness are buried in the object. The soul of the world was free and conscious choice, now the unconscious is king and the world has lost its soul.''[60] So it was by the mid-1960s that Althusser, a professional philosopher and holder of a prestigious teaching post at the Ecole Normal Supérieure, mounted a systematic offensive against Marxist humanism and offered in its place a redefinition of historical and dialectical materialism along structuralist lines.

[60]K. Nair, ''Marxisme ou structuralisme?'' *Contre Althusser*, p. 169.

3

The Althusserian Project

At the very moment when postwar existential Marxism was unified in its rejection of a dialectic of nature and in its attempt to provide history with a phenomenological foundation in human experience, Althusser emerged to declare history a "myth."

The project that Althusser and his colleagues set for themselves is to establish Marxism as a scientifically grounded social theory with no debt to history or to the methods of historical inquiry. This rejection of history and historical modes of thought in general may seem odd, coming as it does from a thinker who professes adherence to the Marxist tradition and whose work may be taken as a kind of reconciliation of the Lenin of *Materialism and Empirio-Criticism* and the structural linguistics of Saussure.[1] Indeed, the originality of Althusser's "structural" Marxism is in having reversed the older materialistic epistemology, for which reality is something "outside the head" (Marx) and truth consists in getting our mental transcriptions to correspond with this reality. For Althusser, there is a sense in which we can never get

[1]Fredric Jameson, *The Prison-House of Language: A Critical Account of Structuralism and Russian Formalism* (Princeton: Princeton University Press, 1972), p. 106.

outside the mind so that we can never attain a direct knowledge of reality. The world of concrete historical reality, then, becomes a kind of Kantian *Ding-an-sich* which we can approach only indirectly through the categories and concepts of the mind. The "real," insofar as it can be said to exist at all, remains the great unknown, inaccessible to knowledge.

The intention of Althusser is to distinguish as sharply as possible between historical knowledge, that is "science," on the one hand, and the lived experience of human agents, on the other. In an allusion to the similarities between historical knowledge proper and knowledge of certain chemical properties, he remarks that history can no more be reduced to the consciousness of historical actors than "the knowledge of sugar is sweet" (*RC*, 106). Just as in the natural sciences, so also in the so-called "sciences of man," knowledge and the way in which it is "produced" is entirely heterogeneous to the object that it is a knowledge of. This distinction will, I hope, become clearer later on. However, for Althusser this recognition of the radical disjunction between concept and object, representation and being, so reminiscent of Kant's "Copernican" revolution in science, constitutes Marx's major theoretical contribution.

While Althusser situates his own work within the Marxist theoretical tradition, he has not hesitated, when necessary, to borrow concepts from a wide range of non-Marxist thinkers in order to elucidate what he takes to be already implicit in Marx's works. This retrospective assimilation of a non-Marxist thinker into Marxism is most sweeping in the case of Spinoza, whom Althusser goes so far as to call "Marx's only direct ancestor" (*le seul ancêtre direct de Marx*) (*RC*, 102). What Althusser borrows from Spinoza is essentially the rationalistic, mathematical approach to the study of society as opposed to the Hegelian historicist model. He even takes the Spinozist conception of God as the "immanent cause" (*causa immanens*) of all things, as a prefiguration of a more secular version of the "structural causality" of the mode of production (*RC*, 187–89). At the epistemological level Althusser's rigorous distinction between the "object of knowledge" (*objet de pensée*) and the "real object" (*objet réel*) is taken straight from Spinoza's distinction between *idea* and *ideatum* (*RC*, 40). Finally, Spinoza's thoroughgoing determinism and belief that even in the least oppressive regimes men will continue to be governed by their passions is taken by Althusser to indicate that even in a future communist society the masses of mankind will be immersed in the fantasms of "ideology" as the necessary medium of their lived experience (*FM*, 232–35).

No less important for his reading of Marx are Freud and Althusser's immediate mentor, Gaston Bachelard. Althusser credits Freud with having opened up a new science of psychoanalysis by delimiting the "unconscious" as its specific object of study (*LP*, 177–201). Indeed, the Althusserian concept of a "symptomatic reading" of Marx, based not only on the proffered word of a text but on the silent or suppressed discourse, is taken directly from Freud's manner of treating dreams and other aspects of what Freud called "the psychopathology of everyday life." The notion that there may be an unconscious in theory as well as in mind and that to comprehend the blanks, gaps, and lacunae of a text a particular theory of reading is necessary is clearly borrowed from Freud's depth hermeneutics as practiced in *The Interpretation of Dreams*. Furthermore, the Althusserian concept of "overdetermination" as a manner of describing the complex set of relationships that hold within a given social whole is taken from Freud's use of the same concept as a way of representing dream thoughts in images (*FM*, 252–53). Even Althusser's attempt to remove the human subject from the center of social inquiry has the added backing of Freudian psychoanalysis, according to which the ego, far from being the unified center of an autonomous self, is in reality "decentered" from the subject, lost in the impenetrable stream of the unconscious. In fact Althusser can be seen as doing for Marx what his contemporary Lacan has done for Freud, that is, brought him up to date by the standards of contemporary social science.[2]

Finally and more directly, Althusser has borrowed from

[2]Roger Garaudy, *Peut-on être communiste aujourd'hui?* (Paris: B. Grasset, 1968), pp. 273–74.

Bachelard the concept of an "epistemological break" to show how the progress of knowledge advances not cumulatively but through massive leaps and dislocations (*RC*, 44–45; FM, 32–34, 37–39). Althusser applies this concept to Marx's rejection of the Hegelian and Feuerbachian philosophies of his youth and the later construction of the basic concepts of dialectical and historical materialism in the works of his maturity. At the origin of all science, there is a break which consists in the "construction" or "production" of a new object. In the case of Marx this new object is the "mode of production," which refers not only to the economy, but to the total combination of "instances" or "levels"—economic, political, ideological, and theoretical—which together produce and reproduce themselves and the relations between them. Also from Bachelard, Althusser adopts the view that theories emerge through a critique of previous theories and not through simple observation and abstraction from experience. As we shall see, this disjunction between concept and reality is of central importance for Althusser's rejection of the classical "problem of knowledge" (*RC*, 35–41).

While the vicissitudes of Althusser's intellectual geneology will be taken up piecemeal as we proceed, his primary claim to our attention is as a philosopher, and it as such that he must be assessed (*RC*, 30–31, 74). While Marx has been read by economists, historians, and politicians, both friend and foe alike, rarely has he been studied by philosophers or those interested in posing the radical questions concerning the precise object of his investigations. Althusser's reading, so he tells us, is an avowedly philosophic one, undertaken by a philosopher in order to establish an adequate epistemological framework within which Marx's scientific discoveries could be theorized:

> We read *Capital* as philosophers . . . we posed it the question of its *relation to its object,* hence both the question of the specificity of its *object,* and the question of the specificity of its *relation* to that object, i.e., the question of the nature of the type of discourse set to work to handle this object, the question of scientific discourse. . . . To read *Capital* as philosophers is precisely to ques-

tion the specific object of a specific discourse, and the specific relationship between this discourse and its object; it is therefore to put to the *discourse-object* unity the question of the epistemological status which distinguishes this particular unity from other forms of discourse-object unity [*RC,* 14–15].

Before we are allowed to proceed to the "object of *Capital,*" Althusser takes us through an intricate maze of problems concerning how we must "read" Marx.

The Problem of Reading

Althusser has become famous for his thesis that the problems of Marxist theory (or any theory for that matter) can be solved only by learning to "read" the texts properly—hence the title of his own work: *Lire le Capital,* "Reading Capital." The problem of reading arises for Althusser because of his conviction that a text does not merely say what it seems to say. This suspicion of the obvious leads him to posit that behind the "explicit discourse" of the text, there is a second "silent discourse" which lies like so many "symptoms" of the unconscious buried deep within the first. The aim of interpretation must therefore be not simply to bring out the literal meaning of the text. The literal meaning, if there is one, becomes a disguise for some deeper more significant meaning or content. It is not enough, presumably, to remain faithful to the letter of the text. Rather it is necessary to press beyond exegesis to that "symptomatic" discourse which lies hidden and which must be examined for the absences, lacunae, and silences that the first conceals (*RC,* 16). Let us see how Althusser attempts to accomplish this aim.

Althusser designates two different levels of reading. The first and inferior is a sort of literal reading "in the spirit of the writer" which attempts to recapture an author's meaning in the way he intended it to be taken. The main presuppositions of this reading to which Althusser objects is that it takes the author to be the sole determiner of the text's meaning, which is in principle objective,

75

reproducible, and accessible to the interpreter coming to it from a different tradition or a different point in time. All that is deemed necessary to recapture what an author could have reasonably intended to communicate is sufficient attention to the text itself, together perhaps with its surrounding context. In Althusser's words, this would reduce exegesis to a matter of "vision," since it consists in merely collating the materials of one text and juxtaposing them to those of another in order to see whether an author "anticipated" some later doctrine, including one of his own, or whether he "failed" to see it at all. "This reduces every weakness in the system of concepts that makes up knowledge to a psychological weakness of 'vision.' And if it is absences of *vision* that explain these *oversights,* in the same way and by the same necessity, it is the presence and acuteness of 'vision' that will explain these '*sightings*': all the knowledges recognized" (*RC,* 19).

The problem with this manner of reading is that it fails to specify the nature of the work performed by Marx upon the texts of political economy. What Marx exercised on Smith and Ricardo was not simply a retrospective historical reading, weighing up the "sights" and "oversights" of each. Rather what he brought about was nothing short of a complete "change of terrain" in terms of which the very problems of political economy were posed. This revolution in method is suggested by the subtitle of Marx's major work, "A Critique of Political Economy." Drawing attention to the Kantian origins of this critical enterprise, Althusser writes: "To criticize Political Economy cannot mean to criticize or correct certain inaccuracies or points of detail in an existing discipline—nor even to fill in its gaps, its blanks, pursuing further an already largely initiated movement of exploration. 'To criticize Political Economy' means to *confront* it with a new problematic and a new object: i.e., to question the very *object* of Political Economy" (*RC,* 158).

The critical work performed by Marx consists, then, in a radical questioning of the "object" of political economy. To question the object of a discipline means not simply to confront it with questions with which it may be unfamiliar, but to confront it with a new "problematic," that is, a whole new way of posing questions. The importance of the problematic (which will be discussed in more detail in the next section) has, of course, been widely debated in a variety of disciplines ranging from literary criticism to the history of science. Indeed, readers familiar with this literature will recognize a family resemblance to Thomas Kuhn's notion of a "paradigm" or a broad set of quasi-metaphysical insights or theories about how the phenomena in some specific domain should be studied.[3] The concept of the problematic of a text is not to be understood here as a "tradition of discourse" that would suggest a certain open-endedness and ability to change. Rather it is taken by Althusser to signify a hierarchical structure of problems that sets internal limitations on what an author can and cannot say. Put in these terms, the problematic serves as a kind of ideational infrastructure to the history of ideas which "determines" the thinking done in the sense that it serves as an ultimate limitation on thought, on the problems that are posed as well as their solutions. It follows, then, that the problematic provides the conceptual boundaries which mark off the thinking of a writer or school of writers. In this respect it resembles, as Fredric Jameson has noted, nothing so much as Collingwood's theory of "absolute presuppositions" particularly in its idealistic character.[4]

It is important to note that we cannot grasp the problematic of a work so long as we refer the whole body of texts, the *oeuvre* of any writer, back to some overarching authorial intention. The problematic is almost always completely "silent" so that it must be disclosed in the same manner as a psychoanalyst "reading" the dreams of his patients. Althusser puts it: "Only since Freud have we begun to suspect what listening and hence what speaking (and keeping silent), *means* (*veut dire*); that this '*meaning*'

---

[3]*The Structure of Scientific Revolutions* (Chicago: University of Chicago Press, 1971), pp. 43–52.

[4]Jameson, *The Prison-House of Language*, p. 137. For Collingwood's theory see his *Essay on Metaphysics* (Chicago: Regnery, 1972), ch. 5.

(*vouloir dire*) of speaking and listening reveals beneath the innocence of speech and hearing the culpable depth of a second, *quite different* discourse, the discourse of the unconscious'' (*RC,* 16).

In fact as Paul Ricoeur and others have indicated, the psychoanalytic encounter, at least in the ideal typical version of it, is an exemplar of the relation between an interpreter and the text.[5] The psychoanalytic experience is first and foremost interpretive, since it is the aim of the analyst to understand the verbalizations of the analysand, to explicate their hidden meanings. However, it is also an objective of psychoanalysis to delve behind the exoteric articulations of the patient to the vast domain of the unconscious in order to see what has become broken off and distorted from public communication. In the process of therapy, the analyst moves constantly from one level or frame of reference to the other in order to explain causally what lies behind the patient's own self-understanding. Only by revealing this deeper level of meaning, this "symptomatic" discourse which has become inaccessible to the conscious mind, can the analyst restore the wholeness and unity of the self, just as the Althusserian interpreter hopes to restore the wholeness and unity of the text.

The implications of this manner of reading now become clear. By focusing on the problematic as the unconscious infrastructure governing the "production" of the text, Althusser wishes to show that it is impossible for even the most careful author to be the sole determiner of the text's meaning. Against the view mentioned above that the writer has some special authority over his meaning, Althusser argues that the writer's avowal of his purpose is unnecessary once we have his text. What for instance Plato intended to show by argument in the *Parmenides* is one thing. What he succeeded in saying is another, which can be distinguished from his point in writing it. The upshot of this is that the finished text acquires an "autonomy" of its own detached from the author's private thoughts and mental

[5]See Paul Ricoeur, *Freud and Philosophy: An Essay on Interpretation,* trans. D. Savage (New Haven: Yale University Press, 1971).

states. As a critique of the unduly mentalistic treatment of concepts like intentionality, this argument is fair enough, but it is by no means self-evident, as Althusser apparently thinks, that writers communicate in terms of these fixed systems of meaning which limit what they can and cannot say. What a writer can say is in principle indeterminate and open to change, and any attempt to force his thought into a closed and static conceptual framework cannot but be misleading. The force of this objection will be seen again later on when we examine Althusser's claim that Marx the young humanist and Marx the mature structuralist are in fact two different authors, who, as it were, merely happen to occupy the same body.

In the meantime, there are several possible objections to this type of "symptomatic" reading of texts.

First, this approach to an author's meaning suggests a type of linguistic determinism in that the terminology a writer uses places strict limitations on what it is possible for him to have intended to communicate. While there is surely some truth in this assertion, on examination it could only be maintained in a closed and deterministic universe where meaning is effectively restricted by certain self-contained frames of reference. But this linguistic determinism cannot begin to explain how a given writer can and indeed often does challenge and go beyond existing linguistic conventions by revising existing meanings and in the process saying something new. It is not the case, as Althusser implies, that meanings are restricted to the problematic or linguistic paradigm in which they are found. What happens is, of course, that language as a dynamic whole is constantly undergoing changes rendering some meanings obsolete and endowing others with connotations that they formerly did not possess. Thus, it would appear that Althusser is guilty of operating with an altogether too static understanding of language which leads him to view the history of thought in terms of restraints and limitations and not in terms of its creative and dynamic propensities.

Second, this approach misleadingly implies that a knowledge of the linguistic system or problematic is a necessary precondition for the understanding of a given text. But what is our point of access to this problematic? If this term means something like "prevailing conventions" or "available linguistic resources," then the only point of access we have to them is through other texts. There is an irreducible circularity at the heart of this approach, since we can only understand texts through a prior understanding of conventions and we can only understand conventions through texts. This reasoning comes very close to the famous "hermeneutic circle," in which the part can only be seen in terms of the whole and the whole in terms of its parts. In any case Althusser is not unaware of this circularity and has in fact attempted to incorporate it into his interpretive strategy for reading *Capital:*

> May I sum up all this in one sentence? This sentence describes a circle: a philosophical reading of *Capital* is only possible as the application of that which is the very object of our investigation, Marxist philosophy. The circle is only epistemologically possible because of the existence of Marx's philosophy in the works of Marxism [*RC*, 34].
>
> This critical reading [of *Capital*] seems to constitute a circle, since we appear to be expecting to obtain Marxist philosophy from its own application. . . . This apparent circle should not surprise us: all "production" of knowledge implies it in its process [*RC*, 74].

This circle may not be a vicious one, although the apparent care Althusser takes to avoid this conclusion would make it seem such.

Third, Althusser is exceedingly obscure about formulating definite criteria for determining interpretive accuracy. Rejecting the view that the meaning of a text, say *Capital*, resides in its author's communicative intent, Althusser seems closer to those thinkers like Hans-Georg Gadamer for whom meaning is not so much discovered as created or "produced," the product of an ongoing dialectic between the interpreter and the text.[6] Accord-

---

[6]*Truth and Method* (New York: Seabury Press, 1975), pp. 263–64.

ingly, there can be no one correct "reading" of Marx. There are only "readings," the result of the inherent productivity of the interpretive act. But by denying that the recovery of an author's intention is significant for the determination of meaning, Althusser leaves himself open to the charge of scrapping all claims for objectivity. One gets the impression that one can simply make up the rules as one goes along. Thus, to the question of why one should recommend his reading of Marx rather than the many others put forward since the late nineteenth century, an appropriate response would be a sort of methodological agnosticism. The adoption of one reading over another seems a matter of arbitrary choice against which scholarly debate is a waste of time.[7]

The last problem is one which faces not only Althusser but much of the recent literature in both the philosophy and the history of the sciences. For if there are no general criteria of interpretive accuracy, or, what comes to the same thing, if our criteria are bound up internally to certain self-contained problematics (Althusser), paradigms (Kuhn), or language games (Wittgenstein), then there is no rational manner by which we can choose between basic theoretical outlooks or adjudicate differences between those of opposing perspectives. For that matter, it becomes very difficult to know how someone coming from one context could possibly hope to make his views intelligible to someone else coming from another, much less hope to convince him of the correctness of those views. The slide from methodological agnosticism to methodological nihilism would seem inevitable. The conviction that there are no facts but only endlessly receding interpretations underscores the nihilism of Althusser's method. As Michel Foucault put it during a colloquium on Nietzsche: "Interpretation can never be brought to an end, simply because there is nothing to interpret. There is nothing absolutely primary to be interpreted, since fundamentally everything is already interpretation; every sign is, in itself, not the

[7]Anthony Giddens, *New Rules of Sociological Method: A Positive Critique of Interpretive Sociologies* (New York: Basic Books, 1976), p. 63.

thing susceptible to interpretation, but the interpretation of other signs."[8] We must now interrogate this conviction further.

"The Indispensable Theoretical Minimum"

No reading, Althusser has maintained, can be entirely "innocent" (*RC*, 14). His own reading, as we have seen, is premised on the assumption that behind the literal meaning of text there lies a second text, the discourse of which is "unconscious" and which must, therefore, be "dragged up from the depths." In order to divulge this hidden esoteric text, however, there are two concepts which Althusser designates as "the indispensable theoretical minimum" to authorize a critical reading of Marx. These two concepts are the "problematic" and the "epistemological break."

The concept of the problematic is used by Althusser to signify "the particular unity of a theoretical formation" (*FM*, 32). It is the overall framework of a system which puts the basic concepts of a theory into relation with one another, determines the nature of each concept by its place and function in this system of relationships, and confers on each concept its peculiar significance. As such, according to Althusser, the problematic of a theory determines the form in which problems can be posed as well as suggests the solutions it is able to provide:

> This introduces us to a fact peculiar to the very existence of science: it can only pose problems on the terrain and within the horizon of a definite theoretical structure, its problematic, which constitutes its absolute and definite condition of possibility, and hence the absolute determination of *the forms in which all problems must be posed,* at any given moment in the science [*RC*, 25].

[8]Michel Foucault, cited in Vincent Descombes, *Modern French Philosophy,* trans. L. Scott-Fox and J. M. Harding (Cambridge: Cambridge University Press, 1980), p. 117.

And he goes on to say:

> This opens the way to an understanding of the determination of
> the *visible* as visible, and cojointly, of the invisible as invisible,
> and of the organic link binding the invisible to the visible. Any
> object or problem situated on the terrain and within the horizon,
> i.e., in the definite structured field of the theoretical problematic
> of a given theoretical discipline, is visible [*RC*, 25].

The problematic, then, delimits the theoretical or ideological
field. It governs what is and what is not to be included within it.
It is, as he puts it, a "determinate unitary structure" unifying all
the elements contained therein (*FM*, 67).

One seemingly peculiar feature of the problematic upon
which Althusser insists is that it plays the active role in the
determination of a theory. Indeed, he attributes functions to it
which other philosophers attribute to the human subject. In words
that we are advised to take "literally," Althusser claims that it is
no longer the individual subject who thinks and who develops
scientific or philosophical theories. It is rather the problematic of
the theory which thinks through him and of which the individual
is but the vehicle of expression:

> The sighting is thus no longer the act of an individual subject,
> endowed with the faculty of "vision" which he exercises either
> attentively or distractedly; the sighting is the act of its structural
> conditions, it is the relation of immanent reflexion between the
> field of the problematic and *its* objects and *its* problems. . . . It is
> literally no longer the eye (the mind's eye) of a subject which *sees*
> what exists in the field defined by a theoretical problematic: it is
> this field which *sees itself* in the objects or problems it defines—
> sighting being merely the necessary reflexion of the field on its
> objects [*RC*, 25].

As will be readily seen, this conception of the problematic
relates back to what was described earlier as the dissolution of an
individual writer's or speaker's intention into the pre-existing

structures of language that define the range of what can or cannot be intended. This view that the knower somehow vanishes in his knowledge, just as the speaker disappears in his language, is not uncharacteristic of Althusserian Marxism. In fact it is designed specifically to counter the main tendency of phenomenology, which has claimed that the object of knowledge has no stable independent existence and cannot be known without reference to the psychological or inner states of the subject, the intentional individual who thinks.

Althusser develops this concept of the problematic in the context of his controversy with the Marxist humanists over the status of the young Marx. Many of these interpreters have argued for a direct continuity between Marx's early ethical writings and his later structural analysis of capitalist production processes. This continuity is said to be guaranteed by the appearance in the later works of certain key expressions such as the "fetishism of commodities," which in turn refers us back to the earlier concept of "alienation." Althusser claims, however, that this supposed continuity between the young and the old Marx is due to a "superficial" reading which takes the visible presence of certain terms at their face value without attempting to penetrate to the level of the problematic that gives these concepts their meaning. "We must go further," he says, "than the unmentioned presence of the thoughts of a living author to the presence of his *potential thoughts,* to his *problematic,* that is, to the constitutive unity of the effective thoughts that make up the domain of the existing *ideological field* with which a particular author must settle accounts in his own thought" (*FM,* 66). Since concepts are only properly understood within the context of their problematic, they should not be regarded as apparently discrete elements which can be isolated by analysis and compared to apparently similar elements borrowed from other problematics. Such an approach Althusser considers both "eclectic" and unscientific, for if the problematics in question are fundamentally dissimilar, any comparison that can be established at the level of the elements will be at best superficial and at worst misleading (*FM,* 46, 55–57).

The overall significance of the problematic, then, is this. Its purpose is to provide a formal, organized coherence to a body of thought from an apparent multiplicity of disparate elements. This approach is designed to counteract the "analytical" or "teleological" approach to the history of ideas, which begins by breaking a body of doctrine down into its constitutive elements and then tracing their development from their first and earliest manifestations to their most mature and systematic expression. While such an approach is no doubt useful in the understanding of why a thinker came to hold the ideas that he did and within what social context, it tells us nothing, or at least nothing of great significance, about the general structure or framework of his thought, the logic of his ideas and the formal relationships that hold between them. Thus, only by bringing out the problematic of a text from behind the visible web of concepts and methods will it be possible to comprehend the thought of a person at its deepest level: "What actually distinguishes the concept of the *problematic* . . . is that it brings out within the thought *the objective internal reference system of its particular* themes, the system of *questions* commanding the *answers* given by the ideology. If the meaning of an ideology's answers is to be understood at this internal level, it must first be asked *the question of its questions*" (*FM*, 67, n. 30).

The problematic is said to be the underlying "unitary structure" of either a theoretical or ideological system. While the distinction between theory and ideology will be taken up in the next chapter, for now we can say that for Althusser there is a radical qualitative difference between formal scientific knowledge and the lived experience from which it arises, which any similarity at the level of the elements cannot but obscure. This rupture, which Althusser sees as the necessary precondition for the founding of any new scientific discipline, is designated by him as an "epistemological break" (*coupure épistémologique*). This break is the point of no return which sanctions the birth of any new science. He uses the concept in a general way to show that the progress of human knowledge is not one of slow, uninterrupted continuity, but is rather punctuated by massive epistemological dislocations:

> We are beginning to suspect, and even to be able to prove in a number of already studied examples, that the history of reason is neither a linear history of continuous development, nor, in its continuity, a history of the progressive manifestation or emergence into consciousness of a Reason which is completely present in germ in its origins and which its history merely reveals to the light of day. . . . The real history of the development of knowledge appears to us today to be subject to laws quite different from this teleological hope for the religious triumph of reason. We are beginning to conceive this history as a history punctuated by radical discontinuities (e.g., when a new science detaches itself from the background of earlier ideological formations), profound re-organizations which, if they respect the continuity of the existence of regions of knowledge (and even this is not always the case), nevertheless inaugurate with their rupture the reign of a new logic, which, far from being a mere development, the "truth" or "inversion" of the old one, *literally takes its place* [*RC,* 44].

This concept of a "coupure" is introduced by Althusser to describe the break between the prescientific world of common sense and ordinary experience, the world of "ideology" as he calls it, and the scientific world of ideas which would reduce the other to a set of mathematically formalized relations. It is just such a break that Marx is said to have initiated not only between himself and his forerunners but between his later works and the ideological conceptions of his youth. Yet, as we shall see in the next section, the break between the young and old Marx was not a "clean" one, with the result that many of the old ideological concepts continue to survive even into the works of Marx's maturity. This creates serious problems for Althusser's reading, since it makes his division between the early and later Marx appear to be merely arbitrary or imposed. This objection, however, is not fatal because it could still be argued that, since the problematic remains "unconscious," Marx himself was unaware of the direction of his own enterprise and for this reason continued to use a

86

conceptual terminology appropriate to the older discarded stand-point. Althusser writes:

> In this process of real transformation of the means of production of knowledge, the claims of a "constitutive subject" are as vain as are the claims of the subject of vision in the production of the visible; that the whole process takes place in the dialectical crisis of the mutation of a theoretical structure in which the "subject" plays, not the part it believes it is playing, but the part which is assigned to it by the mechanism of the process [*RC*, 27].

This conception of science as advancing through certain epistemological ruptures is not Althusser's own, but is borrowed from his mentor, Gaston Bachelard. In attempting to understand what he calls the "nouvelle esprit scientifique," Bachelard raises the problem of what is "scientific progress" and what criteria we can use to distinguish between prescientific and scientific ideas.[9] Explicitly rejecting the older evolutionary model of scientific development according to which truth arises out of the essential untruth that is its precondition, Bachelard proposes a schema that would avoid this "recurrent optimism" of regarding new discoveries as somehow latent in the old and simply waiting to find their proper expression. In contrast to this evolutionist or historicist theory of progress, itself borrowed from Comte's "law of the three states," Bachelard maintains that at the founding moment of any new science there is an essential rupture or "cut" in the theory's development which signifies the emergence of a new level of scientific discourse.

From Bachelard, Althusser has taken over the conviction that reason, the object of philosophy, must follow and obey science. Its aim is not to seek some type of "transcendental" grounding

---

[9]See in particular *La formation de l'esprit scientifique* (Paris: Librairie Philosophique J. Vrin, 1972); and *Le nouvel esprit scientifique* (Paris: Presses Universitaires de France, 1972). For an excellent account of Bachelard's scientific and epistemological theory see Dominique Lecourt, *L'épistémologie historique de Gaston Bachelard* (Paris: Librairie Philosophique J. Vrin, 1969).

87

for science, but to make it conscious of itself as an established mode of proceeding. Science emerges only when the evidence of the senses or the "truths" of everyday life are transformed or displaced such that between experience, on the one hand, and theory, on the other, there is not a continuity but a qualitative leap. The object of science is, then, not something given in experience but something produced or constructed, a "manufactured object" which owes its existence to the overcoming of various "obstacles" which experience throws up in its path.[10] This emphasis upon the constructive or "creative" aspect of science as a series of continual historical caesuras marks the essential difference between the "new rationalism" of Bachelard, Koyré, and their followers, Althusser, Canguilhem, and Foucault, and the older empiricism or positivism of Hume, Mach, and the Vienna School.

Much of this talk of breaks and discontinuities in knowledge will once more bring to mind Kuhn's work and in particular his attack upon the conventional thesis that scientific progress is a form of incremental advance made possible because scientists scrupulously adhere to certain practices governing scientific procedure. In what he calls periods of "normal science" the particular controlling concepts and theories, that is paradigms, which dominate the scientific community perform their function so effectively that they not only guide the community in its choice of problems, but indicate the range of solutions of which these problems are capable. These master paradigms constructed during periods of "extraordinary science" by thinkers like Ptolemy, Galileo, Newton, Laplace, and Einstein enable lesser and later scientists to get on with their work without being distracted by the need to defend the basic principles of the paradigm, its methodology, or the view of the world that it embodies. It is only when certain problems remain unresolved, because they cannot be accommodated within the existing framework, that a "scientific

---

[10]Gaston Bachelard, *The Philosophy of No: A Philosophy of the New Scientific Mind,* trans. G. C. Waterson (New York: Orion Press, 1968), p. 41.

revolution'' takes place and a new paradigm intervenes in place of the older dispensation. Once this new paradigm is institutionalized, it too begins to act as a conservative force within the community, the Hegelian thesis, which will in turn generate its own antithesis and synthesis at a later date.

The difference between the older evolutionary schema and the ''new image of science'' is that writers of an empiricist cast still continue to believe in the knowability of an independently existing external world, while those we have been examining here come to regard science, as did Nietzsche, as a form of artistic production. Accordingly, we can no longer think in terms of standards or controls set by nature and which serve as a guide in the scientist's quest for truth. Rather the only controls one can speak of are those imposed by the particular paradigm or problematic that for contingent purposes the scientist happens to adopt. As opposed to the realist's belief that there is a world ''out there'' waiting to be given conceptual expression, this approach has emphasized the priority of the interpretive framework without which there would be no such thing as an ''out there'' at all. The difficulty with this approach, which we have alluded to already, is that by making the purported facts of experience dependent upon interpretation, we abandon any limits to what we may be prepared to believe or to what may be considered as a fact. What's more, a model of science which puts a premium upon the periodic dislocations and permutations of knowledge makes it difficult even to continue to speak of progress or truth at all. Kuhn even admits as much when he says that ''we may . . . have to relinquish the notion, explicit or implicit, that changes of paradigm carry scientists and those who learn from them closer and closer to the truth.''[11] This is, furthermore, to diminish the once sovereign role played by philosophy in relation to science. For once we disallow the possibility that there are any independent criteria by the light of which we can judge science, then the methodological procedures followed by scientists themselves be-

[11]*The Structure of Scientific Revolutions,* p. 170.

come the only standards to which we can appeal as the test of a theory's accuracy.

It must be added at once that the methodological self-sufficiency of science in relation to philosophy is an inadequate means of guaranteeing its truth. Indeed, for self-professed "anarchists" like Paul Feyerabend, science must abandon as futile any claim to genuine truth. The concept of truth must be replaced by "approximate knowledge" or "what does, or does not, seem appropriate when viewed from a particular and restricted point of view, different views, temperaments, attitudes giving rise to different judgements and different methods of approach."[12] If scientific theories, as well, we might add, as political and moral "truths," cannot be considered true or false, one obvious explanation for why we choose one over another is simply because it either reflects or fails to reflect a particular thinker's tastes or wishes. "What remains are aesthetic judgements, judgements of taste, and our subjective wishes," as Feyerabend puts it.[13] Scientific theories, as this passage seems to imply, are merely creations of the human will, which we can no more think of as being true or rationally justifiable than the myths of primitive tribes or a penchant for chocolate ice cream.

The conclusion we draw from all this is that if all understanding takes place within these closed and self-contained meaning frames, each with its own set of epistemological premises, then any manner of producing conceptual change becomes as good as any other. If people disagree over their basic beliefs about politics, morality, or the nature of the world, there are no neutral or mutually acceptable "facts" to which they can appeal to adjudicate their differences. Philosophy, which has traditionally assumed the existence of such facts, would thus acquire the character of a shouting match. Power, as Foucault has recently argued,

[12]"Against Method: Outline of an Anarchistic Theory of Knowledge," *Minnesota Studies in the Philosophy of Science,* Michael Radner and Stephen Winokur, eds. (Minneapolis: University of Minnesota Press, 1970), 4: 21.
[13]"Consolation for the Specialist," *Criticism and the Growth of Knowledge,* Imre Lakatos and Alan Musgrave, eds. (Cambridge: Cambridge University Press, 1970), p. 228.

would become the *ultima ratio*.[14] In science just as in politics and literature to back one interpretation is to declare war on another. All interpretation is polemical, and there is no such thing as a neutral middle ground. Thus while Althusser never discusses the possibility of inducing an epistemological rupture by force, such a possibility cannot be entirely ruled out.

The problem with this model of scientific development is that it expressly prohibits us from engaging in a number of activities which we characteristically do engage in. Whenever we translate from one language into another, analyze critically the values of societies other than our own, or even when Althusser criticizes other readings of Marx, we (and he) are implicitly assuming the existence of certain common criteria which transcend any one particular context or form of life. If Althusser is to salvage his understanding of Marxism from this type of radical relativism, it can only be by admitting to a great deal more continuity between our basic beliefs than his notion of problematics and epistemological breaks would seem to imply. While there may be profound differences between, say, Newton's and Einstein's systems of science, there are nevertheless direct continuities between them at the same time, that is, they are both systems of science and not sets of political, religious, or ethical beliefs and therefore must be judged in terms of how well they satisfy criteria of scientific scope, accuracy, and so on. The same is true for Marx, who no doubt recast Hegelian modes of thought or classical economics in new and unforeseen ways, but can still be seen as carrying on a distinct tradition that he inherited from the past. This last point has been forcefully stated (if not perhaps a bit overstated) once more by Foucault who says that: "At the deepest level of Western knowledge, Marxism introduced no real discontinuity. . . . Marxism exists in the nineteenth century like a fish in water, that is, it is unable to breathe anywhere else."[15]

Whether or not Marx actually did inaugurate one of these

[14]*Power/Knowledge: Selected Interviews and Other Writings 1972–1977*, trans. Colin Gordon (New York: Pantheon Books, 1980).

[15]*The Order of Things*, trans. A. M. Sheridan Smith (London: Tavistock Publications, 1970), pp. 261–62.

great paradigmatic breakthroughs associated with the great names of scientific thought has yet to be demonstrated. For now it is enough to say that the attribution of such a "coupure" within his own thought runs aground of the *Grundrisse*, the draft copy of *Capital*, which seems to indicate that Marx never did completely renounce his early humanist origins. That is to say, he continued to analyze productive relations not just in terms of how they helped the economy to function, but in terms of what they did to man as man. Consequently, socialism was not just for him a means of increasing man's technical mastery over nature, but a way of increasing his moral mastery over himself. If this link between the early and the late Marx, or between Hegel and Marx, is completely severed, it may be that what we will have left is an entirely new science just like structuralism, but at the expense of evacuating it of any interest it may have for us.

One Marx or Two?

On the basis of these concepts—symptomatic readings, problematics, and epistemological breaks—Althusser has postulated certain distinct stages in Marx's intellectual development. In contrast to the Marxist humanists, for whom Marx's early writings were seen as providing the key for the interpretation of his later works up to and including *Capital*, Althusser has argued that there is a break in Marx's development which categorically separates his mature scientific doctrine from his early philosophical and humanistic origins. There are, then, not one but two entirely different Marxes. As a result, Marx's *oeuvre* is divided into an early ideological humanist period and a later scientific structuralist one. Before questioning whether or not this alleged bifurcation of the Marxian corpus can be defended, let us examine Althusser's typology in some detail (*FM*, 34–37).

(1) The years between 1840 and 1844 are designated by Althusser as Marx's early period. This was the period of the

Rheinische Zeitung, when Marx's thought was dominated not by a Hegelian but by a "Kantian-Fichtean" problematic. Philosophically, this presented itself as a view of man as constituted by freedom and reason, while politically the question turned on a critique of the nonrational system of privileges characteristic of Prussian absolutism (*FM,* 223–24). It was only after 1842, Althusser tells us, that Marx turned away from this sort of ethical idealism toward a "naturalist humanism" of a Feuerbachian variety. Indeed, for works such as *On the Jewish Question* and the *Critique of Hegel's "Philosophy of Right,"* Marx is said merely to have applied Feuerbach's theory of alienation to certain social and political *topoi* before extending it later to the domain of political economy. In contrast to the conventional interpretation that throughout his early period the young Marx was a left-Hegelian, Althusser argues that only in the last text of this period, the *1844 Manuscripts,* did Marx seriously confront Hegel and then only to reject him. "Paradoxically," he says, "if we exclude the Doctoral Dissertation, which is still the work of a student, the Young Marx *was never strictly speaking a Hegelian,* except in the *last* text of his ideologico-philosophical period. . . . So the thesis that the Young Marx was a Hegelian, though widely believed today, is in general a myth" (*FM,* 35).

(2) The epistemological break which separates Marx's works from those of his predecessors as well as from the ideological conceptions of his youth is located by Althusser in the year 1845. This break, which was announced in the *German Ideology* and the *Theses on Feuerbach,* not only includes a "settling of accounts" with his "erstwhile philosophical conscience" but is said to inaugurate the birth of historical materialism as a science. Logically, therefore, all of Marx's works that appeared before this date can be dismissed as scientifically fruitless (*FM,* 155–60). In place of the old philosophical anthropology based upon the notion of a universal human nature or essence of man as an attribute of each individual subject, Marx is said to have founded a theory of politics and history along new conceptual lines. What exactly this new founding consists of will be discussed in due

93

course. For now, suffice it to say that, while Marx established historical materialism as a science, he failed to conceptualize the epistemological novelty of his claims, with the result that many of the old anthropological notions persist even after the supposed break in his thought.

(3) The years between 1845 and 1857 are designated as a transitional period in Marx's thought. This period—which includes such works as the *Communist Manifesto,* the *Poverty of Philosophy,* and *Wages, Price and Profit*—marks the first attempt to develop a conceptual terminology and systematics adequate to his theoretical advances. It was only after 1857 that the period of Marx's maturity is said to begin. Yet even here certain of the earlier ideological terms continue to survive. While Althusser is not always careful to specify what these holdovers consist of, one suspects he is referring to the sort of quasi-Hegelian language found throughout the *Grundrisse* and to those places in the opening chapters of *Capital* where in Marx's own words he here and there "coquetted" with certain Hegelian modes of expression. It is asserted by Althusser that it was not until a year before his death that Marx succeeded in casting off his residual humanism and installing the new scientific problematic in its place in the *Randglossen zu Adolph Wagners 'Lehrbuch der Politischen Ökonomie'* (1882).[16]

The question of one Marx or two is not merely an academic problem of interest to the intellectual historian. It is an eminently political problem. As we have seen, in the years immediately following World War II, a tremendous enterprise of criticism and conversion began, according to which Marxism was interpreted as an ethical system, the origins of which can be traced back to his theory of alienation in the *1844 Manuscripts,* where he first arrived at a critical awareness of the existence of man under capitalism. According to this argument, alienation became the central concept of Marxism, which in turn was seen as a progres-

[16]For some caustic remarks on this typology see Schaff, *Structuralism and Marxism,* pp. 128–40.

sive development over both classical German philosophy and English political economy. Since the debate was inaugurated not by Marxists themselves, but in many cases by Catholics or Existentialists seeking to reconcile Marx with Thomas or Marx with Husserl, the effect was to catch orthodox communists completely by surprise so that with little dissension the young Marx was simply integrated into Marxism without loss of continuity or damage to the "whole" Marx (*FM*, 54–55).

Althusser's response to this search for a single unitary structure to Marx's thought is his theory of the two Marxes. In opposition to the "analytico-teleological" fallacy in the history of ideas, which is always seeking for "germs" or "anticipations" of an idea, Althusser enjoins us to regard each text as a unity in itself organized by a specific problematic or a specific hierarchy of problems which may or may not be identical to that of other texts even by the same author.[17] It is not enough to say, just because the term "alienation" appears in the *1844 Manuscripts* and the apparently similar term "fetishism" emerges over twenty years later in *Capital,* that this is sufficient to establish the integrity of the Marxian corpus. In fact he argues that these concepts have entirely different functions because the problematics which underlie them are so different. Alienation is bound up with an anthropological conception of man as an expressive being who finds his creative propensities thwarted under a system that allows him to develop only one-sidedly or "abstractly." Fetishism, by contrast, refers to the way in which capital as a fixed system of production conceals its mode of operation from the human agents living under it (*FM*, 230, n. 7).

What this crypto-teleology which seeks only continuities and resemblances in the history of thought fails to establish is the "immense theoretical revolution" that Marx is said to have ef-

---

[17]For a sample of this kind of "analytico-teleological" reading see Shlomo Avineri, *The Social and Political Thought of Karl Marx* (Cambridge: Cambridge University Press, 1968), p. 40: "Not only is there not 'caesura' between the young and the old Marx, but the guarantee of continuity has been supplied by Marx himself."

fected upon the sciences. This revolution did not consist, as is sometimes maintained, in a change from idealism to materialism for this would have taken place with Democritus or Epicurus or in modern times with Hobbes or Feuerbach. Nor did it consist in a change from metaphysics to dialectics, as this would have taken place with either Heraclitus or Hegel. Instead, the "epistemological revolution" which Marx is said to have carried out not only upon his predecessors but upon himself consists of the changeover from ideology to science, which is for Althusser the crucial distinction upon which the entire Marxian edifice rests. The break between everyday experience and scientific knowledge is read back into Marx's own discoveries.

Much of what is discussed here turns on what Althusser understands by the philosophical "revolution" supposedly effected by Marx. Althusser recognizes that Marx's break with tradition was not a "clean" one. "Indispensable theoretical concepts," he writes, "do not magically construct themselves upon command when they are needed," so Marx himself lacked the perspective necessary to see what he was doing that he had not been doing before (*RC*, 51). He is, of course, correct that this is not an uncommon occurrence in the histories of both philosophy and science. The great innovators who advance into *terra incognita* have to make up their own conceptual terminology as they go along, and this language necessarily partakes of the nature of the old problematic left behind. "The whole history of the beginnings of science or of great philosophies shows . . . that the exact set of new concepts do not march out on parade in single file; on the contrary, some are long delayed, or march in borrowed clothes before acquiring their proper uniforms—for as long as history fails to provide the tailor and the cloth" (*RC*, 51). In *Capital*, Marx found it difficult to apply the sort of methodology that would have been appropriate to his "unprecedented" discoveries and was forced to fall back upon traditional Hegelian expressions, particularly a terminology embodying a vision of the world as a dialectical process kept going by a hidden logic of contradiction.

Althusser's conception of Marx's "theoretical revolution" runs into difficulties on two counts.

First, one might begin to wonder why, if this celebrated "coupure" was not a "clean" one, Althusser continues to call it a break at all. If certain of the old Hegelian or ideological vestments continue to exist alongside the new before disappearing altogether, it would seem that just as good a case could be made for arguing that far from there being two Marxes there is only one Marx whose development was one of gradual, incremental change. Indeed, by casting off Marx's mature acknowledgments of his debt to Hegel as survivals of an abandoned ideological problematic, Althusser runs the risk, to continue with his own metaphor, of losing the tailor's labor in his coat. One suspects that Althusser has gone too far in attempting to conceptualize the "novelty" of Marx's discoveries. Even if he developed his thought by means of a critique of existing theoretical systems, he still chose to define himself largely in opposition to those systems. "One may choose," as André Liebich has put it, "to call Marx's relation to Hegel one of negative dependency; it is a dependency nonetheless."[18]

Second, and more important, one may wonder whether Althusser's understanding of revolution is a plausible one. The Althusserian (and Bachelardian) conception of revolution is closely bound up with a vision of reality as permeated by a series of discontinuous breaks and ruptures with the past which can be seen as introducing new and unprecedented states of affairs. This view of revolution, as Alasdair MacIntyre has recently demonstrated, is thoroughly Cartesian in character.[19] In the same manner as Althusser, Bachelard, and Kuhn, Descartes in the *Discourse on Method* and the *Meditations* describes an epistemological crisis that attempts to throw into radical doubt every element of human belief such that there can be no relation of con-

---

[18]"Hegel, Marx and Althusser," *Politics and Society,* 9 (1979): 93.

[19]"Epistemological Crises, Dramatic Narrative and the Philosophy of Science," *The Monist,* 4 (1977).

tinuity between the situation that prevailed before the crisis and that which comes into being afterward. Descartes' construction of the *cogito* is just such an effort to portray the self as a ''thinking substance'' disassociated from the tradition and history that formed it. Descartes' attempt fails. Not only must he continue to speak a language, French or Latin, that was familiar to his seventeenth-century readers, but there are certain things that he cannot throw into doubt, namely, the existence of God, without which any talk of doubt would be rendered meaningless. The result is that continuities with the past, no matter how ruthlessly they may try to be suppressed, will re-emerge to assimilate past to future.

This ''Cartesian'' misunderstanding of the revolution initiated by Marx is a direct consequence of a similar misunderstanding of the character of the tradition he rejects. Althusser's understanding of revolutions, epistemological and otherwise, as associated with the search for novelty and the cult of originality cannot but regard any tradition as essentially conservative and unitary, the proverbial ''night in which all cows are grey.'' What this understanding fails to acknowledge is that conflict and incoherences are present within traditions, that traditions are not static and univocal but many-sided and ''dialectical,'' and that changes can occur not only between but within traditions. A tradition in this sense will incorporate innovation and adaptation as part of its self-definition. It allows for elements of both continuity and diversity in the characterization of, say, scientific practices, without which that history would be punctuated by a series of inexplicable and hence irrational ''breaks'' in those practices themselves as well as in the personal lives of its practitioners. The ironical outcome of Althusser's understanding of the relationship between revolution and tradition is that reason, which can only be embodied in those self-contained problematics, is the product of an essential unreason which is at the basis of one of those periodic epistemological crises of science. At the moment of its highest creativity, science is at its most irrational.

It is by no means clear that Marx regarded his own discoveries as representing this type of radical rejection of the tradition of either classical economics or German philosophy. His conception of the relation between tradition and revolution is indeed well captured in Hegel's dialectical approach to history as a process in which the past is continually "aufgehoben" in the threefold sense of being negated, preserved, yet superseded.[20] This approach, which has the advantage of embodying a certain continuity within discontinuity, was not lost even upon the mature Marx, who continued to speak of the "aufhebung des Staates," a phrase quite distinct from Engels' better-known formulation of a "withering away" of the state.[21] This phrase cannot simply be dismissed as a "symptom" of the old prescientific dispensation, but indicates positively Marx's mature dependence upon the central categories of the Hegelian dialectic. This dependence Althusser cannot explain, although he does his best to explain it away. In a passage where he attempts to explicate Marx's position vis-à-vis Hegel, he writes:

> The "supersession" of Hegel *was not at all an "Aufhebung" in the Hegelian sense,* that is, an exposition of *the truth of* what is contained in Hegel; *it was not a supersession of error towards its truth, on the contrary, it was a supersession of illusion towards its truth, or better, rather than a "supersession" of illusion towards truth it was a dissipation of illusion and a retreat from the dissipated illusion back towards reality:* the term "supersession" is thus robbed of all meaning. . . . I hope it is now clear that if we are truly to be able to think this dramatic genesis of Marx's thought, it is essential to reject the term *"supersede"* and turn to that of *discoveries,* to renounce the spirit of Hegelian logic implied in the innocent but sly conception of "supersession" *(Aufhebung)* [*FM,* 77–78, 82].

Without meaning to belabor the point, I find it curious that Althusser continues to describe Marx's development as "dialec-

---

[20]G. W. F. Hegel, *The Science of Logic,* trans. A. V. Miller (London: George Allen & Unwin, 1969), pp. 106–08.
[21]For Engels' formula see *Anti-Dühring* (Moscow: Progress Publishers, 1962), p. 385.

tical.'' By insisting upon the ''blinding novelty'' of Marx's discoveries, he would seem to reject a truly dialectical development in the ordinary sense of the term. This is not to deny the usefulness of occasional conceptual innovation. One could easily grant that every set of problems has from time to time to be reformulated. Yet if these reformulations or reconstructions depart too far from customary or traditional usage, it should come as no surprise if they end by raising more problems than they solve. Such, we have seen, has been the case with Althusser, whose talk of epistemological ruptures in knowledge has led to a form of irrationalism as the foundation of all reason. My view here does not favor a static and unbending view of tradition against a dynamic and innovative one. I only wish to stress that without some underlying continuity that links Marx to his predecessors as well as the mature Marx to his past, his radical conceptual discoveries could hardly be regarded as discoveries at all. A tradition, so conceived, cannot seriously erode the idea of revolution as a means of conceiving the unity of continuity and discontinuity. It can only detract from the fatuous notion that one can clear the ground and start over again without regard to the conditions of one's own genesis.

4

A System of Epistemological Marxism

The nature of the Althusserian enterprise and its place within the broader context of contemporary Marxian debate should now be clear. This enterprise, we have seen, is based upon a reading of the Marxian corpus at once critical and rigorous. While Althusser's reading contains distinct stages, behind all the diverse problems considered and answers posed, it has remained unified in a single direction—"the investigation of Marx's philosophical thought" *(FM,* 21). The task of defining the novel and peculiar character of Marx's philosophy has remained the cornerstone of the entire Althusserian edifice. *"What is Marxist philosophy? Has it any theoretical right to existence? And if it does exist in principle, how can its specificity be defined?"* *(FM,* 31).

The need for a critical examination of this sort stems, according to Althusser, from the very nature of Marx's achievements. These achievements involve the founding of two distinct disciplines, which are worked out to varying degrees in Marx's writings. There is first a science of history and politics, which Althusser designates by the traditional name "historical materialism," and second a philosophy of that science, or "dialectical materialism" *(FM,* 33). But while Marx's science of history was developed at length in *Capital* and other writings, his philosophy was left unfortunately in abeyance, existing, so we are told, alongside of or within his historical texts in a largely untheorized "practical state" (*FM*, 174). This philosophy represents the "absence" in Marx's texts that Althusser's "symptomatic" reading would discover. The importance of this philosophy will become clearer later on. Suffice it to say for now that without a properly articulated dialectical materialism to reflect upon and set limits to the conditions of theoretical inquiry, the science of historical materialism will be left to develop spontaneously without the adequate methdological and epistemological tools necessary to chart the directions of its advance. For this reason, then, "the theoretical future of historical materialism depends today on the deepening of dialectical materialism" (*RC*, 77).

Althusser's claim is, then, that historical materialism is the science inaugurated by Marx in *Capital*. Indeed, the signal importance of historical materialism is that it represents the founding of a new scientific discipline comparable to Thales' discovery of mathematics and Galileo's discovery of physics. The absence of an articulated philosophy that could disclose the "logic" or "method" of this science is no accident. Philosophy always follows in the wake of scientific revolutions, which explains why the philosophy of Marxism had to wait almost a century to receive its commission. This theoretical dependence of philosophy on science, characteristic we might add, of most species of positivism, is maintained throughout all of Althusser's work but is nowhere more emphatically stated than in the Foreword to the English edition of *For Marx:*

> I should add that, just as the foundation of mathematics by Thales "induced" the birth of Platonic philosophy, just as the foundation of physics by Galileo "induced" the birth of Cartesian philosophy, etc., so the foundation of the science of history by Marx has "induced" the birth of a new, theoretically and practically revolutionary philosophy, Marxist philosophy or dialectical materialism. The fact that, from the standpoint of its theoretical elaboration, this unprecedented philosophy still lags behind the Marxist science of history (historical materialism) is explained by histor-

ico-political reasons and *also* simultaneously by theoretical reasons: great philosophical revolutions are always preceded and "borne along" by the great scientific revolutions "active" in them, but long theoretical labour and long historical maturing are required before they can acquire an explicit and adequate form [*FM*, 14].

The conception of philosophy advanced in this passage is entirely consonant with the whole neo-Kantian reduction of philosophy to methodology. Philosophy is no longer understood as an independent inquiry into the nature of things. It is for science to state what is and what is not. Philosophy is only "borne along" by science and must content itself with addressing second-order problems of scientific discourse. Following Bachelard and the whole school of French epistemology, Althusser states that philosophy simultaneously directs itself to both a theory of science and a history of that theory. As Althusser's collegue Pierre Machery has put it: "Today, philosophers are those who do the history of theories and at the same time the theory of this history . . . to philosophize is to study in what conditions and to what conditions scientific problems are posed."[1]

There is, however, an initial problem with this conception. By positing dialectical materialism as the philosophy of historical materialism, Althusser sets into motion a self-referential system in which he derives an epistemology from *Capital* and then justifies the latter's claim to scientific status with the assistance of this same epistemology. The result is, of course, to immunize science altogether from the epistemological criticism and control of philosophy. Instead of seeking the empirical foundations for science or asking how is science itself possible, Althusser is prepared to take for granted the existence of science as a "theoretical practice" and to reduce philosophy to a theory of this practice, or as we are now prepared to say, to a "theory of theoretical practice." Before we can interrogate this unique conception of Marx-

---

[1]*Lire le Capital* (Paris: François Maspero, 1965), 1: 216.

ist philosophy any further, however, we must pause to get straight what Althusser means by a "practice."

Practice

The fundamental core of Marxist philosophy is the concept of practice, where this is understood to mean the production and reproduction of social life. The "primacy of practice" is intended by Althusser to show that societies typically present themselves as composed of distinct and irreducible levels of practice, of which at least four "instances" can be discerned. Thus Marx is said to have founded a "historico-dialectical materialism of praxis: that is, a theory of human practice (economic practice, political practice, ideological practice, scientific practice) in their characteristic articulations, based on the specific articulations of the unity of human society" (*FM*, 229).

The various modes of "articulation" or combination of these practices comprise the overall "social formation" or "mode of production." The latter term has a special significance for Althusser, indicating not the economy alone, but the entire configuration or combination of practices and the relations among them. The state or condition of the overall system is a function of the particular way in which these four practices interrelate. Indeed, with one important exception, the entire conceptualization is reminiscent of Talcott Parsons' division of the social "system" into the economic, political, cultural, and social subsystems. And as with Parsons also, explanation is satisfied when the functions of each of these subsystems and their particular interactions are exhaustively described.[2]

[2]On the similarity between Althusser, Parsons, and functionalist theory see Alfred Schmidt, "Der strukturalistische Angriff auf die Geschichte," *Beiträge zur marxistischen Erkenntnistheorie,* Alfred Schmidt, ed. (Frankfurt: Suhrkamp, 1969), pp. 209, 265; Anthony Giddens, *Central Problems in Social Theory: Action, Structure and Contradiction in Social Analysis* (Berkeley: University of California Press, 1979), pp. 50–53; see also David Easton, "The Political System Besieged by the State," *Political Theory,* 9 (1981): 303–25.

A System of Epistemological Marxism

The isolation of certain distinct and "autonomous" types of human practice does not blind Althusser to the need for a "general definition of practice" within which these different modalities of social life can be conceived. If the practices are not unified by a common substance, they at least share a "homologous form," which Althusser describes as follows:

> By *practice* in general I shall mean any process of *transformation* of a determinate given raw material into a determinate *product*, a transformation effected by a determinate human labour, using determinate means (of "production"). In any practice thus conceived, the *determinant* moment (or element) is neither the raw material nor the product, but the practice in the narrow sense; the moment of the *labour of transformation* itself, which sets to work, in a specific structure, men, means and a technical method of utilizing the means. This general definition of practice covers the possibility of particularity: there are different practices which are really distinct, even though they belong organically to the same complex totality. Thus, "social practice," the complex unity of the practices existing in a determinate society, contains a large number of distinct practices [*FM*, 166–67].

In *For Marx*, Althusser makes use of a tripartite division to elucidate further the common form the practices share. Each practice entails the transformation of a given raw material or object (Generality I) by means of a labor process involving laborers and means of production (Generality II) into a specific product (Generality III). But within this formal similarity, there is a real dissimilarity of content separating these four practices. Economic practice involves putting to work labor power and means of material production to transform natural materials into socially useful products. Political practice works on its own type of raw material, given social relations, to produce its own type of product, new social relations. Ideological practice transforms existing modes of representation and perception by which social agents organize conceptually their experience into new perspectives and outlooks. And finally theoretical or scientific practice combines its own objects and means of production to create its own products—

knowledge. Of these last two modes of practice, Althusser writes: "Ideology is not always taken seriously as an existing practice: but to recognize this is the indispensable prior condition for any theory of ideology. The existence of a *theoretical practice* is taken seriously even more rarely: but this prior condition is indispensable to an understanding of what theory itself, and its relation to 'social practice' are for Marxism"*(FM, 167).*

This last point, the existence of an autonomous practice of theory, is, we shall see, one of the most problematical features of Althusserian Marxism. For if theory is truly autonomous of the other practices which constitute the social whole, then what is the source of its claim to be in touch with the reality which precedes it and of which it is the second-order expression? What also of the relation between theory and practice, the claim of theory to guide and inform practical life? Althusser's answer to these questions is, briefly, that there is no such unity between theory and practice, at least as this is ordinarily understood and that theory bears no relation to any other practice save itself. To put it another way, we might say that the unity of theory and practice takes place not *between* the various "levels" of social production, but first of all *within* each of them.

> It is perfectly legitimate to say that the production of knowledge which is peculiar to theoretical practice constitutes a process that takes place *entirely in thought,* just as we can say, *mutatis mutandis,* that the process of economic production takes place entirely in the economy, even though it implies, and precisely in the specific determinations of its structure, necessary relations with nature and other structures (legal-political and ideological) which, taken together, constitute the global structure of a social formation belonging to a determinate mode of production [*RC,* 42].

This, of course, leaves the reader entirely unsatisfied, since it appears to finesse the whole question of theory and practice out of existence through a play on words. Obviously theory takes place entirely within thought just as economic production takes place entirely within the economy. No one ever thought otherwise. But to say this is a mere analytical definition and as such a tautology. It leaves altogether untouched the more troublesome problem of the relation between the various practices within the "global structure" of the social formation and what holds them together as a formation.

In any case the structural autonomy of the different practices is intended to lead to a richer and more complex understanding of Marxism than that offered by previous commentators. In particular it is directed against those orthodox Marxists who would reduce all the basic forms of human-life activity to the economic, explaining all else as merely epiphenomenal or "superstructural." In contrast to this restriction of production to material production, Althusser insists upon the real differences between the levels of practice as the key to the understanding of the social whole. "We must recognize," he says, "that there is no practice in general, but only distinctive practices" for "there can be no scientific conception of practice without a precise distinction between the distinct practices" (*RC*, 58). Under the guise of asserting the breaks between the various levels of practice, Althusser is able to guarantee the autonomy of theoretical reflection. The great advantage of this approach is that it rescues Marxism from the sterile reductionism which conceives all practice along economic lines. Its great disadvantage is that in place of the primacy of the economic, it substitutes a broader, some might say "pluralistic," conception of society, resembling not so much Marxian as Parsonian sociology.

There are further difficulties as well. The concept of practice represents the alpha and omega of Althusserian Marxism. It governs not only the conditions pertaining to the production of social life but the production of theoretical knowledge also. The function this concept is intended to play is not difficult to discern. It is intended to supply Althusser with an apodictic starting point from which all further investigation might be carried out. The problem is that there is always something necessarily arbitrary about such starting points. "The basis for the whole tripartite Althusserian architecture," André Glucksmann has remarked, "thus arises fully armed from the simple but forced use of a dictionary. It 'happens' that everything is production, it 'happens' that every production is divided into three. That is how it is." This criticism, while damaging, is not fatal. We cannot ask an a priori principle to account for its own genesis precisely because an a priori principle has no genesis, at least not an empirical genesis. Glucksmann admits this much. "True," he continues, "no *a priori* truth is deducible, but it can be examined."[3] Our task must be, then, to examine the use to which this concept is put in order to determine whether the claims made on its behalf are justified or not.

The Problem of Knowledge

"To conceive Marx's philosophy in its specificity . . . is to conceive knowledge as production" (*RC*, 58). In thus describing knowledge itself as a type of production, Althusser has in mind two aims, one positive, the other critical. His positive goal is to highlight the "autonomous" character of theory. Theory, to be sure, shares with the other practices a common or homologous form, but in contrast to the other practices it works on its own raw materials (an existing stock of concepts) by means of a set of analytical tools in order to produce a new knowledge or science. The autonomy of theory is logically tied to another feature of science—its "internalist" criteria of verification. Knowledge is not verified either empirically by reference to "fact" or "brute data" or pragmatically as an expression of certain social needs or interests. Rather it is said to contain its own canons and protocols of validation that are strictly "internal" to itself alone.

The claim that "knowledge is production" is used also as a polemical weapon against two prevailing epistemologies, or theories of knowledge. The first is empiricism, which was founded

---

[3]"A Ventriloquist Structuralism," *New Left Review*, 72 (1972): 71.

by Hume but may be traced back to Locke's "plain historical method" enumerated in the *Essay Concerning Human Understanding,* which takes as its point of departure the psychological origins of knowledge in perception. By an analysis of the genesis of all knowledge in perception, empiricists were forced to consider the psychological preconditions of knowledge even prior to its validity. The second school is historicism, which radicalized the teachings of the empiricists by demonstrating (or attempting to demonstrate) that even our powers of perception, previously regarded as constant whatever the differences in time, place, and circumstance, are themselves socially or culturally determined. Since man is in his essence a socially and historically determined being, it follows that his mind and the very categories of his thought will be subject to constant fluctuation and change.[4]

The importance of these two rival epistemologies will be treated more fully below, although we can already see why Althusser insists that scientific knowledge must be above all taint of either empiricism or historicism. For if the changing substance of reality is allowed to infect the conceptual models used to grasp and explain it, the result will be to make science itself impossible. It becomes necessary, therefore, to treat the product or "object of knowledge" apart from the context of its production. This, it should be said, is not merely a distinction that Althusser is foisting upon Marxism. In fact in the Afterword to *Capital,* volume one, Marx makes exactly this distinction, anticipating the later distinction between the "context of discovery" and the "context of justification." In answering a number of critics who he believed erred in describing his "dialectical method," Marx distinguishes between his "mode of presentation" (*Darstellungsweise*) and his "mode of inquiry" (*Forschungsweise*). The mode of presentation, the logical structure of the inquiry, he argues, must be kept radically apart from its conditions of gene-

---

[4]For an excellent account of the transition from empiricism to historicism in contemporary political theory see Eugene F. Miller, "Positivism, Historicism, and Political Inquiry," *American Political Science Review,* 3 (1972): 796–817.

sis. "Of course," he says, "the method of presentation must differ in form from that of inquiry. The latter has to appropriate the material in detail, to analyse its different forms of development, to trace out their inner connection. Only after this work is done, can the actual movement be adequately described."[5]

In this passage Marx emphasizes the distinction between the *Darstellungsweise* and the *Forschungsweise* in order to avoid an unreflective historicism in which knowledge simply runs parallel to the chronological order of events. Some critics like Lucio Colletti have suggested that Marx's intention here is to "invert" the order of theory construction or the logical deduction of Marx's categories and the actual temporal sequence by which they were produced.[6] Indeed this interpretation would appear to be vindicated by the very next paragraph in Marx's Afterword, in which he suggests that not only is his use of the dialectic different from that of Hegel but is its "direct opposite." Thus rather than use a logico-deductive order, directly reflecting the historical genesis of reality, thought would project itself backward so "the subject matter is ideally reflected as in a mirror." The problem with Colletti's interpretation here is that it is insufficient to establish the specificity of the Marxian dialectic. As Althusser has consistently maintained, this metaphor of "inversion" is not of Marxist origin but goes back to Feuerbach's "transformative method" (*FM*, 35–36, 89–91, 107–9, 173–75, 180–82, 190–92).

Althusser's task of reconstructing a specifically Marxian epistemology has been considerably complicated by the fact that, with the exception of a few scattered observations, Marx himself never directly reflected on the problem of the validity of knowledge claims. Jürgen Habermas has suggested, plausibly in my view, that Marx failed to do so because he too readily assimilated the structure of his own thought to that of the natural sciences.

[5]Page 19.
[6]*Hegel and Marxism*, trans. Lawrence Garner (London: New Left Books, 1973), pp. 113–37.

Taking these sciences as the paradigm for knowledge, rather than as only one possible form of cognition, there was no reason for this science in turn to reflect back upon the conditions of its own validity. In *Knowledge and Human Interests* he goes so far as to hold not only Marx but Hegel responsible for the "dissolution" of epistemological reflection upon the conditions of possible knowledge, turning it into a kind of methodological reflection on already established fields of thought.[7] There is, I think, much truth in this judgment even if it does cut against Althusser's denial of any positive or lasting influence of Hegel on Marx. While Althusser does not acknowledge it as such, Hegel's polemic against traditional epistemology or "first philosophy" in the Introduction to the *Phenomenology of Mind* is too close to his own repudiation of the "problem of knowledge" to go without a word of comment. If I am right in this claim, the radical disjunction between Hegel and Marx asserted by Althusser may itself require revision.

In the *Phenomenology,* Hegel attempted to replace traditional epistemology with what he called the "phenomenological" self-reflection of mind. Traditional epistemology, as this was understood by modern philosophy from Descartes to Kant, sought to ascertain the conditions of knowledge even prior to our acceptance of already acquired cognitions. Epistemology was conceived in this sense as a "critical" enterprise since it not only sought a firm foundation on which acquired knowledge could be made to stand but sought to establish limits beyond which it could not go. In summarizing this traditional conception of philosophy Hegel remarks: "It is natural to assume that before philosophy enters on its subject proper—namely, actual knowledge of reality—it must first come to an understanding of knowledge itself."[8] This program is a familiar one. Without a firm foundation

---

[7]*Knowledge and Human Interests,* trans. Jeremy J. Shapiro (Boston: Beacon Press, 1971), esp. ch. 1.

[8]*The Phenomenology of Mind,* trans. J. B. Baille (London: George Allen & Unwin, 1971), p. 131.

on which it may be grounded, the whole purpose of modern science will appear as irrational or lacking any justification as knowledge.

Hegel's polemic against this conception of philosophy proceeds by two stages. First taking Kant and the activist conception of mind to task, Hegel remarks that if we conceive knowledge as "an instrument by which we apprehend reality" we will inevitably end by distorting the reality we seek to grasp. Likewise, however, if we adopt a passive Humean conception of mind as "a medium through which the light of the truth reaches us," this medium will imperceptibly end by filtering the truth in such a way that we will not be able to grasp what it is in itself.[9] While Hegel does not develop these remarks at much length, his overall point is simple and decisive. The theory of knowledge which regards itself as an inquiry into the conditions of possible knowledge is itself a type of knowledge. It cannot, therefore, lay claim to some privileged position vis-à-vis existing knowledges without falling into circularity.

Hegel brings this point out particularly well in a reference to Kant from the *Lectures on the History of Philosophy:* "What is demanded is thus the following: we should know the cognitive faculty before we know. It is like wanting to swim before going in the water. The investigation of the faculty of knowledge is itself knowledge, and cannot therefore arrive at its goal because it is this goal already."[10]

Every consistent epistemology is caught in this circle. Take for example Hume and the school of classical empiricism, who argue that everything that is to count as knowledge must be capable of verification through perceptual experience. The aim is to establish some principle or criterion of what can and cannot count as authentic knowledge. But since the Verification Principle cannot itself be verified on perceptual grounds, it must of

[9]Page 131.

[10]*Lectures on the History of Philosophy*, trans. E. S. Haldane and Frances H. Simpson (London: Routledge & Kegan Paul Ltd., 1955), 3: 428.

necessity fall prey to circularity since its presupposes precisely what it is intended to establish. The same is true for Descartes' theory and classical rationalism, which aspires to an understanding of such clarity or "self-evidence" as to carry within it the certainty of the undeniable. But the principle of self-evidence cannot be used in turn to establish the principle of self-evidence without giving way to circularity or to some other unspecified criterion that can establish it.

Hegel's approach to knowledge, then, is to abandon traditional epistemology and to appeal directly to "science" (*Wissenschaft*) as an already constituted "form" (*Gestalt*) of knowledge. But this approach would appear to give rise to difficulties. For if science is already constituted or has "come on the scene," then how do we know this? Moreover, what are the claims by which it has established itself as a knowledge? Hegel himself recognizes these as real problems. He remarks that no "investigation and test of the reality of knowledge" seems possible "without some presupposition which is laid down as an ultimate criterion."[11] But what, we might ask, could such a criterion be without falling back into the same circularity mentioned above? His answer is that knowledge itself provides its own criterion by which it is to be judged so as to render any type of "first philosophy" superfluous. "Not only in this respect" are "concept and object, the criterion and what is to be tested ready to hand in consciousness itself" but, Hegel asserts, we do not even have to do the testing "since consciousness tests and examines itself, all we are left to do is simply and solely to look on."[12]

This conception of knowledge testing itself or providing its own criteria or standards of acceptability strikes us as odd. Nevertheless, Hegel takes it seriously. He tries to clarify his point as follows. Traditional epistemology presents knowledge as involving a distinction between itself on the one side and the thing which it is a knowledge of on the other. In other words, knowl-

[11]*Phenomenology*, 139.
[12]Page 141.

edge at least appears always to be a knowledge of something outside itself. The task would seem, then, to bring about as close a possible harmony or correspondence between our concepts which are "for us" and reality as it is "in itself." But Hegel wants to suggest that this dichotomy is wrongly posed or is only a dichotomy in appearance. The distinction between "for us" and "in itself," appearances to the contrary notwithstanding, is not a distinction between a self-contained subject and a self-contained object, but is a distinction that takes place *within* knowledge itself. The suggestion is not to see whether the object corresponds to its concept or the concept to its object, but to examine the various forms of consciousness as they have appeared phenomenologically to us in terms of the criteria internal to them. This procedure of an internal or immanent examination of knowledge will allow us to see whether knowledge lives up to its own self-imposed standards of adequacy without foisting some external or merely presupposed standards on it.

This brief excursus into Hegel's critique of traditional epistemology should help us to understand Althusser's defense of the autonomy of historical materialism or Marx's "theoretical practice." Like Hegel, he is concerned with the way in which "science" presents itself and wants to know what are the grounds of its justification. And like Hegel also, he believes that these grounds cannot be discovered by purely a priori investigation into the nature and limits of knowledge but will make themselves known only by probing already existing modes of cognition. Like many "positivists" Althusser assumes the methodological self-sufficiency of science and, as we have seen, denies the necessity of asking whether science itself is possible.

Like everything else in the Althusserian universe, science is a form of practice the first "moment" of which consists of the "raw materials" or evidence out of which knowledge is produced. The raw material presents itself first as a series of discrete mental events or commonplace concepts. The point to be noted here is that evidence never presents itself as a world of "facts" or "objects" open to direct inspection, but rather as an already existing world of concepts and linguistic entities. It is not something immediately "given" but is a world already mediated by interpretation and judgment of an "ideological" nature. The raw material of theoretical practice is a type of thought, but thought at a very low level of mentation—what (following the phenomenologists) we might call the position of the "natural attitude" or of "prethetic" reflection. This natural attitude may be characterized as essentially prescientific or pretheoretical not only because it exists prior to the coming into being of science but because it is presupposed in all of our thinking about science.[13]

Characteristically, Althusser displays little concern with the diverse origins and natures of these commonplace concepts that form the basis for knowledge. It is an inert, pliant kind of stuff, fashioned by the exigencies of experience and the needs of society. He is adamant, however, that these concepts are not scientific. The work of any science consists in "elaborating its own scientific facts through a critique of the ideological 'facts' elaborated by an earlier ideological theoretical practice." To elaborate these "facts" is, moreover, "to elaborate its own 'theory' since a scientific fact—and not the self-styled pure phenomenon—can only be identified in the field of theoretical practice" (*FM*, 184). Thus, whereas theoretical practice may begin with existing systems of representation, its aim is to produce a "corpus of concepts" which both "rejects the old one even as it 'englobes' it, that is, defines its 'relativity' and the (subordinate) limits of its validity" (*FM*, 185).

These passages are obscure, and it is not immediately evident what Althusser is arguing against. On closer inspection, however, it becomes clear that he is attacking a traditional conception of the relation between knowledge and reality. This traditional conception is at the basis of a conceptual problematic known as "empiricism," according to which the fundamental building blocks of knowledge are sense data acquired through experience.

[13]Cf. Maurice Merleau-Ponty, *The Phenomenology of Perception*, trans. Colin Smith (New York: Humanities Press, 1962), p. viii.

These data are understood as basic units of information which are not the products of prejudgment or interpretation precisely because they are the foundations on which all judgments and interpretaions are made. The attractiveness of the empirical model has been, of course, its attempt to ground all knowledge in a set of ''logical facts'' or ''atomic propositions'' that could be taken as incorrigible because they lie outside our subjective intuitions or insights and against which our intuitions and insights can be checked. Verification of knowledge, then, must be grounded ultimately in the acquisition of facts whose credibility cannot be undermined by offering further interpretation or reasoning because such facts are the brute data from which further interpretation and reasoning proceeds. The problem with the empiricist conception of knowledge, as we have already seen, is that the Verification Principle itself cannot be empirically verified, in which case it either presupposes the knowledge whose truth it claims to establish or must have recourse to some further set of criteria by which that truth can be judged. Circularity or regress seem to be the conclusions to which empiricism leads.

But this is not all Althusser has to say about empiricism. The empiricist conception of knowledge is tied logically by Althusser to another problematic known as ''historicism.'' Empiricism could retain its viability so long as the facts or the brute data of experience could be regarded as constant. So long as these data remained fixed, they could yield knowledge that could be taken as true independently of time, place, and circumstance and subject only to revision in the light of further experience. Once these data were conceived as themselves subject to change, however, such knowledge could no longer be guaranteed. And if reality is subject to continual change, so must the categories of the mind that seek to grasp and explain it. By insisting on the historicity of the mind, then, historicists were led to argue that each age or epoch or culture has a truth relative to it alone or develops a unique ''world view'' or *Weltanschauung* created by philosophers and artists reflecting upon the special circumstances of their own time. Whereas empiricists could speak of truth as representing a congruence between subject and object or in terms of an agreement or correspondence between thought and things, historicism could argue no such thing. In fact early historicists under the influence of Nietzsche regarded the search for truth as impossible. Since everything is in a process of eternal flux, any attempt by the mind to conceptualize this flux would result in an arrest of experience and therefore in a distortion of it. Accordingly, the very concepts of scientific thought came to be seen as "reifying" or "objectifying"—an attempt to turn what is sheer movement into a stable and predictable order subject to mathematical manipulation and control.[14]

Curiously, Althusser identifies Engels as the chief culprit responsible for the propagation of this problematic. By reducing all knowledge to the same coming into being and passing away that characterizes the "material life process" in general, Engels eliminates any independent basis for thought. Thus in the Preface to the third volume of *Capital* he could say that, "It is self-evident that where things and their interrelations are conceived, not as fixed, but as changing, their mental reflections, the concepts, are likewise subject to change and transformation." And similarly in a passage from the *Anti-Dühring* he states: "To science definitions are worthless because always inadequate. The only real definition is the development of the thing itself, but this is no longer a definition" (cited in *RC*, 113).

This type of mind-numbing historicism fits in well with the widely shared belief that different theories are always directed at or addressed to particular social groups. Accordingly, the cognitive validity of a theory derives not from its explanatory power but from its ability to assist in the formation of the world views of the group or groups in question. There can be, then, no indepen-

---

[14]See Lukács, *History and Class Consciousness,* pp. 110–49; Max Horkheimer, "The Latest Attack on Metaphysics," *Critical Theory: Selected Essays,* trans. Matthew J. O'Connell et al. (New York: Seabury Press, 1972), pp. 132–87; Jürgen Habermas, "The Analytical Theory of Science and Dialectics," and "A Positivistically Bisected Rationalism," *The Positivist Dispute in German Sociology,* G. Adey and D. Frisby, eds. (London: Heinemann, 1976).

dent or neutral criteria in terms of which these world views can be assessed since our very epistemic principles are themselves part of a distinct history shaped by the influence of the same political and cultural traditions which it ought to be their task to judge. Since our basic epistemic standards are just part of our tradition and have no absolute basis or transcendent warrant, the only means we have of adjudicating between them is by invoking some pragmatic criterion such as success in practice or assisting a class in the attainment of its specific goals or ideals. Marxism is said to be "scientific" therefore because it assists the proletariat in their struggle for power. But once these specific aims are achieved, the theory itself becomes redundant and as such is destined to disappear.

One frequent objection to Marxism was that while it submitted competing theories to historical analysis showing the limited horizons within which they developed and the particular needs which they served, it failed to carry through this program consistently and apply it to itself. Mannheim, for example, has shown that this type of thoroughgoing historicism was impossible for Marx for it would have revealed that his own doctrine was just as partial and ideologically biased as those he criticized.[15] It was Lukács who eventually used this radical historicism to show that Marxism itself was not outside the stream of history that it sought to comprehend. In an essay entitled "The Changing Function of Historical Materialism," we read:

> The substantive truths of historical materialism are of the same type as were the truths of classical economics in Marx's view: they are truths within a particular social order and system of production. As such, but only as such, their claim to validity is absolute. But this does not preclude the emergence of societies in which by virtue of their different social structures other categories and other systems of truth prevail. To what conclusion should we then come? Above all we must investigate the social premises of

[15]*Ideology and Utopia,* trans. Louis Wirth and Edward Shils (New York: Harcourt, Brace and World, 1936), pp. 276–78.

the substance of historical materialism just as Marx himself scrutinised the social and economic preconditions of the truths of classical economics.[16]

The same radical historicism, we note, underlies the problematic of Sartre's *Search for a Method*. Here Sartre designates Marxism as the preeminent philosophy of our age. Since philosophies are great "moments" or episodes in the history of thought and culture, their own time "apprehended in thought" as Hegel put it, they cannot be "gone beyond" until the conditions that produced them have themselves been surpassed. The same is true for Marxism, which Sartre takes to be absolute or "unsurpassable" for us, but not unsurpassable simply. The suggestion, arguably more Nietzschean or Heideggerian, is that even the truths of Marxism are only relative, truths "as such," set against the continually changing horizons of history. When Marxism does finally disappear, Sartre confidently predicts that "a philosophy of liberty will takes its place," although he also freely admits that as yet "we have no means, no intellectual instrument, no concrete experience which allows us to conceive of this freedom or of this philosophy."[17]

The entire thrust of Althusser's analysis is away from the search for either epistemological foundations or the social context of knowledge and toward something closer to Hegel's method of internal or immanent critique of consciousness. By an internal or immanent critique I mean an approach to knowledge which seeks to avoid the pitfalls of both classical empiricism, with its search for a set of fixed "guarantees" by which knowledge can be verified, and radical historicism, which would dissolve all fixed reference points for truth or accept them only in the provisional sense of truths "as such." Althusser's response to these two sides of the "problem of knowledge" is to argue that we need not assume that there are *either* fixed guarantees *or* none at all, but that knowledge contains within itself its own immanent criteria

[16]*History and Class Consciousness,* pp. 228–29.
[17]Pages 7, 30, 34.

with which to validate its product. The result is something like a phenomenological analysis of science as an autonomous form of theoretical practice distinct from the processes that brought that consciousness itself into being. This characterization makes it clear that epistemological thinking for Althusser does not aim at grounding or discovering transcendental foundations for knowledge. Rather he presupposes the existence of this knowledge as his data and would help us to attain some kind of clear self-consciousness about it.

The idea, then, that theoretical practice contains its own internal criteria of reflective acceptability is for Althusser the major epistemological discovery of *Reading Capital:*

> *Theoretical practice* is indeed its own criterion, and contains in itself definite protocols with which to *validate* the quality of its product. . . . No mathematician in the world waits until physics has *verified* a theorem to declare it proved, although whole areas of mathematics are applied in physics: the truth of his theorem is a hundred percent provided by criteria purely *internal* to the practice of mathematical proof, hence by the *criterion of mathematical practice*, i.e., by the forms required by existing mathematical scientificity [*RC*, 59].

By insisting that theory supplies its own internal criteria of validity, Althusser is enabled to avoid the pitfalls of the traditional theory of knowledge. More positively, by adopting the standpoint of an internal critique Althusser not only provides a possible alternative to empiricist and historicist epistemologies, but is in accord with much of the recent work in this area. In his later works Wittgenstein, for example, argued that epistemic standards must be sought not in some sort of "metalanguage" or first philosophy but within established ways of proceeding. The use of language itself provides criteria of reflective acceptability so that it is necessary only to check our judgments against existing linguistic standards to see whether or not we are justified in making them. While we shall see later on just where Althusser's account of theoretical practice differs from ideology or from the world of the natural attitude or ordinary language, where he joins issue not only with Hegel but with Wittgenstein is in seeing all thought, even science, as arising ultimately out of ordinary perceptual judgments or a world that is to some extent already preinterpreted.

Clearly there is much in Althusser's view to recommend it, although there is also much that is unclear. First it could be argued that, while the logico-mathematical procedures he refers to may be valid for certain restricted areas of scientific inquiry, they cannot be true for history which is bound by the demands of fact or evidence. If there is no body of hard factual evidence that is taken to be objective and independent of the inquirer into it, then we have no compelling grounds on which to distinguish fact from fantasy. This objection is no more than what is called the correspondence or foundational view of truth. Althusser could respond that to regard the world of fact or evidence as having an independent existence "outside the head" (Marx), against which the truth and falsity of our statements can be checked, is to misdescribe what a fact is. No matter how it might appear, the world of fact is never merely a "given," something that exists whether or not anybody takes notice of it. Facts for Althusser have to be established or "produced" and then only after a lengthy process of thinking and judging has gone on. A fact cannot, therefore, be used to test the adequacy of a theory because it is only within the framework or "problematic" of a theory that facts are brought to light. Facts themselves have to be expressed and once this happens the world of fact is transformed. It is transformed by being interpreted.

To some extent, Althusser's problems derive from the philosophical source from which his theory is culled. The statement that truth is its own criterion is taken directly from Spinoza's *Ethics*, in which, Althusser points out, we can read that truth is the criterion both of itself and falsehood (*veritas norma sui et falsi*) (*ESC*, 132–41). The force of this aphorism is to show that an idea or statement is never true or false simply as it stands. An idea is regarded as false if it does not fit in or cohere with other ideas of the same sort. Accordingly, ideas can be at best relatively false, false in comparison to a more coherent set of beliefs. It follows, then, that the truth of an idea consists in its systematic character, that it is fully integrated or logically "concatenated" into a perfect order of ideas. But Spinoza could hold to this position only by enlisting the support of a rigorously monistic metaphysics in which all truths are seen as part of a single system. "The order and connection of things is the same as the order and connection of ideas."[18] There is no possibility, then, that the order of thought may ever fall away from or fail to correspond to the order of things, since there is a preexisting harmony between them. They are both modes or attributes of a single underlying substance. The result of holding on to this coherence theory of truth is, of course, that science or reason itself must lose its "autonomy" with that which it is called upon to explain. It must become, then, entirely passive or contemplative in relation to its object. As we shall see, Althusser is at pains to extricate himself from the implications of this "radical inwardness," although his insistence on the Spinozistic origins of his thought pushes him in this direction. The question he does not answer is whether it is possible to contend with Spinoza that truth rests in logical coherence without committing himself to the system of metaphysics of which that claim is a part.

The result of Althusser's insistence on the "internal" criteria of truth is to sever theory from the controls of evidence, thus rendering theory itself immune to empirical falsification. In a number of passages from *Reading Capital,* Althusser stresses the absolute independence of theory from fact. "We must once again," he says, "purify our concept of the theory of history, and purify it radically, of any contamination by the obviousness of empirical history, since we know that this 'empirical history' is merely the bare face of the empiricist ideology of history. . . .

---

[18]*Ethics,* Part II, Prop. 7: "Ordo et connexio idearum rerum idem est, ac ordo connexio rerum." For some interesting remarks see Umberto Eco, *La struttura assente* (Milano: Bompiani, 1968), p. 360.

We must grasp in all its rigour the absolute necessity of liberating the theory of history from any compromise with 'empirical' temporality" (*RC*, 105). At the same time, we must also free ourselves from the power of a "prejudice . . . which is the basis for contemporary historicism and which would have us confuse the object of knowledge with the real object by attributing to the object of knowledge the same 'qualities' as the real object of which it is the knowledge" (*RC*, 106). Accordingly, historians and other readers have continually misunderstood *Capital* in their attempts to find "correspondences" between the logico-deductive order of Marx's categories and the real historical development of the subject matter.

> They did not see that history features in *Capital* as an object of theory, not as a real object, as an "abstract" (conceptual) object and not as a real-concrete object; and that the chapters in which Marx applies the first stages of a historical treatment either to the struggles to shorten the working day, or to primitive capitalist accumulation refer to the theory of history as their principle, to the construction of the *concept* of history and its "developed forms," of which the economic theory of the capitalist mode of production constitutes one determinate "region" [*RC*, 117].

The question remains for Althusser to answer that if truth resides simply in internal consistency or the logical order of propositions, then what of the situation in which we are confronted with competing theories, all more or less coherent within their own terms, and each claiming to provide us with the truth about a particular phenomenon that we seek to understand. How are we to judge between theories when the very criteria we seek are said to be "internal" to the systems that need to be evaluated? On this account it would seem to be impossible to choose rationally between say a scientific and a theological account of the origin and the development of the species or between a Marxist and a liberal conception of the state, since each could plainly be held to contain its own immanent logic and criteria of intelligibility. The point is that, unless our conceptions are at some level tied down to fact, our whole construction could be rigorously coherent *and* still be a delusion.

Althusser's response is simply to dismiss the whole problem of knowledge, that is, the verification and empirical validation of truth claims as "ideological." In his own words: "We can say, then, that the mechanism of production of the knowledge effect lies in the mechanism which underlies the action of the forms of order in the scientific discourse of the proof" (*RC*, p. 67). But this offhand dismissal of the whole validity problem by no means succeeds in answering our questions. Without some specified rules of procedure independent of the practice in question, not only will we be unable to decide between competing accounts but we will be thrown back into a morass of epistemological relativism or anarchy.

We encounter here another problem. For not only does Althusser's theory of internal criteria lack the constraints of external evidence, but it tells us nothing about how criteria themselves change over time. Interestingly, Althusser's position is not unlike that of Peter Winch in his book *The Idea of a Social Science*.[19] In discussing the differences between theology and science Winch claims that "intelligibility takes many and varied forms" and that there is no "norm for intelligibility as such." "For instance," he writes, "science is one such mode and religion is another; and each has criteria of intelligibility peculiar to itself. So within science or religion actions can be logical or illogical. . . . But we cannot sensibly say that either the practice of science itself or that of religion is either illogical or logical; both are non-logical."[20] Just as Althusser remarks that no mathematician requires physics to verify his theorems, so is Winch suggesting that both science and theology have their own criteria of intelligibility, each peculiar to itself and as such each must be

---

[19]*The Idea of a Social Science and Its Relation to Philosophy* (London: Routledge & Kegan Paul, 1968).
[20]Pages 100–101.

judged purely "internally" or in its own terms. These criteria can tell us, for instance, what is to count as true or false, logical or illogical, within the disciplines or modes of life in question. But the criteria cannot tell us whether the disciplines themselves make sense. Each discipline merely *is* and as such must be accepted. We could easily imagine Althusser agreeing with Wittgenstein's dictum, "What has to be accepted, the given, is—so one could say—forms of life."[21]

But this acceptance of "forms of life" or existing practices glosses over the immense discrepancies that can arise within forms of life, language games, or theoretical practices. The criteria operative at any one time are not monolithic. They not only may contain internal incoherences and contradictions, but may be challenged by rival practitioners of the same discipline. Thus Alasdair MacIntyre has said in response to Winch that "at any given date in any given society the criteria in current use by religious believers or scientists will differ from what they are at other times and places. Criteria have a history."[22] But if criteria change, what this suggests is that they may not at any one time be considered all of one piece so that to refer to them as though they were is misleading. The more important question is why at some points in history the criteria of intelligibility are regarded as tolerable and even necessary for social well-being, while at others the anomolies and incoherences that the criteria exhibit become so great as to sanction an "epistemological revolution."

Finally, Althusser's insistence on the "radical inwardness" of our criteria leads to the severence of theory from practice, an analysis totally at odds with Marx's more pragmatic conception of truth.[23] The basic point of departure for all of Marx's epis-

[21]*Philosophical Investigations,* trans. G. E. M. Anscombe (New York: Macmillan, 1968), p. 226.

[22]"Is Understanding a Religion Compatible with Believing?" *Rationality,* Bryan R. Wilson, ed. (Oxford: Basil Blackwell, 1979), pp. 66–67.

[23]For an excellent account see Leszek Kolakowski, "Karl Marx and the Classical Definition of Truth," *Toward a Marxist Humanism: Essays on the Left Today,* trans. Jane Z. Peel (New York: Grove Press, 1968), pp. 38–66.

temological reflections is the conviction that the relations between the human species and its environment are fundamentally
relations of need. The human mind is ruled by practicality; it is
adjudged not by its ability to recreate at a second-order level a
first-order world of *pragmata,* but by its practical function of
helping us to satisfy both our biological and our socially acquired
needs. As Marx indicates in a number of texts, reality itself is a
human creation, and theory—man's "practical consciousness,"
his awareness of the world of things—is defined by its ability to
assist him in appropriating reality as the sum total of the possible
objects of desire. Thus in the *German Ideology* we find statements like, "consciousness is . . . from the very beginning a
social product and remains so as long as men exist at all" and
more specifically that "language is as old as consciousness, language is practical consciousness that exists also for other men
. . . language, like consciousness, only arises from the need, the
necessity, of intercourse with other men."[24] The implication is
that not truth but success in practice, success in helping us to
acquire the objects of need, is the primary epistemological category. Success in the accomplishment of certain objectified ends
proves the truth of our knowledge; failure forces us to reject or to
modify it. Indeed the idea of a purely "theoretical practice"
unconnected to the satisfaction of need would have struck Marx
as a typically idealist fantasy.

There may be good reasons for rejecting Marx's instrumentalist or pragmatist conception of knowledge. But without demonstrating its ties to social practice, Althusser's internal criteria
remain subject to the same problems that Marx leveled against
Hegel and the German idealists of his own day. Unlike Marx's
pragmatism, which regards knowledge as the result of an interaction between our cognitive faculties and the state of material
reality within which they develop, for Althusser the entire development takes place within language. To be sure, he provides us

[24]*German Ideology,* pp. 49–50.

with a perfunctory assurance that material reality does exist, but then goes on to treat theory formation in complete abstraction from this reality. The result is a species of idealism which denies the materialist ''primacy'' of being over consciousness. This idealism consists not in the denial of an external material world, but in the positing of a self-generating conceptual universe which imposes itself upon the phenomena of social existence. There is, then, no interplay or ''dialectic'' between social being and social consciousness, but rather, as with all systems of idealism, the former is entirely engulfed within the latter. In this respect Althusser would have no difficulty in agreeing with the verdict of Michael Oakeshott, who writes: ''Nowhere is there to be found a form of experience which is not a form of thought. There is . . . no experiencing which is not thinking, nothing experienced which is not thought, and consequently no experience which is not a world of ideas.''[25]

The charge of idealism is not merely an epistemological one unconnected to political practice. For if in order to be scientific, a theory must be validated by its own ''internal criteria,'' like those applied in a mathematical theorem, the result, as Waldeck Rochet has warned, will be a Marxist theory ''elaborated and developed by specialists in philosophy, well trained in abstract reasoning, but without any real ties with social practice.''[26] In other words, the final authority on matters of theory would no longer be political but scholarly, not the *bureau politique* but the *bureau des savants*. This statement cannot simply be put down to the layman's suspicion of the clerisy. There is a real sense for Althusser that theory must remain pure or above any contamination by the ''ideology'' or the practical attitude by which ordinary agents come to make sense of their experience. This distinction between science and ideology, or theoretical and ideological

---

[25]*Experience and Its Modes* (Cambridge: Cambridge University Press, 1933), pp. 25–26.

[26]''Le marxisme et les chemins de l'avenir,'' p. 20.

practice, can be made on both epistemological and ontological grounds. They are both forms of knowledge as well as dimensions of social reality. Let us see on what this distinction turns.

Ideology

One of the chief tasks which Althusser assigns to dialectical materialism is its assistance in preserving scientific discourse from all manner of ideology. What exactly an ideology is and how it differs from science is a question we must now pause to consider.

Perhaps the crucial difference between scientific and ideological discourse turns on their respective cognitive statuses. An ideology is said to be characterized by a certain blindness regarding its own presuppositions. "The way the problems are posed" determines an ideology: "An ideology (in the strict Marxist sense of the term—the sense in which Marxism is not itself an ideology) can be regarded as characterized in this particular respect by the fact that *its own problematic is not conscious of itself*." An ideology is, therefore, "unconscious of its 'theoretical presuppositions,' that is, the active but unavowed problematic which fixes for it the meaning and movement of *its problems* and thereby of their solutions" (*FM*, 69).

This distinction is not, I think, particularly revealing. Simply on historical grounds science has never been noted for its attentiveness to its own presuppositions or at least no more than other nonscientific areas of discourse, such as theology, morals, or politics. Thomas Kuhn, for example, has argued that science itself is only possible once the critical examination of presuppositions is held in abeyance.[27] Scientific progress is only possible when presuppositions are taken for granted or are not seriously challenged by scientific practitioners. Even as Plato indicates in the *Republic*, mathematics, the prototypical science for Althusser, assumes certain hypotheses which the mathematician is

[27]Kuhn, *The Structure of Scientific Revolutions*, pp. 23–42.

not free to challenge, or if he does he fails to be a mathematician. Thus the openness to free self-examination is not an earmark of science and cannot be used to distinguish it adequately from ideology.

If ideology cannot be distinguished from science on cognitive grounds alone, we might look at the respective social function of each to clarify the matter. What distinguishes science, formal knowledge, from ideology is not that the one is true and the other is not. Strictly speaking, questions of truth and falsity do not apply to the sphere of ideology since the primary function of ideology, say a set of moral norms or a system of religious beliefs, is not explanatory but practical, to help us live in the world. To use the language of Merleau-Ponty, ideology is "lived" as much as it is known. Ideologies, therefore, can only be assessed functionally, that is, in terms of how well they respond to certain basic human needs.

One particularly useful manner of classifying ideologies has been suggested by Raymond Geuss in his insightful work *The Idea of a Critical Theory*.[28] Here Geuss distinguishes three ways in which the term "ideology" can be fruitfully employed. The first is what he calls the "descriptive" use of the term, which will typically include such things as the beliefs held by members of a group, the concepts they use, the attitudes, predilections, and dispositions that they exhibit. In this broad omnibus sense, every human grouping by virtue of the fact that it is a human grouping will have an ideology to which its members will characteristically subscribe. The second sense of the term is "pejorative" since ideology is here taken to be a form a "false consciousness" or delusion which needs to be combated or rectified by some form of "Ideologiekritik." Ideology here is clearly related to its Marxist usage in which ideologies are bodies of doctrine used to justify or legitimize existing relations of dominance and oppression. Finally we can speak of ideology in its "positive" sense. Ac-

---

[28]*The Idea of a Critical Theory* (Cambridge: Cambridge University Press, 1981), ch. 1.

cording to this view ideologies are not merely "out there" in the world to be discovered, but have to be created or invented; it is a *verité à faire*. The positive conception of ideology is clearly related to the Leninist theory of ideology as created by a vanguard party which introduces into the proletariat from the outside a new set of beliefs and attitudes which are not the beliefs and attitudes that this class would "spontaneously" develop but which are held nonetheless to be appropriate to its objective situation.

Althusser's conception of ideology participates in all three of these usages. First Althusser uses the term in a perfectly descriptive sense to indicate a fact of social life, a characteristic practice which societies everywhere exhibit. An ideology in this sense is a system of ideas or representations that dominates the mind of either a group of individuals within society or even an entire society. "Ideology," he says, "is a system (with its own logic and rigor) of representations, (images, myths, ideas, or concepts, depending on the case) endowed with a historical existence and role within a given society" (*FM*, 231). An ideology in this sense is not a random collection of traits that can be considered in isolation, but a well-organized system of beliefs which serves to reinforce or reproduce the existing set of social relations. What distinguishes ideology as our lived practical attitude toward the world from the objective knowledge provided by science is that rather than clarifying or explaining reality, ideology has to be treated as a part of that reality which is in need of explanation. At the epistemological level, then, ideology is tied to the realm of those commonplace concepts and beliefs which, we have already noted, constitute the first moment in the production of knowledge.

The main thrust of ideology in this sense is directed away from the view that it is either the specific creation of class society or that ideology is an expression of the interests of one particular class within society. Far from limiting the working of ideology to class society only, Althusser extends its sphere of operation to every possible form of society, even a classless one. "Ideol-

ogy," he says, "is as such an organic part of every social totality" (*FM,* 232). As the medium of lived experience, human
societies can no more do without ideology than they can do
without their economic or political structures. "All human societies secrete ideology as the very element and atmosphere indispensable to their historical respiration and life" (*FM,* 232). And
elsewhere we read that "man is an ideological animal by nature"
(*LP,* 160). In opposition, then, to both the liberal and the Marxist
theory that we already have or will in the near future have attained to an "end of ideology," Althusser says that "only an
ideological world outlook could have imagined societies without
ideology and accepted the utopian idea of a world in which ideology (not just one of its historical forms) would disappear without
trace, to be replaced by science" (*FM,* 232). Thus, even in a
communist society, ideology would remain the medium within
which people experience their world. "Historical materialism,"
he asserts in an even more emphatic manner, "cannot conceive
that even a communist society could ever do without ideology"
(*FM,* 232).

At a certain level these remarks are beyond reproach. If we
accept that ideology has been part of past human societies, then it
follows that it has been "indispensable" since we cannot replace
any part of what is already past. But if he is suggesting that the
ideological consciousness not only was but is and will continue to
be "indispensable," then he has moved from a rather banal and
uncontentious statement of fact to a large and by no means in-
controvertible imputation of value. But ideology can only be
considered indispensable in this sense if it can be shown to fulfill
some intrinsic human need. This may be either some deep-rooted
psychological need, such as the necessity for the individual to
think of himself as a free and independent center of initiative, an
agent, or some more general social need, such as the necessity for
society to continue to reproduce its own conditions of existence.
In either case, though, one ends up by attributing to ideology a
definite normative status. We can see now how far we are from
Marx's original conception of ideology as a species of delusion

and falsehood; in the hands of Althusser it has become a functionally necessary feature of society as such.

This effort to treat ideology not as a function of a class or of certain sectional interests that are pitted against others but as a property of social systems as a whole testifies to the influence of Durkheim and the tradition of "holistic" sociology on Althusserian Marxism. Ideology loses all connection with group interests within a social order and is transformed into an amorphous "collective consciousness" that acts as a social fluid inculcating predominant values and beliefs. These values and beliefs in their turn lend legitimacy to society rather than to the domination of one particular class within it.

But if Althusser has given his Marxism a Durkheimian twist, he has also given his Durkheim a Freudian turn. Ideology, he tells us, is like the unconscious—"immutable" in its structure and operation (*LP,* 151–52). While specific ideologies change in conjunction with the process of historical change, there can be no end of ideology even with the transcendence of socialism over capitalism. The permanence of ideology is explained as a feature of its "practico-social" function of binding men together in society. It functions (in Gramsci's words) as a "social cement," the indispensable core of social cohesion: "In a society without classes, just as in a class society, ideology has the function of securing the bond between men in the ensemble of the forms of their existence, the relation of individuals to their tasks fixed by the social structure."[29]

Beyond this merely descriptive use of the term, Althusser uses ideology to designate a mode of deformed or inadequate apprehension closer to Geuss' "pejorative" sense. This "deformation" of consciousness is related by Althusser directly to the "opacity" of the social formation:

> The deformation of ideology is socially necessary as a function of the very nature of the social whole: more specifically as a function of its determination by its structure which renders this social

[29]Althusser, cited in Rancière, *La leçon d'Althusser,* pp. 229–30.

whole opaque to the individuals who occupy a place in it determined by this structure. The representation of the world necessary to social cohesion is necessarily mythical, owing to the opacity of the social structure.[30]

It must be admitted that little is offered here to support this claim. Here, however, we see where Althusser differs most radically from classical Marxism, in which ideologies are above all else instruments of class domination, "the ruling ideas . . . of the ruling classes."[31] Ideologies in this sense inevitably put forward a distorted and one-sided image of the world, since they are called upon to represent sectional interests as universal ones. Only in a classless society did Marx envision a situation in which men could at last dispense with ideology as an aspect of the "prehistory" of the species. Only there could the conditions for complete intelligibility and transparency be achieved. Althusser, by contrast, regards this instrumental use of ideology as impossible since the class that uses it is as much its captive as the class upon which it is used. Two passages, the first from *Capital* and the second from *For Marx* should help to illustrate this difference. Marx writes:

> Let us now picture to ourselves, by way of change, a community of free individuals, carrying on their work with the means of production in common, in which the labour power of all the different individuals is consciously applied as the combined labour power of the community. . . . The social relations of the individual producers, with regard both to their labour and to its products, are in this case perfectly simple and intelligible, and that with regard not only to production but to distribution.[32]

And from Althusser:

> If the whole social function of ideology could be summed up cynically as a myth (such as Plato's "beautiful lies" or the tech-

[30]Page 231.
[31]Marx, *German Ideology*, p. 67.
[32]*Capital*, 1: 78–79.

niques of modern advertising) fabricated and manipulated from the outside by the ruling class to fool those it is exploiting, then ideology would disappear with classes. But as we have seen that even in the case of a class society ideology is active on the ruling class itself and contributes to its moulding, to the modification of its attitudes to adapt it to its real conditions of existence (for example, legal freedom)—it is clear that *ideology (as a system of mass representations) is indispensable in any society if men are to be formed, transformed and equipped to respond to the demands of their conditions of existence* [*FM,* 235].

The difference in images here is striking. From Marx we get a picture of society in which all opacity has been dispelled, that is, where social relations have acquired the simplicity and intelligibility of the self-evident. But this picture of a "community of free individuals" is undercut by Althusser's insistence on the inevitability and even utility of the ideological perspective whatever the political regime "if men are to be formed, transformed and equipped to respond to the demands of their conditions of existence." The conception we arrive at is that even under the most moderate or least oppressive regime, men will continue to live their lives under the sway of illusion and myth. Ideology exists, and exists necessarily, because of certain functional necessities of the social formation. That these necessities could ever cease to exist is itself said to be an illusion characteristic of the ideological mind as such.

The question still to be answered, though, is why it is that human beings are necessarily condemned to live in this opacity, cut off from an understanding of the real conditions by which their lives are determined. This opacity is due to the inability of science or rational knowledge to generate substantive principles of action. Science must abdicate its responsibility in this role to the realm of ideology. The difference between them hinges upon the respective function each fulfills. Ideology serves the practical end of adapting individuals to their social roles so as to make them more responsive to the needs of society. "Ideology as a system or representations, is distinguished from science in that in it the practico-social function is more important than the theoretical function (function as knowledge)'' (*FM*, 231). This distinction between the primarily practical ''interests'' at work in ideology and the purely theoretical ''interests'' of science is expressed with particular force when Althusser writes: ''It is a peculiarity of every ideological conception . . . that it is governed by 'interests' beyond the necessity of knowledge alone'' (*RC*, 141). So defined, this distinction entails two consequences. First, the theoretical function is not itself a practical or social one so that to function theoretically is not to function socially. And second, only interests internal to knowledge—knowledge for its own sake—and not any social or political interests are at work in the development of science. The conclusion toward which we are inexorably drawn is that human interests and scientific interests are totally opposed to one another. Logically, then, Marxism *qua* science has to be divorced from all normative interests, even an interest in socialism.

We can now see that the necessarily obfuscatory character of ideology is related to the ''practico-social'' function it is called upon to perform. This function, as Althusser describes it, is performed through a process of ''hailing'' or ''interpellating'' individuals as ''subjects.'' The category of the subject, like that of ego or consciousness, is said to be ''constitutive of all ideology'' or ''all ideology has the function (which defines it) of 'constituting' concrete individuals as subjects'' (*LP*, 160). Accordingly, the notion of ''a subject endowed with a consciousness'' who ''freely forms or recognizes ideas in which he believes'' and acts in conformity with those ideas must be regarded as an ''absolutely ideological 'conceptual' device'' (*LP*, 157). The central idea here is that only through this constitution of the individual as a ''centre of initiatives, author of and responsible for its actions'' can the life of society as well as the reproduction of the relations of production be guaranteed and secured (*LP*, 169).

Let us leave to one side the obvious objection that ideology which is focused on the concept of subjectivity is not peculiar to society as such but to one particular form of society, to wit, Western individualist or liberal society. The process of "hailing" or "interpellating" man as "a free subjectivity," far from necessary to sustain society, would be regarded in many non-Western or precapitalist societies as extremely destructive of the relations of "reciprocity" and "redistribution" around which those societies turn.[33] But leaving this objection aside, Althusser's claim that what established Marxism as a science is not that it articulated the interests of any one class, namely the proletariat, but that it did not conceptualize society from the perspective of any of its members, is either to misunderstand or misrepresent Marx's own theory of ideology. Marx did not criticize theories as ideological because they fostered certain human interests, but because they solidified the class domination of society. What distinguished Marxism from previous theories is not that it abandoned the standpoint of class altogether, or the "practico-social" interests of a class, but that it sought to delegitimize the nature of class rule and hence sought to undermine class ideology.

Indeed, Althusser's attempt to detach theory from the standpoint of human interests is questionable in the extreme. As many philosophers of the social sciences have noted, the very subject matter of social and political inquiry is constructed by the choice of what is essential for us, that is, by reference to the values, standards, and interests of the particular thinker standing at a particular point in time. History is largely a matter of perspective, how we choose to look at it and what we choose to look at. There is no Archimedian point standing outside history, some set of "theoretical interests" internal to science alone, divorced from the merely practical or value-laden concerns of social agents themselves. The historian may, as it were, choose between values or interests, but he cannot, by virtue of the fact that he is a human being, choose to be without them. Oddly enough Al-

---

[33]Karl Polanyi, *The Great Transformation: The Political and Economic Origins of Our Time* (Boston: Beacon Press, 1967), ch. 4.

136

thusser arrives, albeit from a different direction, at a position not dissimilar to that of Mannheim. Only the "intellectuals" are able to rise above the competing clash of values and ideologies and grasp the true nature of the social process from a "total orientation" precisely because in their capacity as theorists their interests transcend the limitations of any party, nation, or class.[34]

Furthermore, there is the problem alluded to earlier that, once theory is divorced from all human interests, we necessarily lose the vital connection between theory and practice. So long as the distinction between science and ideology, true and false consciousness, is conceived as a rigid dichotomy, so long will Marxian theory remain cut off from the realities of the world of politics and the class struggle. Indeed, in place of the Hegelian and dialectical view of truth as always emerging out of or mixed up with illusion and error, Althusser establishes another "coupure" between Marxism as a body of scientific concepts which is true for theoretical purposes on the one hand and the ideology of the masses which is useful for purposes of social integration on the other.[35] The attitude underlying this rigid dichotomy between science and ideology is one which could be variously described as both positivist and metaphysical. It is positivist insofar as it presupposes a sharp and unbridgeable gap between ideas and beliefs pertaining to a false consciousness and those comprising a true one. It is metaphysical inasmuch as it operates with a set of purportedly timeless or abstract categories, namely, ideology or bourgeois ideology on the one side and Marxian thought on the other.

There is evidence, however, that in some of his more recent work Althusser has sought to overcome what he now describes as the "theoreticist" formulations of his earlier studies (*FM*, 15). Responding to some of the more "politically-oriented critics,"

[34]*Ideology and Utopia*, p. 161.
[35]Garaudy, *Peut-on être communiste aujourd'hui?*, p. 271: "Ainsi l'on arrive aisément à considérer que l'idéologie est bien assez bonne pour le mainement des masses en réservant la Théorie pour les technocrates de la philosophie."

Althusser has argued that science cannot remain neutral or on the sidelines but must take a more activist role within the class struggle. In a formula that is invoked continuously to distinguish ideology in this more activist or what we have called earlier more "positive" sense, Althusser refers to the "Marxist-Leninist thesis" that "puts the class struggle in the front rank" and explicitly castigates his earlier texts for having failed to do so (*ESC*, 130, 141–42, 146, 148, 166). The suggestion is that Marx was able to advance his theory of history and society only by virtue of his prior commitment to the cause of the working class. The revised conception of theory as a "weapon" in the class struggle should be clear from the following passages:

> This science cannot be a science like any other, a science for "everyone." Precisely because it reveals the mechanisms of class exploitation, repression and domination, in the economy, in politics and in ideology, it cannot be recognised by *everyone*. This science, which brings the social classes face to face with their truth, is unbearable for the bourgeoisie and its allies, who reject it and take refuge in their so-called "social sciences": it is only acceptable to the proletariat, whom it "represents" (Marx). That is why the proletariat has recognised it as its own property, and has set it to work in its practice: in the hands of the Workers' Movement, Marxist science has become the theoretical weapon of the revolution [*LP*, 7–8].

> To understand *Capital* . . . it is necessary to take up "proletarian class positions," i.e., to adopt the only viewpoint that makes *visible* the reality of the exploitation of wage labour power, which constitutes the whole of capitalism [*LP*, 96].

These passages are regarded by those "politically oriented critics" mentioned above as being "beneficial" and as representing Althusser's "most important contribution to Marxist theory."[36] This would appear to be a rash judgment, given Althusser's general reticence to say anything concrete about exactly

[36]Joe McCarney, *The Real World of Ideology* (New York: Humanities Press, 1980), p. 74; Callinicos, *Althusser's Marxism*, p. 88.

how theory "intervenes" in the class struggle. The very suggestion that any intervention is necessary at all would seem to imply that Marxian theory, the elaboration of the correct proletarian standpoint, is not indigenous to the working class but has to be introduced or "imported" from the outside by members of a vanguard party (many of bourgeois origin) (*RC*, 141). It is clear, then, that what Marxian theory is called upon to do is not merely to elaborate or articulate the "spontaneous" or natural attitude of the masses, for this would in all likelihood yield only some further form of "bourgeois ideology." It becomes the aim of Marxian theory and those trained in it to *construct* the beliefs and attitudes appropriate for the proletariat to have. The task of the vanguard party must be to create those attitudes and beliefs that best enable the working class to restructure society in accordance with their "true" or "real" interests.

Nevertheless, if we are looking for a closer specification of what will make the "proletarian class position" more transparent or less subject to the charge of being another form of false or obfuscatory consciousness, we will be disappointed. Whatever his alleged "self-criticisms," the concept of ideology still carries a largely pejorative signification (*ESC*, 126, 151, 157). Indeed, the claim that theory "intervenes" in practice only serves to reinforce the basic idealism of Althusser's original position. Norman Geras has aptly put it:

> To reduce the whole process by which Marxist theory was produced to a theoretical activity autonomous of the political practice of the working class and political conditions which were its indispensable, if not sufficient, conditions of production, is to perpetrate a reduction as grave as any of those castigated by Althusser himself. Its final effect is to make the relation between Marxist theory and the working class a unilateral and purely pedagogic one: the intellectuals "give" the class the knowledge it needs. This is only the final consequence of every idealism: elitism. When knowledge celebrates its autonomy, the philosophers celebrate their dominance.[37]

---

[37] "Althusserian Marxism," pp. 83–84.

There is only one problem with Geras' summation. This concerns the use of the term ''pedagogic.'' To say that Althusserian ''theoretical practice'' has a pedagogical relation to the working class would seem to suggest that it is like a ''critical theory'' in the Frankfurt School sense, that is, a theory intended to produce enlightenment, emancipation, or self-reflection in the agents to whom it is addressed. It is in fact much closer to a ''traditional theory'' that objectifies society and history in the same manner that physics does for the natural world, that is, to turn it into a domain of potential *manipulanda* by so many elite technicians. This view of politics as so much raw material to be worked up into a finished product is a natural formula for a Leninist rule by an elite. It might be suggested, of course, that what Althusser has in mind is a scientific theory which is not manipulative, but which could help us adjust more harmoniously to the course of events in the manner of engineering or medicine. But this would be to make theory dependent upon history in the manner of historicism. Marxist theory, for Althusser, does not have a ''pedagogic'' function but a technical one. It has nothing to do with *praxis* in the sense of action but is exclusively a *techne,* the building or construction of the foundations of socialism. Marxist theory aims, then, at the creation of that ''immortal commonwealth'' that Bacon and Hobbes quite rightly believed to be the product of modern technology.

5

Marxism and the Problem of History

Any adequate interpretation of Althusser must at some point come to terms with his account of Marx's "science" of history. Marx's "science" is a mode of analysis which seeks to explain the relations between the economic "base" of society and the legal, political, and ideological "superstructure" which is said to arise from and "correspond" to it. These concepts along with two others—productive forces and relations of production—provide us with the basic rudiments of what Althusser calls "historical materialism."

In exploring the novelty of Althusser's account we shall have to examine two other widespread interpretations of Marxism that he rejects. The first is the economistic version, so named because it regards the productive forces of society as directly determining all the other spheres of social, political, and cultural life. The Fundamentalist Thesis, as I will call it, amounts to a form of technological determinism defended by most proponents of "orthodox" Marxism, which seems to be making a revival in our own day. The second theory regards base and superstructure not as externally or contingently connected to one another but as internally related or mutually determining attributes of the same social totality. The Internal Relatedness Thesis, so named by

Bertell Ollman, has been adopted, as we shall see, in various forms in the works of writers as diverse as Lukács, Gramsci, and the members of the Frankfurt School. And the third theory is that of Althusser himself, who has tried to bridge the gap between the first two by suggesting that, while the productive forces of society remain determinant "in the last instance," this determination is still compatible with a considerable degree of "autonomy" for the superstructure. The twin principles of determination "in the last instance" by the base and the "relative autonomy" of the superstructure will be called the Overdetermination Thesis and will be examined in detail later on.

The Fundamentalist Thesis

The first and best-known articulation of historical materialism is found in the Preface to Marx's 1859 *Contribution to the Critique of Political Economy,* the crucial passage of which runs as follows:

> In the social production of their life, men enter into definite relations that are indispensable and independent of their will, relations of production which correspond to a definite stage of development of their material productive forces. The sum total of these relations of production constitutes the economic structure of society, the real foundation, on which rises a legal and political superstructure and to which correspond definite forms of social consciousness. The mode of production of material life conditions the social, political and intellectual life process in general. It is not the consciousness of men that determines their being, but, on the contrary, their social being that determines their consciousness.[1]

The Fundamentalist Thesis appears to rest on at least three presuppositions. First, every society is divided into different levels or strata that can be organized hierarchically in the following order: (1) forces of production (*Produktivkräfte*), (2) relations of production (*Produktionverhältnisse*) or the economic structure

[1]*Selected Works* (Moscow: Foreign Language Publishing House, 1958), 1: 362–63.

(*ökonomische Struktur*) or the real foundation (*die reale Basis*) of society, (3) the legal and political superstructure (*juristischer und politischer Überbau*), and (4) forms of social consciousness (*gesellschaftlische Bewusstseinsformen*). The second presupposition is that processes in any of the higher subsystems are determined in the sense of causal dependency by the subsystems below it and ultimately by the forces of production. And the third presupposition is that this causal determination is entirely one way or unidirectional, so that the base determines the superstructure and not vice versa. These three presuppositions taken together amount to a form of technological determinism most commonly associated with Plekhanov, Kautsky, and Bukharin.

It is noteworthy that not even the most orthodox defenders of the Fundamentalist Thesis have been able to defend it consistently. This is due to the difficulty of isolating the productive forces, or technology, as a cause independent of the relations of production, or the division of labor. Consequently, many Marxists have been led to argue that there is some kind of "interaction" or "mutual conditioning" between base and superstructure or that the base only asserts itself "in the last instance." Yet no matter how insistent one may be about the reciprocal causality between these factors or how removed the economic might be from its final determination, these formulations merely serve to underscore the initial "regional" separation of the spheres into isolated and self-enclosed entities. Karl Kautsky recorded the difficulty of this position when he remarked:

> Only in the final analysis is the whole legal, political, ideological apparatus to be regarded as a superstructure over an economic infrastructure. This in no way holds for its individual appearance in history. The latter—whether of an economic, ideological, or some other type—will act in many respects as infrastructure, in other ways as superstructure. The Marxian statement about infrastructure and superstructure is unconditionally valid only for new appearances in history.[2]

[2]*Die materialistische Geschichtauffassung* (Berlin: J. H. W. Dietz, 1927), 1: 817–18.

Kautsky's reservations about the Fundamentalist Thesis do not, however, succeed in elucidating in what sense the forces of production can be attributed primacy in history. The difficulty with attributing causal primacy to the productive forces is the core of H. B. Acton's objection to orthodox historical materialism. To assert that the forces of production determine the relations of production is to assume that one factor "*x*" can be isolated and differentiated from another factor "*y*" that can be seen to follow from it sequentially or temporally. The problem here stems from the difficulty of separating out one factor or element from the totality of social conditions in which it is found and then elevating this factor to the "cause" of those conditions. It is difficult to conceive much less to observe the forces of production as something apart from the legal, moral, and political relationships among men. In this sense it is difficult to say that productive forces can be regarded as "causes" or even "influences" on other noneconomic factors.[3]

The Fundamentalist Thesis depends for its viability on just how we understand the determinative influence of the productive forces. Marx's normal word for determine is "bedingen" or "bestimmen," which derives from the Latin "determinare," which means literally "setting bounds" or "setting limits."[4] An important aspect in the understanding of determinism is the idea of externality, that is, of some independently specifiable agency, in this case the productive forces of society, that can control or decide the outcome of a process or action apart from the contributors to or participants in that process. In this sense productive forces can be said to "block" or "select out" all features of the superstructure that do not "correspond" or comply with it. The force of the term "correspond" must here be understood in a quasi-functional sense. Societies get the superstructures they do because what does not correspond to or comply with the produc-

---

[3]See for instance H. B. Acton, *The Illusion of an Epoch* (London: Cohen and West, 1955), p. 167.

[4]Raymond Williams, *Marxism and Literature* (Oxford: Oxford University Press, 1977), p. 84.

tive forces has already been blocked out as inappropriate, and what has already been blocked out obviously did not comply. With this emphasis on the externality of the productive forces in exerting their influence, it is not difficult to see how Marxism came to be understood as a deterministic system in which a set of fixed and independently specifiable objective factors are regarded as setting the conditions within which all else happens.

This form of "technological determinism," with its insistence upon the absolute primacy of productive forces over productive relations and of bases over superstructures, has been given renewed impetus in recent years, due largely to the work of G. A. Cohen.[5] More thoroughly than other interpreters, Cohen has put forward a sophisticated defense of the functional dependence of the economic structure and superstructure on the technological apparatus of society. He says: "To say that being determines consciousness, means at least in part: the character of the leading ideas of a society is explained by their propensity, in virtue of that character, to sustain the structure of economic roles called for by the productive forces."[6] Cohen rests his case for the "causal primacy" of productive forces upon two suppositions about human nature in general. The two assertions are first that human beings are somewhat "rational" and second that they can use their rationality to improve materially their situation. These two suppostions are cojoined with the observation that the condition in which most human beings find themselves is one dominated by material scarcity, that is, requires material improvement.[7] The premise here is that there is a natural tendency grounded in the conditions of human rationality or intelligence as such, and independent of social or historical circumstances, to expand and improve upon the productive forces in order to conquer the conditions of scarcity. Since Cohen believes that productive forces have a tendency to expand "in the normal run of

[5]*Karl Marx's Theory of History: A Defence* (Princeton: Princeton University Press, 1978).
[6]Page 279.
[7]Page 152.

things," at any given stage of their development only those social relations will obtain that serve to facilitate the further improvement of the technological substratum of society. This "extra social" or "supra-historical" principle of technology, around which the whole is (functionally) constrained to adjust, constitutes, for Cohen, the core of Marx's technological determinism.[8]

It is not clear from Cohen's analysis why he ascribes pride of place to technology and not rationality. One imagines that this would conflict with his "materialism," which regards the content of human reason as determined by nonrational material forces, scarcity. In order to make good his claim, Cohen points to a number of passages from *Capital* and the *Grundrisse* in which Marx speaks of the technological and material base as a sort of free cause analytically distinct from the social and historical form in which it develops. Cohen writes:

> We are arguing that the familiar distinction between forces and relations of production is, in Marx, one of a set of contrasts between nature and society. Commentators have failed to remark how often he uses "material" as the antonym of "social," and how what is described as material also counts as the "content" of the same form. . . . The upshot of these oppositions and identifications is that *the matter or content of society is nature, whose form is the social form.*[9]

It has been suggested that the distinction between "natural" and "material," on the one side, and "social" and "historical," on the other, is false because the passages cited in support of it are used by Marx not to defend but to attack this abstraction.[10] My point is, however, that by conceiving the productive forces of a society as narrowly as he does, Cohen's argument ends by giving more weight to the technological base than it can be made

[8]Pages ix, 285.

[9]Page 98.

[10]See Ellen Meiskins Wood, "The Separation of the Economic and the Political in Capitalism," *New Left Review,* 127 (1981): 70–74.

to bear. Technique may be analytically separated from the social relations of production and other moments of the superstructure, but then to assume that this analytical distinction refers to two substantively separate objects or regions of activity physically divisible from each other in the real world is to fall prey to the type of reification so often decried by Marxist theoreticians themselves. Indeed, it is this fear of confusing our epistemological categories with ontological ones that has led many Marxist thinkers to reject the whole base/superstructure and forces/relations of production dichotomies as misleading.[11] Technique is, no doubt, an important phenomenon in accounting for historical change, but to abstract it from social relations, division of labor, and the like, within which it is always found, is to fall prey to the type of "fetishism" criticized by Marx as characteristic of bourgeois social science. The fact is that we never find the forces of production existing outside of specific social relations, and in reality the two overlap to a considerable degree. One need only think of how in ancient Greece, for instance, slaves were considered to be a productive force. But slavery can only be understood in terms of a wealth of social relationships that ensure the status of a slave. Or we can see how in modern society science functions in many ways not as a derivitive but as a cause of developments in economic technique. These point to the limits of the Fundamentalist Thesis by demonstrating a considerable degree of overlap, or what Melvin Rader has called "multiple countings" between basic and superstructural phenomena.[12]

It should be said that for all the analytical sophistication and expertise of the modern proponents of the Fundamentalist Thesis, they do not escape the pitfall that vitiated the older formulations. In identifying the forces of production with a natural or material substratum in contrast with its social and historical form, Cohen and others end by abstracting one feature of the social whole and

[11]Williams, *Marxism and Literature*, p. 78.
[12]*Marx's Interpretation of History* (Oxford: Oxford University Press, 1979), pp. 28, 72.

making it responsible for the development of all the others. Interestingly, Georg Lukács makes this point in a brilliant review article of N. Bukharin's *Historical Materialism,* whose own version of technological determinism attempted to explain all of human development by reference to one fixed principle. Lukács writes:

> But technique as the self-sufficient basis of development is only a dynamic refinement of this crude naturalism. For if technique is not conceived as a *moment* of the existing system of production, if its development is not explained by the development of the *social* forces of production (rather than the other way round), it is just as much a transcendent principle, set over against man as "nature," climate, environment, raw materials, etc.[13]

Lukács' point can, I think, be put this way. We must not mistake technique, which is at most analytically prior, with the actual movement of history, in which social relations dominate. It is at least arguable that modern technique is the consummation of modern relations of production, not its cause. The result of Cohen's (or Bukharin's) privileging of technique is that it is unable to explain how technique itself changes except by positing certain unexplained (and in certain respects very non-Marxian) assumptions about human nature as such. To cite Lukács once again:

> Nobody doubts that at every determinate stage of the development of the productive forces, which determine the development of technique, technique retroactively influences the productive forces . . . but it is altogether incorrect and unmarxist to separate technique from the other ideological forms and to propose for it a self-sufficiency from the economic structure of society.[14]

The conclusion we reach is that productive forces do not

[13]"N. Bukharin's 'Historical Materialism,'" *Political Writings, 1919–1929,* Rodney Livingstone, ed.; trans. Michael McColgan (London: New Left Books, 1972), p. 137.
[14]Page 137.

comprise a "self-subsistent world" that can be separated from other categories such as consumption, distribution, and exchange, much less from the various modes of social cooperation and from the application and development of certain bodies of social knowledge. These processes are in fact indissoluble and not simply links in a causal sequence—not that these categories may not be isolated and described for purposes of analysis. But then to think that they refer to separate compartments of real life is to commit a simple category mistake. The chief weakness, then, of the Fundamentalist Thesis is not that it simplifies history, which is always richer and more complex than any theory of history can represent it as being. It is that it mistakes the theory for the object it seeks to explain.

The Internal Relatedness Thesis

A different approach to historical materialism has recently been suggested by those theorists who focus not on causal or external connections between base and superstructure but on the internal relatedness of the various social practice within the same totality. The virtue of the Internal Relatedness Thesis is that it refuses to treat the various levels, instances, or factors of social formations as constituting more or less self-enclosed or regionally separated spheres of activity. No matter how insistent adherents of the Fundamentalist Thesis may be about the "interaction" or "reciprocal causality" of base and superstructure, they cannot avoid, as I have tried to suggest, the fragmentation and reification of reality, which treats the categories of thought as though they were categories of reality. What distinguishes the Internal Relatedness Thesis from the Fundamentalist Thesis is that it regards social relations not as cause of other factors within the whole, but as Spinozistic attributes which coexist along side one another as parts of a larger whole or totality.

The language of totality has recently become quite common and has much to recommend itself over the layered notion of a base and a consequent superstructure. The concept of totality was introduced into the Marxist idiom by Lukács, who had originally taken it from Hegel and German Idealism.[15] In the hands of idealist philosophers the concept was taken to indicate the reconciliation and harmony between the various opposed and contradictory features of a society or any organic whole. The critical thrust of the concept was its insistence that the features of a totality are not isolated or discrete variables that are logically independent of one another. Rather it is the characteristic feature of the category of totality that its parts cannot be separated out analytically and studied in isolation, but are bound to one another by bonds of mutual and irreducible interdependence. Unlike the Fundamentalist Thesis, which is based on a Humean model of causality which tries to isolate the different components of a causal sequence, the Internal Relatedness Thesis is much closer to the Hegelian conception of a "concrete universal" where to alter one relation is to alter the whole of which that relation is a part.

There are good reasons for attributing some version of the Internal Relatedness Thesis to Marx. On numerous occasions Marx remarks that only in terms of its relations with other things can social reality be made intelligible. Thus, in the methodological introduction to the *Grundrisse,* Marx berates the political economists for treating the categories of production, consumption, and distribution "abstractly," that is, as self-contained spheres which can be studied in and of themselves. He writes: "Production is . . . at the same time consumption, and consumption is at the same time production." Similarly he says that a change in any one relation or set of relations is bound to bring about changes in all the others. "A change in distribution changes production. . . . Mutual interaction takes place between

[15]See Lukács, *History and Class Consciousness,* p. 27: "It is not the primacy of economic motives in historical explanation that constitutes the decisive difference between Marxism and bourgeois thought, but the point of view of the totality."

the different moments." "This," Marx concludes, "is the case with every organic whole."[16] There are other passages where Marx seems unwilling to limit the Internal Relatedness Thesis to human phenomena alone and seems to accord it the status of a more general cosmological theory encompassing the whole of organic nature. In a passage from the early *Economic and Philosophic Manuscripts* we read: "The sun is the object of the plant—an indispensable object to it confirming its life—just as the plant is an object of the sun, being an expression of the life awakening power of the sun, of the sun's objective essential power."[17] In other words what Marx is suggesting in these passages is that the connection between objects which most of us would tend to regard in causal terms is best understood as an "expression" of what each "naturally" is.

The category of totality is also logically tied to the idea of "mediation," which suggests an active process of intercession between opposites or adversaries.[18] Mediation must be understood here in marked contrast to the method of empiricism or the causal judgments of science examined in the last chapter. Now empiricism provides the epistemological basis for the "correspondence" theory of the superstructure or the "reflection" theory of cognition. This reflection theory presupposes that there is some independently specifiable "material" or "objective" world which is in turn reflected at a second-order level in the world of "consciousness," that is, art, religion, philosophy, and science. The superstructure so conceived is an essentially passive transcription of the base. Real knowledge, science, will provide an accurate representation of the "laws" governing the material processes of society, while ideologies are those bodies of beliefs that present "false" or "distorted" pictures of the world. In either case, though, it is supposed that the entire superstructure

---

[16]*Grundrisse: Foundations of the Critique of Political Economy,* trans. Martin Nicolaus (Harmondsworth: Penguin Books, 1973), pp. 99–100.

[17]*Early Writings,* p. 207.

[18]Williams, *Marxism and Literature,* pp. 97–98.

and the "corresponding forms of consciousness" exist as so many reflexes, echoes, and phantasms of some primary process of reality.

It should be clear that the idea of mediation is radically incompatible with any doctrine of reflection. The concept of mediation aims to overcome the dualistic conception of base and superstructure as categorically distinct areas of reality by bringing out the complex web of internal relations that binds them together. The superstructure, then, can no longer be regarded as a secondary phenomenon at a remove from the material base, but must be seen as constitutive of those material processes which it is said to reflect. Accordingly, no aspect of reality may be studied without relating it to the conceptual whole. Indeed, this view of the totality is often called "dialectical," inasmuch as it becomes extraordinarily difficult to prohibit every relation from potentially "spilling over" into and even becoming every other relation. Bertell Ollman has summed this view up particularly well: "Through its internal ties to everything else," he says, "each factor is everything else viewed from this particular angle, and what applies to them necessarily applies to it, taken in this broad sense. Thus, each factor has—in theory—the potential to take the names of others (of whatever applies to them) when it functions as they do, that is, in ways associated with their core notions."[19] Indeed Ollmann even cites Pareto's dictum that "Marx's words are like bats: one can see in them both birds and mice" to underscore that not only things but our mental perceptions of them radiate out in all different directions.

The minimum requirement of the Internal Relatedness Thesis is that we recognize the dialectical penetration of the various aspects of the social whole. If the proponents of this thesis are correct, it cannot but have a profound effect on our understanding of theory. For on this account, we cannot understand theory, or

---

[19]*Alienation: Marx's Conception of Man in Capitalist Society* (Cambridge: Cambridge University Press, 1977), p. 23.

crucially misdescribe it, if we attempt to grasp it as as a quasi-autonomous power or practice apart from the overall life processes that constitute a society. Here again Lukács might serve as our guide as a thinker who tried to grasp the active processes of mediation at work between the emergence of the modern sciences of nature, on the one hand, and the rise of capitalist relations of production, on the other. In *History and Class Consciousness,* Lukács tries to establish the absolute homogeneity of nature between the emergent natural sciences and the development of a bourgeois society. "The idea," he says, "formulated most lucidly by Kant but essentially unchanged since Kepler and Galileo, of nature as the 'aggregate of systems of the laws' governing what happens" must be regarded as a "development out of the economic structures of capitalism." "Capitalist society," he affirms, "is predisposed to harmonize with scientific method." Galileo's call for "scientific exactitude" and the essential mathematization of nature can only be considered in relation to the recognition that "capitalism tends to produce a social structure that in great measure encourages such views" and that "it is in the nature of capitalism to process phenomena in this way."[20]

These remarks of Lukács could be amplified at greater length. However, the substantive charge is that science, once regarded as the crowning ornament of human achievement, is now seen as intrinsically bound up with the enslavement of man engendered by capitalism. By its very nature, science is animated by an "interest" in domination and control which invariably includes control not only of nature but of human beings as well. Science thus becomes an ideological institution of the bourgeois world, sharing essentially the same structure as it does. Lukács significantly reveals the source of this critique in the *Lebensphilosophie* of late nineteenth-century German romanticism when in a citation from Tönnies he remarks: "Scientific concepts which by their ordinary origin and their real properties are judgements by means

[20]Pages 136, 7, 5–6.

of which complexes of feeling are given names, behave within science like commodities in society."[21]

The gist of this attack upon science or "traditional theory" was continued by two of Lukács' disciples, Horkheimer and Adorno, in their joint work *The Dialectic of Enlightenment*. Here they portray the "deductive form of science" as expressing "hierarchy and coercion." The Enlightenment, which began with Bacon's efforts to free men from the *idola* of the cave and culminated in Kant's clarion call for men to cast off their "self-incurred immaturity" and to "have the courage to use your own intelligence," is now said to serve capital, to have become positivistic, and to anticipate fascism.[22] The irony of this critique is that while it originally sought to emancipate men from their conditions by making them aware of hidden sources of coercion, it has in effect produced the opposite of the result intended. By emphasizing the internal relatedness and homogeneity between science and modern productive technique, they have attributed a rational efficiency and solidarity to the world that precludes the possibility of change. The internal dynamics of the Enlightenment with its twofold forces of science and capitalism have drawn a closed circle that appears to allow no escape. The result of accepting this thesis must lead to a repudiation either of revolution or of reason. The first was accepted by Weber and his heirs, for whom the "iron cage" of capitalism has produced a race of "specialists without spirit, sensualists without heart."[23] In the face of overwhelming technical superiority, the only recourse is to passivity and resignation. The second has been adopted by Marcuse in his notion of the "Absolute Refusal."[24] This is not so much a revolution as Marx understood it, a libera-

[21]Page 131.

[22]Trans. John Cumming (New York: Seabury Press, 1972), pp. x, 13, 24, 84, 193.

[23]Max Weber, *The Protestant Ethic and the Spirit of Capitalism*, trans. Talcott Parsons (New York: Charles Scribner's, 1958), pp. 181–82.

[24]Herbert Marcuse, *One-Dimensional Man: Studies in the Ideology of Advanced Industrial Society* (Boston: Beacon Press, 1966), pp. 255–56. For a

tion from the work day, but a total negation of what exists. Since what exists is largely the product of science and technology, this "Promethean" rebellion must therefore be a nihilistic negation of what exists. It must be a transcendence of the very stuff of history.

It should be said that there is both a strong and a weak sense in which one can take the Internal Relatedness Thesis. The weak version attempts to salvage some stable ground for reason or science despite the alleged insight into the internal relatedness of all things. This is the version adopted by Hegel and to some extent by Marx and Engels, which holds that history itself is a rational process guided by some intelligible necessity. But this view is possible only because history is said to culminate in an "absolute moment" at which time the nature of the process would be revealed as rational. By coupling reason and history, it becomes possible to retain something like the original belief in science or philosophy without falling prey to radical historicism or relativism.

The extreme version of this thesis, however, is that because capitistic relations of production are so intimately bound up with a certain conception of reason or science, it is impossible to repudiate the one without at the same time repudiating the other. This view is fatal to Marx, who retained some conception of the independence of science, although it is not necessarily fatal simply. Nietzsche, for example, argued that science itself is only a myth created by Western man and as such can lay no greater claim to truth than can any other theory. So long as that myth is believed to be true, it remains a useful one, useful that is for the preservation of life and culture. It is only when science itself is called into question, only when it is seen as simply one creation among others, that it loses its life-giving or life-enhancing power. This, for Nietzsche, is the deadly but inescapable truth of history,

---

withering critique of this see Lucio Colletti, "From Hegel to Marcuse," *From Rousseau to Lenin: Studies in Ideology and Society,* trans. John Merrington and Judith White (London: New Left Books, 1972), esp. pp. 135–40.

deadly because it is destructive of all those errors and illusions that are so necessary for life.[25]

It follows, then, that all art and all science are built upon myth or at lest presuppose myth for their foundation. All culture, one might say, is a massive attempt to avert attention from the truth contained in relativism, that everything is subject to coming into being and passing away.[26] The vitality of culture requires a kind of blindness to history and likewise a firm dedication to principles of thought and action that must be regarded as non-historical. For Marx, who retained the Hegelian belief in the rationality of the historical process, it was possible to avoid this problem because socialism was regarded as that "absolute moment" in which the rational and the real would become one. But for those members of the Frankfurt School who, like Nietzsche, had turned the historical critique back upon itself, no such solution was possible. Not only is history unfinished; it is unfinishable. The recognition of this truth may be, as has been suggested, either enervating or exhilarating. It may be enervating because even socialism will be deprived of any foundation in the nature of things or the historical process. It will become just one more

[25]*Beyond Good and Evil,* trans. Walter Kaufmann (New York: Random House, 1966), pp. 11–12: "The falseness of a judgment is for us not necessarily an objection to a judgment. . . . The question is to what extent it is life-promoting, life-preserving, species-preserving, perhaps even species-cultivating . . . renouncing false judgments would mean renouncing life and a denial of life."

[26]That Nietzsche took the doctrine of historicism and turned it into a cosmic phenomenon called the "eternal recurrence" is well known. What is less well known is that Engels subscribed to a version of the same creed. See *Dialectics of Nature, Selected Works* (Moscow: Foreign Language Publishing House, 1958) 2: 72–73: "It is an eternal cycle in which matter moves . . . a cycle in which every finite mode of existence of matter . . . is equally transient, and wherein nothing is eternal but eternally changing, eternally moving matter. . . . We have the certainty that matter remains eternally the same in all its transformations, and that none of its attributes can ever be lost, and therefore, also, that with the same iron necessity with which it will again exterminate on the earth its highest creation, the thinking mind, it must somewhere else and at another time again engender it."

creation among infinite others. It may be exhilarating precisely because it is groundless, because it is not an objective necessity, or because it is a free creation of the will. This sort of cheerful nihilism constitutes the spiritual core of much of the Marxist humanism of our own day—and which, as we shall see in Chapter 6, Althusser has done much to dilute.[27]

The Overdetermination Thesis

Althusser's theory of overdermination is in a sense a combination of both the Fundamentalist and the Internal Relatedness Theses. It tries to retain the notion of a social formation as constituted of distinct and regionally separated "levels" or "instances" in which the economic remains determinant, but also recognizes a reciprocal or mutually determining relationship between base and superstructure in which the latter manages to enjoy a considerable degree of "autonomy." In attempting to steer a middle course between "economism" or "mechanism" on the one hand and the Hegelian "expressive totality" on the other, Althusser attributes especial importance to the older Engels' qualifications of his and Marx's earlier views, stating that it is only "ultimately" or "in the last instance" that the forces of production are determinant.

The most important piece of evidence that Althusser adduces for the Overdetermination Thesis is Engels' letter to Joseph Bloch in which he denies that either he or Marx had ever claimed that "the economic element is the only determining one" and goes on to suggest that those who have, have transformed the substantive theses of historical materialism into "a meaningless, abstract, senseless phrase." Nonetheless, Engels is willing to admit that Marx and he are "partly to blame for the fact that the younger people sometimes lay more stress on the economic side than is due

[27]For the influence of Nietzsche on the "Left Nietzscheans" of our own day see George Friedman, *The Political Philosophy of the Frankfurt School* (Ithaca: Cornell University Press, 1981), pp. 62–70.

it,'' but he attributes this overemphasis on the economic to the heat of debate when there was not always the time or place to develop ''the *other elements* involved in the interaction.''[28] Engels is even more explicit about the limits of determinism in other letters from this period. Writing to Conrad Schmidt he attacks the ''younger writers in Germany'' who adopt ''historical materialism'' in order to compress their historical knowledge into ''a neat system as quickly as possible.'' And anticipating Sartre's later conception of the dialectic as a ''heuristic'' principle, Engels states that ''our conception of history is above all a guide to study, not a lever for construction after the manner of the Hegelian.''[29] In another letter to Schmidt he expresses an awareness of the autonomy of the state and ideology as factors independent of the economic base. He explains that ''new political power, which strives for as much independence as possible . . . is endowed with a movement of its own.'' While ''economic'' factors remain dominant, he argues that the ''ideological outlook reacts in its turn upon the economic basis and may, within certain limits, modify it.''[30]

Engels reemphasizes this point a year before his death in a letter to Starkenburg of 1894. Here he maintains that ''the ultimately determining element in history is the production and reproduction of real life,'' but goes on to qualify this with the following proviso: ''Political, religious, juridical, philosophical, literary, artistic, etc. development is based on economic development. But all these react upon one another and also upon the economic basis. It is not that the economic situation is cause, solely active, while everything else is only passive effect. There is, rather, interaction on the basis of economic necessity, which ultimately always asserts itself.''[31]

Althusser regards these passages as of ''decisive'' importance for the clarification of historical materialism (*FM*, 117).

[28]*Selected Works*, 2: 488–90 (emphasis mine).
[29]Page 487.
[30]Pages 492, 494.
[31]Page 504.

What these passages claim is the importance of "other" factors which are not purely economic, and that Marx and Engels knew the limitations of determinism all along. Unfortunately, Engels' formula is left somewhat vague because the phrase "ultimately determining" is not unambiguous. The question remains that if the economic does not solely or uniquely determine the character of a society, what, then, does it do? And if the determination "in the last instance" by the base is compatible with the "relative autonomy" of the superstructure, what does the qualifier "relative" add? It does not tell us whether the productive forces are to lose their hitherto privileged position within the Marxian canon and, if they do, how Marxism is to be distinguished from its chief competitor, liberal pluralism. This is the problem which Althusser hopes to resolve through the use of the concept of "overdetermination" (*FM*, 89–116, 209–10, 216–17).

The concept of overdetermination is taken over by Althusser from Freudian psychoanalytic theory, where it is used to show how several simultaneous factors each with some explanatory power can contribute to the formation of symptoms.[32] A dream, for instance, is said to be overdetermined if it has multiple sources of determination which make it susceptible to several possibly contradictory interpretations. It is in this sense of multiple sources of determination that converge on a single result that the term has been used by the classical scholar E. R. Dodds to describe the Herodotean view of history.[33] While history, for Herodotus, is on one level the outcome of human acts and purposes, it is on another the work of divine *phantos* or the jealousy of the gods working in and through human deeds. A similar use of the term is also to be found in the work of the anthropologist E. E. Evans-Pritchard, who tells us that among the Azande belief in death from natural causes and belief in death from witchcraft do

---

[32]See Sigmund Freud, *The Interpretation of Dreams*, trans. James Strachey (New York: Avon Books, 1965), pp. 182–83, 327–30, 341–43.

[33]*The Greeks and the Irrational* (Berkeley: University of California Press, 1973), pp. 30–31.

not necessarily exclude one another.[34] In any case the general sense of the concept is that more influences go into producing an event than are necessary to explain it.

Althusser uses the overdetermination concept in both a polemical and a constructive sense. As a polemical weapon, it is aimed against both the fundamentalist and the internal relatedness models of base and superstructure relations. Against the fundamentalist version Althusser questions how a single determinant—the state of economic technology—can possibly cause or explain so wide a variety of cultural, political, and intellectual practices. If it is asserted, for instance, that Greek political life was determined by its slave economy, how does one explain the existence of slavery elsewhere without the politics of the city state. Likewise, if Catholicism is understood as merely epiphenomenal to the feudal mode of production, how then does one explain both the existence of Catholicism in other nonfeudal economies or for that matter the existence of other feudalisms, say Japanese, without Catholicism? At most it appears that the economic mode of production is a necessary but by no means a sufficient condition for the emergence of various superstructural properties. The point is not to devise some abstract explanatory hypothesis which either ignores or abstracts from the actual complexity of social life, but rather to institute a more subtle theory of causality more attuned to the logic of events.

In opposition to the internal relatedness model, Althusser cavails against the Hegelian conception of the totality or the concrete universal. The concept of totality, we recall, assumes the mutual and irreducible interdependence of the parts of a whole. Each part is but an "expression" of the inner essence of the totality itself. Thus in the *Philosophy of History,* Hegel could describe the whole of world history as a series of epochs following neatly one after the other each expressing some unique princi-

[34]*Witchcraft, Oracles and Magic* (Oxford: Oxford University Press, 1937), p. 73.

ple of spiritual development. The whole of ancient Rome, for example—its economy, polity, laws, morals, arts, and religion—could be regarded as but variations of the principle of the "abstract legal person" derived from Roman law. Similarly, in the modern world, the principle of "subjectivity" is taken as equally pervasive (*FM,* 102–3, 203–4; *RC,* 94–95, 103–4). Instead of conceiving society as a dense set of interlocking practices along Hegelian lines, Althusser regards it as a "global structure" in which the various "regional structures"—economy, politics, ideology—combine to produce and reproduce themselves and the relationships among them. The concept of a global structure is here used as a technical term which refers to the overall functioning of the social system as a whole. By minimizing the role of the economy in determining the total configuration of the global structure, the economy is put on a level with the other structures within the whole except that the various regional structures are arranged in a hierarchical and asymmetrical pattern in which the economy continues to predominate if only "in the last instance." The force of this last phrase will be examined below, although Althusser's general point seems simple enough to grasp. We can no longer speak of a single monolithic History (with a capital "H"), but only of a variety of histories each with its own peculiar "rhythm" and "temporality" of development. The result is a more complex "differential historicity" based upon the overdetermination between the parts and the whole (*RC,* 108–9).

These negative remarks should already indicate in outline the positive theory that Althusser wishes to recommend. The repudiation of the monocausal model of base and superstructure relations is intended by Althusser to underscore what he takes to be a more complex or "overdetermined" relationship that obtains between the various levels of the social whole. Even though the productive forces of a society may exert a powerful causal influence, they are not alone determinative because technique can never be abstracted from the social relations of production within which it is entwined. There is always a multiplicity and coalescence of causes from the various levels of society such that we can never observe the economic functioning in its "pure state" but only as mediated by other aspects of the whole.

> The economic dialectic is never active *in the pure state;* in History, these instances, the superstructures, etc.—are never seen to step respectfully aside when their work is done or, when the Time comes, as his pure phenomenon, to scatter before his Majesty the Economy as he strides along the royal road of the Dialectic. From the first moment to the last, the lonely hour of the "last instance" never comes [*FM,* 113].

What this really amounts to is an attempt to rewrite the Marxian theory of contradiction. In its original form Marx had argued that the contradiction between productive forces and the social relations of production was the source of tension that eventually produces change. Changes taking place at the productive base of society would bring about corresponding changes at the other levels of society like political and juridical relations. But Althusser has now tried to suggest that contradictions inherent in the material base are *supplemented* by contradictions inherent in the superstructure as well, each of which evolves and develops at its own rate. This is the "law" of uneven development (*FM,* 207–10, 212–14). The whole thus appears as a unity of contradictions whose principle aspect is the economic but which is "overdetermined" in the process by key elements of the superstructure:

> The "contradiction" is inseparable from the total structure of the social body in which it is found, inseparable from its formal *conditions* of existence, and even from the *instances* it governs; it is radically *affected by them,* determining, but also determined in one and the same movement, and determined by the various *levels* and *instances* of the social formation it animates; it might be called *overdetermined in its principle* [*FM,* 101].

The whole can best be understood, then, as an "accumulation of contradictions'' which builds up to a point at which time the mechanism of social collapse is finally triggered off:

> If . . . a vast accumulation of ''contradictions'' comes into play *in the same court*, some of which are radically heterogeneous—of different origins, different sense, different *levels* and *points* of application—but which nevertheless ''merge'' into a ruptural unity, we can no longer talk of the sole, unique power of the general ''contradiction'' [*FM*, 100].

The concept of overdetermination is, I believe, a useful way of handling contradictions as well as emphasizing the actual complexities of historical experience. In its most positive form this concept recognizes multiple sources of contradiction at work rather than the isolated forces of productive technique. In this respect it is a valuable corrective to the fundamentalist's denial of any authentic interaction between base and superstructure. Negatively, Althusser never tells us what are the equivalent contradictions—equivalent, that is, to that between the forces and relations of production—that arise within the superstructure. It is hardly adequate to assert that all the elements of the superstructure evolve and develop according to their own ''differential historicity'' without giving some further specification of what this might mean. Let us pursue this further.

Althusser uses the Overdetermination Thesis to account for the crucial problem of regime transformation. The key to regime transformation depends upon the cumulative build-up of general contradictions which triggers the collapse. In some countries one particular constellation or ''conjuncture'' of events will prove explosive and in other situations a quite different mix will be required. Thus Althusser makes much of Lenin's statements about the unique constellation of events that made possible the October Revolution of 1917 (*FM*, 99). On the basis of this testimony, a number of seemingly unrelated events—the outbreak of the war, the collapse of Tsarism, the availability of Lenin and the Bolshevik party—all converged on the same end. Being the "weakest link" in the chain of "advanced countries," Russia combined just those elements in such a way as to make it ripe for revolution.

The consequence of the Overdetermination Thesis is that it prohibits a priori even the possibility of a general or comparative analysis of the emergence of the causes of social revolution. Since every event is unique, the outcome of a constellation of local circumstances that will never appear in the same form again, he is not providing us with something like a "covering law" or an "anatomy" of revolution, but rather telling us why any such explanatory schema is impossible. Thus when Althusser writes that a socialist revolution "could only break out . . . in Russia, in China, in Cuba, in 1917, in 1949, in 1958, and not elsewhere; and not in another 'situation,' " this assessment is not intended as a starting point for a theory of revolution in general (*FM*, 207). In fact no attempt is made to explain how the contradictions with which those societies were wracked were in any way similar to, or for that matter, different from those societies which did not undergo a radical change. All we are told is that if a revolution does break out then the general nexus of contradictions must have reached the point of combustion, but there is no telling what particular constellation of factors will lead up to the crisis.

We encounter the same difficulty if we turn to the Althusserian explanation of the emergence of fascism during the interwar period. In his *Fascism and Dictatorship,* Althusser's disciple Nicos Poulantzas argues that the emergence of fascism can only be understood as a response to the crisis of capitalism in its "imperialist stage."[35] This imperial stage is believed to provide the necessary framework for the emergence of this phenomenon. But why, we should like to know, did the global crisis of capitalism lead to fascism in some countries (Germany, Italy, and Spain), to socialism in others (Russia), and to the continued survival of liberal democracy in still others (Great Britain and the United States)? Poulantzas' answer to this important question is

[35]Trans. Judith N. White (London: New Left Books, 1974), p. 17.

only to repeat Althusser's formula that the first group must have combined the general contradictions of capitalism in such a way as to make them particularly susceptible to the "fascist solution," while the others never produced the mix in just this way. But what is to count as just this way is never explained. Despite his assertion that there were "a whole series of reasons" that led to the appearance of fascism, there are no general criteria adduced to explain why the "immense accumulation" of contradictions led in some places to fascism and in others to quite different outcomes. All we are told by way of explanation is that these various alternatives appeared in those societies that were ripe for those respective outcomes.

It is important to note what this interpretation of the Marxian dialectic is intended to put forward and what, apparently, it seeks to deny. What is being claimed is that structural change is always the outcome of a surprising number of heterogeneous elements, every one of which is indispensable to the success of the enterprise in question. In this sense uniqueness and not overdetermination would be a better term for the process. In other words, since breaks in historical continuity obey no "law," it would become incredibly difficult, not to say impossible, to construct statistical regularities and generalizations which can then be used for the control and manipulation of events. Ironically, it follows that a Lenin or any architect of social change can never have a reliable blueprint for action. What we find is an understanding of revolutions as highly improbable complexes of events that can only be understood after the fact. Revolutionary situations, it appears, can only be grasped retrospectively in the way that Hegel's owl of Minerva takes flight with the falling of dusk.

The main difficulty with the Overdetermination Thesis, as I see it, turns on just how much "autonomy" the principle of determination "in the last instance" by the base is willing to cede to the superstructure. What gave the Fundamentalist Thesis its force was the weight it gave to one specific set of factors in the explanation of social change. But Althusser's reformulation of the theory of contradiction leads to an almost equal weighting of both basic and superstructural factors. The result is that it becomes impossible to distinguish between primary causes without which an event could not have taken place and secondary causes which perhaps only incidentally contribute to it. As I have already suggested, the term overdetermination is perhaps not altogether felicitious as it implies that, had any of the circumstantial factors that produce an event not been present, the event would have happened anyway, whereas the context of Althusser's discussion makes clear that every factor is absolutely contributory, so that we cannot abstract certain features from a situation and rank them in some relative order of importance. It appears that we must be content with a form of descriptive empiricism in which base and superstructure are accorded more or less equal status. The ultimate impact of this multi-causal, overdetermined model of society is to replace the fundamentalist emphasis on the causal primacy of the productive forces with a species of functionalist pluralism.[36]

There is in fact good evidence for appending this label to Althusser. Not only does he tend to equalize base and superstructure relations, but like most systems functionalists he tries to explain social practices and institutions not in terms of their origins or genesis but in terms of their ability to foster the maintenance and ''reproduction'' of society that prevents it from coming apart. Explanation for Althusser is satisfactory when each of the regional structures of a social formation is described not only in terms of its place but in terms of its function in securing the overall stability of the whole. The emphasis throughout is on what forces tend toward systems maintenance rather than toward systems change.

A crucial aspect of Althusser's rapproachment with functionalism has turned on his commitment to a type of methodological holism and his corresponding devaluation of the role of individual motives and intentions in history. Turning his atten-

---

[36]See Roger Garaudy, ''A propos des Manuscrits de 1844,'' p. 119; Frank Parkin, ''The Academicizing of Marxism,'' *Dissent*, 2 (1980): 172–80.

tion away from the question of "who makes history?" he has asked "how is the reproduction of the relations of production secured?" (*LP*, 141). Althusser contends that the problem of the order and articulation of society will remain elusive so long as the answer is sought at the level of conscious human volition and will. The intentional behavior of social subjects plays no role in his form of functionalist determinism. Instead he refers to a "mechanism" which produces this result as the "society effect," that is, a device the result of which is overall social stasis or equilibrium.

> Marx regards contemporary society (and every other past form of society) both as a *result* and as a *society*. . . . But contemporary society is not only a result, a product: it is *this* particular result, *this* particular *product*, which functions as a *society*, unlike other results and other products which function quite differently . . . what Marx studies in *Capital* is the mechanism which makes the result of a history's production exist *as a society;* it is therefore the mechanism which gives this product of history, that is precisely the society-product he is studying, the property of producing the "*society effect*" which makes the result exist *as a society*, and not as a heap of sand, an ant-hill, a workshop or a mere collection of men [*RC*, 65].

The society effect is able to achieve its results, the reproduction of the relations of production, largely through the twin pillars of the coercive state apparatus and perhaps more significantly through the ideological machinery which seeks to instill common norms and values as a way of guaranteeing a stable and cohesive social order. Althusser borrows this distinction between the state and the "ideological state apparatus" from Gramsci, for whom society perpetuates itself through a combination of state power, with its police, military, courts, and prisons, and ideological control instilled through the family, schools, media, culture, and even language itself (*LP*, 141–42, 148). Gramsci's theory of "hegemony" is intended to demonstrate how social cohesion is achieved through a whole range of institutions, both public and private, which attain their goal without anyone willing it as such. Such institutions as the state and ideology derive their functions not by virtue of their relationship to a particular class, even the dominant ones, but to the whole of society. This remains true even though the beneficiaries of these institutions will invariably be the dominant classes.

What are we to make of these remarks? First, the question of the order and reproduction of society is not exhaustive of the nature of historical processes. Upheaval and disorder also require explanation. But Althusser's relatively greater insistence on what holds societies together and allows them to persist in a stable manner is designed to forestall precisely these questions. When a large-scale structural transformation does occur, such as the Russian Revolution, it is only explained as a *hiatus irrationalis* that can be neither predicted nor controlled. Since such moments of transformation are always the product of a unique local confluence of circumstances, they fall outside social theory strictly speaking. Second, both Gramsci's theory of hegemony and Althusser's theory of overdetermination give considerably more to the superstructure in securing the reproduction of society than is true of classical Marxism. Whereas Marx regarded that the fundamental character of society was conferred by the dominant mode of production, both Gramsci and Althusser give more or less equal weight to the complementary modalities of state power and ideology in securing this end. Third, we might wonder whether the explanation of political phenomena like state and ideology in terms of their ability to ensure social cohesion is really an explanation at all. Althusser rejects any ''instrumentalist'' conception of the state as simply a pliant tool in the hands of the dominant class. While this class may subjectively seek to possess both the state and its ideological apparatus, these have a relative independence of their own apart from considerations of class. Likewise, he rejects the conception of the state as a neutral mediator exercising power independently of all social classes. To regard the state in this role of mediator is to turn it into a ''subject'' or a collective actor with a will of its own. But once we eliminate these two alternatives, what else is left? If the state is neither an instrument in the hands of a class nor an actor that can control the various classes independent of them all, we can say, as Poulantzas does, that it is a ''relationship of forces'' that aids in the reproduction of society. But this is only to tell us what the state does (or does not do) to the things around it. It does not tell us what it is in itself.

If Althusser can be said to have made an original contribution to social and political theory, it turns on his conception of the relation of the superstructure to the economic base. Whatever its appearances to the contrary, he denies that the concept of over-determination necessarily commits him to a methodological pluralism. The autonomy of the superstructure is only ''relative,'' not ''absolute,'' and does not exclude the ultimate primacy of the economic. He tries to solve this puzzle by adopting a distinction between ''determinant'' and ''dominant'' instances of a social formation. While the productive base is the determinant instance, it is not necessarily the dominant one. For example, in European countries of the Middle Ages, religious relations appeared to dominate. And in the types of primitve societies studied by Lévi-Strauss, kinship relations appear as dominant. In neither case, however, does this contradict the principle that economic relations are still determinant if only ''in the last instance.'' This distinction between determinant and dominant members of a social totality is said to provide us with ''a new conception of . . . the structure-superstructure complex which constitutes the essence of any social formation'' (*FM,* 111).

In place of both the mechanical reduction of all parts of the social formation to the material or technological base and the equalization of all its parts through a web of internal relations, Althusser adopts the principle of the hierarchical organization of society divided into determinant, dominant, and subordinate instances, each with its own degree of ''specific effectivity.'' This structured totality is called by him a ''structure in dominance.''

That one contradiction dominates the others presupposes that the complexity in which it features is a structured unity, and this structure implies the indicated domination-subordination relations between contradictions. . . . Domination is not just an indifferent *fact,* it is a fact *essential* to the complexity itself. That is why complexity implies domination as one of its essentials: it is inscribed in its structure. So to claim that this unity is not and cannot be the unity of a simple, original and universal essence is not . . . to sacrifice unity on the altar of "pluralism"—it is to claim something quite different: that the unity discussed by Marxism is *the unity of the complexity itself,* that the mode of organization and articulation of the complexity is precisely what constitutes its unity. It is to claim that *the complex whole has the unity of a structure articulated in dominance* [*FM,* 201–2].

This reasoning makes it possible to distinguish or rank the various levels of the whole according to their relative importance.

If every contradiction is a contradiction in a complex whole structured in dominance, this complex whole cannot be envisaged without its contradictions, without their basically uneven relations. In other words, each contradiction, each essential articulation of the structure, and the general relation of the articulations in the structure in dominance, constitute so many conditions of the existence of the complex whole itself. This proposition is of the first importance. For it means that the structure of the whole and therefore the "difference" of the essential contradictions and their structure in dominance, is the very existence of the whole; that the "difference" of the contradictions . . . is identical to the conditions of the existence of the complex whole. In plain terms this position implies that the "secondary" contradictions are not the pure phenomena of the "principal" contradiction, that the principal is not the essence and the secondaries so many of its phenomena, so much so that the principal contradiction might practically exist *without* the secondary contradictions, or without some of them, or might exist *before* or *after* them. On the contrary, it implies that the secondary contradictions are essential even to the existence of the principal contradiction, that they really constitute its conditions of existence, just as the principal contradiction constitutes their condition of existence. As an example, take the complex structured whole that is society [*FM*, 204–5].

The kind of unity described here is neither organic nor mechanistic. It is neither an undifferentiated whole where everything is intimately related to everything else nor a mere congeries of intersecting forces. It is rather a "structured whole" in which one can distinguish between determinant preconditions and dominant functions.

> In it, the "relations of production" are not the pure phenomena of the forces of production; they are also their condition of existence. The superstructure is not the pure phenomenon of the structure, it is also its condition of existence. . . . Please do not misunderstand me: this mutual conditioning of the existence of the "contradictions" does not nullify the structure in dominance that reigns over the contradictions and in them (in this case, determination in the last instance by the economy). Despite its apparent circularity, this conditioning does not result in the destruction of the structure of domination that constitutes the complexity of the whole, and its unity. Quite the contrary, even within the reality of the conditions of existence of each contradiction, it is the manifestation of the structure in dominance that unifies the whole. *This reflection of the conditions of existence of the contradiction within itself, this reflection of the structure articulated in dominance that constitutes the unity of the complex whole within each contradiction,* this is the most profound characteristic of the Marxist dialectic, the one I have tried recently to encapsulate in the concept of "overdetermination" [*FM*, 205–6].

There are two general conclusions I would like to draw from my account of Althusser's Overdetermination Thesis. First, as these passages reveal, we discover an emphatically nonhistorical attitude to the problem of the dialectic. Society is presented herein as a "complex structured whole" which "cannot be envisaged without its contradictions." What is more, the presence of contradiction is not to be accounted a feature of an historically defective mode of existence, but rather as "inscribed in its [society's]

structure'' and as the ''manifestation of the structure in dominance that unifies the whole.'' Thus Althusser could be said to be
dehistoricizing the dialectic at the very point where Marx claimed
to have discovered it. While both Hegel and Marx operated with
a philosophy of history which teaches the progressive resolution
of contradiction, Althusser operates with a social ontology that
regards the fact of contradiction as an ''essential articulation of
the structure.'' In this sense he is operating with a model of
society that can be appropriately described as ''metaphysical'' in
precisely the sense meant by Marx and Engels. He attributes a
permanent content or validity to features found in historically
specific forms of society.

Second, for all his attempts to resolve the problem, there is a
persistent tension, if not to say mutual incompatibility, between
the two principles of determination in the last instance by the base
and the relative autonomy of the superstructure. For if the economic is determinant even in this reduced sense, then the autonomy of the superstructure automatically becomes vitiated. But if
the relative autonomy of the superstructure is taken as the decisive feature, then the causal primacy of the productive forces
loses whatever privilege it had within the Marxian canon. With
the absence of empirical materials to support his case, one won-
ders how far Althusser would be willing to push the autonomy
claim. Does he really believe that the legal institutions of feudalism, say, could coexist along with a market economy based upon
the free movement of labor? Or could a market economy really
support a political apparatus based upon certain classical conceptions of virtue and the value of political participation? Here it
seems that when pushed to their limits one or the other has to
give, and if it is the economy that always ''ultimately'' asserts
itself, why then bother with the autonomy claim at all? In the
final analysis Althusser's Overdetermination Thesis does not escape but rather reproduces the problems of the two accounts of
base and superstructure that we have already examined.

As a final word, it must be said that Althusser's ''mutual
conditioning'' of base and superstructure appears suspiciously

like the type of neo-Weberian functionalism or systems theory he claims to condemn. To say that historical change is brought about by many factors at work simultaneously is an argument compatible with almost any non-Marxist social theorist working within the political mainstream. Althusser is not unaware, however, of the ambiguity of his two principles of determination in the last instance by the base and the relative autonomy of the superstructure and has referred to them as "two ends of the chain" (*FM*, 111). Whether he has succeeded in joining these ends or merely calling our attention to them is a matter left unresolved in his work. At the very least, these principles remain obscure, hovering, as I have suggested, somewhere between metaphysics on the one hand and a pluralist functionalism on the other.[37]

[37]Giddens, *Central Problems in Social Theory*, p. 159.

6

The Structural
Science of History

Althusser's main claim to our attention is based on his attempt to establish a rapproachement between Marxism and structuralism.[1] Since structuralism can be regarded as nothing more than a word for scientific method, we can best begin to grasp its meaning by contrasting it to the existential-phenomenological method it aspires to surpass.

Althusser's attitude toward structuralism is, curiously, the mirror image of Sartre's toward existentialism. In the *Search for a Method,* Sartre began by making the claim that Marxism is the

---

[1] Works of general interest on structuralism include Jean-Marie Auzias, *Clefs pour le structuralisme* (Paris: Seghers, 1967); Raymond Boudon, *The Uses of Structuralism* (London: Heinemann, 1971); Richard T. and Fernande de George, eds., *The Structuralists: From Marx to Lévi-Strauss* (New York: Doubleday, 1972); J. B. Fages, *Comprendre le structuralisme* (Toulouse: E. Privat, 1968); Michael Lane, ed., *Structuralism: A Reader* (New York: Basic Books, 1970); David Roby, ed., *Structuralism: An Introduction* (Oxford: Oxford University Press, 1973); François Wahl, ed., *Qu'est-ce que le structuralisme?* (Paris: Editions du Seuil, 1968). For journals with special issues on the subject see "Problèmes de structuralisme," *Les Temps Modernes,* 246 (1966); "Structuralisme: Idéologie et méthode," *Esprit,* 360 (1967); "Structuralisme et marxisme," *La Pensée,* 135 (1967).

"unsurpassable" philosophy of our time, next to which existentialism is merely an ideology living on and exploiting the domain established by this philosophy. Nevertheless, existentialism can be important for Marxism as a way of "recovering" man within history. Marxism has become a largely scholastic system of concepts and categories incapable of grasping the concrete particularities of individual experience. The comprehension of experience can in turn be achieved only through the introduction of teleological concepts such as "intentionality," which Sartre borrowed from Husserl. Thus only by grafting a new method, that of existentialism, on to the Marxist stem will it be possible to rescue the dialectic from the weight of positivist determinism and restore it as a method of historical research.

Althusser, by contrast, has claimed that Marxism is a "science" and that structuralism is a mere "ideology" (*RC,* 7). But for him structuralism can be important for its attempt to show that the real emphasis of Marxism is not on man, not human actions which can be made intelligible through a phenomenological description of states of consciousness, but on structures which are not resolvable into the expressions of human agency and which are themselves unknown or "unconscious" to the agents whose actions they determine. These structures can in turn only be discovered through a "deconstructive" analysis, that is, one that aims not to describe the given as it appears to us through the "natural attitude" or common sense, but one that seeks to break it down into its component parts in order to disclose the basic elements or combination of elements out of which the given is constructed. What structuralism claims to have discovered—or rather recovered—is the Parmenidean dictum, not that being receives its meaning only in and through the free act of the ego, but simply that being *is* and as such is "subjectless." The advantage of this insight is that, since structures are devoid of meaning and consequently value-free, they can easily be turned into a fit object for scientific investigation. The result, as Henri Lefebvre has noted, is a "neo-eleatic" approach that ranks order higher than change and which denies the thesis that it is man who makes history.[2]

Certain disclaimers to the contrary notwithstanding, Althusser's claim has consistently been to establish a Marxist science of history along structuralist lines. Long before the linguistic analyses of Saussure or the treatment of kinship systems by Lévi-Strauss, Marx, so we are told, set out to describe the whole of social life in terms of structures and their interrelations, differentiating types of societies on the basis of assumed correspondences (or noncorrespondences) between infrastructures and superstructures and claiming to account for the rise and fall of societies by tracing the appearance and development of contradictions between these structures. It is this attempt to account for societies not in terms of men and their histories but through certain underlying structural patterns and relations that is said to have made Marx into a structuralist *ante diem*. The Althusserians are fond of quoting from Marx's sixth *Thesis on Feuerbach* to show that he was a structuralist before the fact. "The human essence," Marx says, "is not an abstraction inherent in each individual . . . it is the ensemble of social relations." It is the turn away from history and toward structure which Althusser claims constitutes Marx's "immense theoretical revolution" and which set the stage for all later structuralist thought.

Structuralism may be a new word upon the intellectual scene, although if we look beyond the appearances of the word we shall discover a mode of thought that reveals a distinguished lineage going back not only to writers like Marx and Freud but even further back to Kant and Spinoza. The modern concept of structure, however, was developed by thinkers in a number of the social-science disciplines but most notably linguistics.[3] It has been maintained that structuralism is really about the substitution

[2]"Claude Lévi-Strauss et le nouvel eléatisme," *Au-delà du structuralisme,* pp. 261–313.

[3]See Jonathan Culler, "The Linguistic Basis of Structuralism," *Structuralism,* Roby, ed., pp. 20–36.

of linguistics for history. Ill-disposed critics have even been known to suggest that the cure is worse than the disease. Whether or not this is true, the obvious attraction of structuralism has been its claim to lay bare the most general features of our conceptual makeup without falling prey to historicism. In any case a few of the central methodological tenets of structural linguistics can be isolated as providing a key to the entire structuralist enterprise of which Althusser is a part.

In the first place, the newer trend in structural linguistics promised to replace the older historical philology by the study of entire linguistic systems. The study of language systems means the priority of *langue* over *parole*. These terms have no very precise English equivalents, although *langue* has occasionally been translated as "language system" to convey the network of grammatical regularities which underlies any natural language, while *parole* has been rendered as "language behavior" to indicate the actual speech acts produced by native speakers on particular occasions. In concentrating on the total system of signs that composes a language as opposed to the spoken word, structuralist linguistics was calling attention to the fact that the structure of the entire system determines the position of every element within it and that change in the meaning of any element will alter the meaning of everything else within the system. The priority of the whole over the parts is thus a central feature of all structuralist thought.

Next, the structure of language (or of any cultural artefact) was sought, not on the surface level of empirical reality, but below or behind it. What the naive observor sees is not the structure, but the evidence and product of the structure. In this respect the structure of language was considered to be "unconscious" or "invisible," since the individual language user can consistently and constantly apply its phonological and grammatical laws in his speech without ever necessarily knowing what he is doing. Moreover, these structures are held to be the product of an innate, that is genetically rather than socially or culturally determined, reason inherent in all men. This inherent quality or capacity is so designated as to limit the possible range of language systems so that the set of all possible languages will probably be very large but finite. Their apparent diversity should not hide the fact that behind them are certain invariant and recurring features that are subject to a method of mathematical notation whose possible permutations can not only be calculated but predicted.

Finally, we arrive at the third point, which is the attempt to study language not diachronically through temporal change but synchronically through static and ahistorical relations. These relations can be characterized as "outside time" or "given" or "perpetually present." The belief that language possesses a certain timeless quality in spite of occasional modifications of its elements pointed out the inherent limitations of any historicist or evolutionist approach. By isolating language from its social and historical context, structural linguistics hoped to grasp the immanent laws underlying language systems which hold them together in a coherent and functional whole.

The difficulty with formulating a universally acceptable definition of structuralism or isolating a few central tenets of structural method, as I have just tried to do, is that the result is likely to be so general as to be useless for any very precise explanatory purposes. Moreover, if the concept of structuralism can be defined by reference to a host of other concepts like "system," "relations," "whole," "coherence," and "function," then it is difficult to see why we should bother with the concept of structure at all. The fact is that there is no central core or unique essence of structuralism to which all structuralists adhere but rather a number of different aspects that some share with others but not necessarily in the same way or for the same reasons. In this sense structuralism forms a kind of family in exactly the way understood by Wittgenstein, that is, "a complicated network of similarities overlapping and criss-crossing: sometimes overall similarities, sometimes similarities, sometimes similarities of detail."[4] What we must attempt to do, then, is to avoid definition in the sense of reduction to a set of basic assumptions shared by all structuralists and see how the term is used by Althusser and others who fall within the same family. Only then will we be able to get a better picture of what Althusser's "structural Marxism" is all about.

Marxism and Structure

The concept of structure is used by Althusser in *Capital* as a way of indicating Marx's "scientific" achievements. These achievements are purportedly based upon the analysis of capitalism not as a dynamically evolving but as a relatively fixed system of production. The mode of production is examined, accordingly, as a system or model, the structure of which determines the position of every element within the whole. Every mode of production will arise from a finite and, as it happens, small number of terms which are always and everywhere the same, the only variation being their mode of combination. As we shall see, while Marx's starting point, the specific "object" of *Capital*, is the capitalist mode of production in particular, Althusser construes this analysis into a universal theory of the "basic forms of unity of historical existence," in other words, into a theory of modes of production everywhere. Rather than providing us with any sort of phenomenological description of capitalism and the work place, Marx is said to have concerned himself with the rudimentary principles of any possible history.

The aim of Althusser's structural Marxism is to provide a model of the social sciences based upon a combination (*Verbindung*) of a limited number of variables that can be mathematically manipulated. "Marx's aim," as Balibar says, "was to show that the distinction between different modes is necessarily and *sufficiently* based on a variation of the connections between a small

[4]*Philosophical Investigations*, p. 32.

number of elements which are always the same. The announcement of the connections and their terms constitutes the exposition of the primary theoretical concepts of historical materialism" (*RC*, 225). And referring very probably to this passage in Balibar's exposition, Althusser writes: "But it is clear that the theoretical nature of this concept of 'combination' may provide a foundation for the thesis . . . that Marxism *is not a historicism:* since the Marxist concept of history depends on the principle of the variation of the forms of this 'combination'" (*RC*, 177).

The deconstruction of Marx's achievements in *Capital* begins by setting out a table of "invariant" elements said to be characteristic of all modes of production. This table contains the invisible "atoms of history" which consists of a combination of three elements set into play by two relations (*RC*, 215). Schematically, these are as follows:

1. the laborer or direct producer (work force),
2. the means of production (object and means of labor),
3. the non-laborer appropriating surplus value.

These three elements are combined by two relations:

4. relation of real appropriation,
5. property relation.

The conception of history that emerges from this deconstruction is that of an eternal recombination of a finite body of elements that provide the a priori building blocks of any possible mode of production. The idea is that while these elements remain constant their mode of combination varies so that it might be possible, at least in principle, to determine not only the types of societies that have existed but those that ideally might exist. Thus Althusser confidently asserts: "By combining or interrelating these different elements we shall reach a definition of the different modes of production which have existed and can exist in human history" (*RC*, 176). The process of change is limited, then, to a small repertory of ideal terms. History, it appears, resembles nothing so much as the perpetual reshuffling of a fixed pack.

The most striking feature of this conception is its subordination of the historical question of how economic structures come into being and pass away to the structural question of their internal functioning. This subordination is a principle common to more or less all who consider themselves structuralists. Marx, so we are told, did not make the question of the origin or historical evolution of social relations the primary object of his science of economic forms. What he was interested in was the "order and connection" (Spinoza) of these relations within a given society, what makes them hold together and function as a society. Only after the logic or internal working of these relations is analyzed can we move on to the study of their temporal dimension. This synchronic approach to modes of production is most forcefully stated by Marx in the introduction to the *Grundrisse,* where he defines the order in which it is necessary to study bourgeois production relations:

> It would therefore be unfeasible and wrong to let the economic categories follow one another in the same sequence as that in which they were historically decisive. Their sequence is determined, rather, by their relations to one another in modern bourgeois society, which is precisely the opposite of that which seems to be their natural order or which corresponds to historical development. The point is not the historic position of the economic relations in the succession of different economic forms of society. Even less is it their sequence "in the idea" (Proudhon). Rather, their order within modern bourgeois society.[5]

This procedure of describing the internal functioning of a network of relations prior to their development over time can be seen even more clearly if we turn to one more example from Marx, this time from his earlier polemic against Proudhon, *The Poverty of Philosophy.* Here Marx explicitly criticizes the attempt to understand society historically, which invariably seeks to ascribe causal efficacy to those relations which exist earlier in time. Instead, what he proposes is a more functional analysis

[5]Pages 107–8.

which shows how the various parts of society are logically inter-related in the present and manage to coexist simultaneously.

> M. Proudhon considers economic relations as so many social phases, engendering one another, resulting one from another like the antithesis from the thesis, and realizing in their logical se-quence the impersonal reason of humanity. The only drawback to this method is that when he comes to examine a single one of these phases, M. Proudhon cannot explain it without having re-course to all the other relations of society; which relations, how-ever, he has not yet contrived to engender by means of his dialec-tic movement. When, after that, M. Proudhon, by means of pure reason, proceeds to give birth to those other phases, he treats them as if they were newborn babes. He forgets that they are of the same age as the first. . . . The different limbs of society are converted into so many separate societies, following one upon the other. How, indeed, could the single logical formula of move-ment, of sequence, of time, explain the structure of society, in which all relations co-exist simultaneously and support one another?[6]

The explanation of a mode of production, in other words, must be found not in its circumstances of origin but in the persistence of its effects.

Even if it were true, as these passages seem to suggest, that Marx refused to grant priority to history over structure, it does not follow that Althusser's conclusions are immune from crit-icism. The first problem arises from his pretension to determine conceptually the invariants of all modes of production. If these five elements are to be taken literally as the central features of any possible mode of production, then they can be derived legit-imately only from a sort of transcendental deduction of the cate-gories in the manner of Kant. But Althusser does no such thing. Instead of a real deduction he derives these "basic concepts of historical materialism" through a comparative analysis of only

[6]*The Poverty of Philosophy* (New York: International Publishers, 1962), pp. 110–11.

three modes of production which have existed in history: Asiatic, feudal, and capitalist. Yet it would seem that to jump from these five factors, based on a simple inductive generalization from only three actual cases to a theory of modes of production in general, is a very large jump indeed. Assimilating them to the Kantian categories, Althusser wants to show that these five elements exist as a priori constitutive features of the economic which can be used for sorting out and organizing empirical evidence, but his comparative method is incapable of establishing this.

There is the further difficulty of actually having to account for all possible modes of production by means of these five elements. It is highly doubtful whether these five terms are sufficient to determine all the possible modes of production without introducing other implicit differentiating principles. The problem is that these categories are purely formal in nature so, when it comes down to actual cases, can tell us little about the actual content of history much less account for particular events.

More significantly, the structural analysis of modes of production works well so long as society is functioning smoothly and where all the relations continue to support one another. It breaks down, or at least becomes severely strained, when having to account for historical change, the problem of structural displacement or transformation. Althusser admits as much when he says: "Just as we can say that we possess only the outline of a Marxist theory of modes of production . . . we must say that Marx did not give us any theory of the transition from one mode of production to another" (*RC,* 197). Instead, therefore, of focusing on major structural changes between different modes of production, Althusser locates the strength of Marx's analysis in his concentration on the inner "consistency" of structures, their continued production and reproduction over time. "The capitalist production process," Marx writes, "considered in its inner-connexion (*Zusammenhang*) or as reproduction, produces not only commodities, not only surplus-value, but it also produces and eternalizes the social relation between the capitalist and the wage-earner" (cited in *RC,* 269). The capital-labor relation is seen as the element of the economic structure which remains constant whatever other variations might occur. The discovery and definition of this logical constant which "eternalizes" capitalist production relations has given Althusserian Marxism a conservative cast which it shares with much of the recent structural-functionalist sociology.

Of course, Althusser does not wish to deny change altogether. Were it otherwise, his ideas could scarcely merit our attention. Rather the question is whether he regards the states of relative permanence as primary and those of periodic crisis as secondary or the other way round. His answer is clear. Just as Parmenides and his school found it difficult if not impossible to conceive of motion, so have Althusser and the structuralist camp found it increasingly difficult to conceptualize historical change. From the fact that history, the eternal stream of becoming, cannot be apprehended, it follows that it can only be grasped as a series of static cross-sections which can be isolated and compared to one another as well as to earlier and later configurations of the same object whether this be an economic system, a language group, or a game. Each can only be studied as a discrete system with a set of internally imposed limitations on its number of permutations and combinations which have no necessary or genetic links to other systems.

If history presents itself as nothing more than a series of discontinuous possibilities, it follows further that we can no longer speak of a linear succession or evolution of societies toward some final culmination or end. To use these terms presupposes some type of meaningful or "teleological" purpose at work giving history an inner unity or purpose. But having rejected any type of teleological or progressivist historicism, Althusser is forced to argue that what unity history possesses is only the sum total of all its possible structural permutations. Consequently, he leaves himself open to the charge of moral relativism or indifference to the question of whether one mode of combination is in any sense better than any other. Socialism could not be adjudged as any more rational than capitalism or earlier economic forms, but only as one of a small and in principle determinable combination of a quasi-Kantian set of invariants.

Althusser's inability to account for the problem of transformation might be attributed to the conception of economic structure with which he operates. Rather than regarding structures as a type of ideal order that the scientist introduces in order to reduce the multiform flux of phenomena to simplified images, he endows them with an objectivity independent of the conceptual models used for explaining them. Thus while structures cannot be "seen" they can at least be inferred through their effects or manifestations which are empirically observable. In contrast to the conceptual empiricism of classical economics, Althusser writes: "The relations of production are structures—and the ordinary economist may scrutinize economic 'facts': prices, exchanges, wages, profits, rents, etc., all those 'measurable' facts, as much as he likes; he will no more 'see' any structure at that level than the pre-Lavoisierian chemist could 'see' oxygen in 'dephlogisticated' air" (*RC*, 181). Structure has in this sense the same status for Althusser that the concept of the "unconscious" had for Freud: neither is open to direct observation but can only be deduced from certain outward forms of behavior.

It is arguable that Althusser is unable to account for transitions because he is operating with an essentially "objectifying" or "reifying" conception of structure. By reification I mean exactly what Marx meant by that term, that is, conceiving a relationship between human agents as a relationship between things. Roger Garaudy, for one, complains that Althusser's reifying conception of structure is due to a rudimentary linguistic confusion:

Unfortunately this is because the word "structure" is a substantive instead of a verb. When we use a substantive we are always inclined to look behind it for something substantial. We end by treating structure as a thing and not as providing information about an action which has no existence apart from the men who perform them, or their writings, the structure of myth in their conduct or their beliefs. In short, it is important not to sacrifice

185

the producer and his acts of production to the product. This is one of the major teachings of Marx's *Capital* when he warns against the illusion of "commodity fetishism."[7]

For Garaudy, the concept of structure is useful but only as a conceptual shorthand or "model" not unlike a Weberian ideal type that allows the scientist to capture the distinct and characteristic features of a given class of phenomena. Marx, he says,

> never turned structuralism into a philosophy as if structure were the only reality. His own dialectical conception of structure in the social sciences first of all never forgets that structure is a human artifact as is every scientific "model," every product and every institution, every cultural phenomenon; consequently, he never separates abstractly, metaphysically, structures from the fundamental social practices which engender them or from the concrete, lived individual practices which these structures inform.[8]

Garaudy and other critics of structuralism are correct in one respect. Althusser does operate with a "metaphysical" or more properly ontological conception of structure as a subjacent reality distinct from ordinary empirical social relations. The exclusive concentration on ordered processes as distinct from the human practices that produce them has led to a political immobilism which amounts to a repudiation of both classical Marxism and history. There is, however, one important respect in which this criticism of Althusser is deficient. Without some idea of structure, it is difficult to see how history, which is otherwise composed of a multiplicity of conflicting aims and "projects," can result in ordered processes rather than an "arbitrary destructured log-jam" (to use Perry Anderson's apt phrase).[9] Althusser has had no difficulty in showing that his critics have invariably fallen back upon some notion of a preestablished harmony or an

---

[7]*Perspectives de l'homme: Existentialisme, pensée catholique, structuralisme, marxisme* (Paris: Presses Universitaires de France, 1969), p. 237.

[8]Page 369.

[9]*Arguments within English Marxism*, p. 51.

Hegelian "cunning of reason" to explain the apparent discrepancy between subjective intentions and objective outcomes. By concentrating on structures, he could at least claim to show that there is an institutional order that is distinct from and even opaque to the conscious intentions and volitions of the social subjects who occupy its places.

What both parties to the debate fail to do is to come up with a means of synthesizing both diachrony and synchrony within a single system. Of the two, however, Althusser comes closer to furnishing a satisfactory solution. His description of the "historical fact" as one which "causes a mutation in the existing structural relations" is clearly an attempt to reunite the twin processes of stability and change (*RC*, 102). Even this, though, is not quite sufficient for his purposes. The restriction of historical research to what brings about structural changes simply eliminates through an apparently arbitrary piece of legislation a great deal of what historians and ethnologists ordinarily do. Likewise the definition of a fact as what "causes" structural changes eliminates from consideration those events which do not so much induce but merely assist in maintaining social equilibrium. The difficulty Althusser runs into here can, I believe, ultimately be traced back to his choice of words—"mutation"—a concept borrowed not from structuralism but from the older evolutionary paradigm which it was attempting to replace. The result indicates a gradual process of adaptation rather than moments of revolutionary "displacement."

A more promising attempt to account for the relationship between diachrony and synchrony is suggested through Althusser's use of the term "structural causality." The question he seeks to answer is how the subjacent synchronic world of economic structure is related to the diachronic world of human behavior, or, put another way, how the structure of a mode of production is related to actual economic transactions in the marketplace. Insofar, Althusser tells us, as Marx was aware of the need for a concept to describe this relationship, it exists in his work only "in the practical state." If we are to find a concept capable of thinking through this problem with all the rigor it deserves, we must go back beyond Marx to Spinoza, "the only theoretician who had the unprecedented daring to pose this problem and outline a first solution to it" (*RC,* 197). Only in Spinoza do we find a concept capable of accounting for the relationship between a structure which is a "hidden" or "absent" cause and its effects. This concept is called structural causality.

What Althusser calls a structural cause is a literal transposition of what Spinoza termed an "immanent cause" (*causa immanens*). In the *Ethics,* Book I, Proposition XVIII, Spinoza remarks that God is the immanent and enduring, not the transient, cause of all things. In this cryptic passage which contains the germ of Spinoza's critique of scriptural theology, he is rejecting a conception of causality which sees God as the creator who set the world in motion by a unique act or set of acts which occurred at some specifiable point in the past and then ceased altogether. This popular conception of the diety as a sort of divine artificer seemed to Spinoza to be a fiction of the imagination, for when analyzed logically it could be shown to contain self-contradiction. The most obvious contradiction is that, if God is conceived as a first cause distinguishable from the objects he creates, then by definition he cannot be infinite and all-powerful since there exists something outside of him that limits his power and perfection. When God is viewed as the immanent cause and not the transient cause of the world, this problem vanishes. To say that God is the immanent cause is not to locate him outside the natural whole, but to pinpoint his activity squarely within the order of nature to which everything must be referred as the ground of its explanation. Nothing, on this account, can be conceived outside the natural order of things, which is nothing other than God since this would be to introduce some unique and miraculous act or event. Following Spinoza's logic, we arrive at the position that everything must be conceived as determined by certain necessary causes, the chain of which extends back to infinity, and this vast theatre of causes and effects he calls God or nature.

Althusser's notion of structural causality is merely a secularized version of Spinoza's immanent cause once the transposition from God to the mode of production is carried out. The mode of production is the immanent, not the transient, cause of all things.

> This implies . . . that the effects are not outside the structure, are not a pre-existing object, element or space in which the structure arrives to *imprint its mark:* on the contrary, it implies that the structure is immanent in its effects, a cause immanent in its effects in the Spinozist sense of the term, that *the whole existence of the structure consists of its effects,* in short that the structure, which is merely a specific combination of its peculiar elements, is nothing outside its effects [*RC,* 188–89].

To make sense of this passage, it is necessary to understand first what Althusser is arguing against. The "transient" or "linear" view of causality would approximate something like the fundamentalist version of base and superstructure relations discussed in the last chapter. On this account, what goes on in the economic base "determines" what goes on in the noneconomic superstructure, making any relation between them one of external association or adjacency. This type of causal model fits well the Humean and positivist thesis according to which we should in principle be able to describe the antecedents and consequents of a causal chain in complete independence of one another. There must be no essential reference to the consequent in describing the antecedent since this would imply some sort of closer internal relationship between them. By emphasizing, on the contrary, that the mode of production is a structural and not a transient cause, Althusser wants to suggest a more homogeneous view of the social whole, not as analyzable into discrete units but as a set of functionally interrelated parts. The economic structure is not a transient cause separable from its effects (like the God of scriptural theology) but a structural cause which can be seen working only in and through its effects.

Althusser uses the concept of structural causality to show how the mode of production functions as the "absent cause" or what

Marx called the "hidden mystery" behind the appearance of the commodity on the marketplace. What deeply fascinated Marx was why in capitalist society the object of labor is represented as a commodity, that is, why the amount of labor time expended in the production of a thing should become embodied as an expression of its value. This is the "hieroglyph" that previous political economists had simply failed to "decipher." "Political economy," Marx states, "has never once asked the question: why this content adopts this form, why labour is represented (*sich darstellt*) by value?"[10]

The real cause of the appearance of the commodity on the marketplace was not present in ordinary economic transactions, but absent, and like the Freudian unconscious, could only be inferred through its effects. It was systematically concealed by the visible processes of circulation, exchange, and consumption. This is not to suggest that these processes are merely illusory or are in some sense less than real. Rather they give rise to certain illusions which in turn work to conceal rather than to reveal the true cause, the production process, whose effects they are. As Marx says: "These imaginary expressions arise . . . from the relations of production themselves."[11] This is to suggest that no amount of ordinary empirical or phenomenological description of the worker or the work place will reveal the mode of production, the "absent cause," which is nowhere visible but which is everywhere present in its effects. What Marx tells us is that society in general, but capitalist society in particular, is characterized by a certain degree of opacity which, so to speak, creates the necessity for a method which will penetrate to the reality behind the appearance and then by a reverse process explain why this reality should take on the specific appearance that it does.

Althusser's account of the structural causality of the mode of production is at the same time both too strong and too weak. It is too weak inasmuch as it fails to show how the mode of produc-

---

[10]*Capital*, 1: 80.
[11]*Ibid.*, 1: 537.

tion actually exerts its determinant influence. It does not so much determine actual economic behavior as it does the form or appearance of the behavior. In this sense, structural causation means something like "circumscribes" or "sets limits to" the types of productive relations one is likely to find in a society. It is too strong, inasmuch as it is asserted as some sort of unequivocal principle of explanation. What we usually mean when we say that something is the cause of something else is that there is a certain observed pattern of regularity or uniformity between one event or series of events and some subsequent event or series of events. Such explanations are usually held to be either verifiable or falsifiable through some set of empirical procedures. But by removing the concept of structural causality from such empirical contexts, in which it could be usefully employed, and elevating it to the level of an "absent cause" capable of explaining not one particular class of things but "the development of things in general," Althusser once more exhibits that tendency to turn economic structures into a metaphysical entity removed from the conditions of human praxis and subjectivity.[12]

Althusser's identification of the mode of production as an "absent cause" by no means casts doubt upon the enterprise of metaphysics. It is merely to call attention to the fact that when the concept of cause is extended to account not for particular types of things but the existence of things "in general," the totality of things, the result is to evacuate the term of all explanatory power since what is used indifferently to explain everything must in the end explain nothing. Because the concept of the mode of production claims to explain so much, it must, like the God of Spinoza, be left out of any particular account precisely because it affords no rational explanation of any one thing. At best the structural causality of the mode of production must be seen not as providing

[12]See Glucksmann, "A Ventriloquist Structuralism," p. 88: "Not merely does the concept of structural causality tell us nothing of its origins, for no structural analysis really founds it, but it actually says nothing of itself, just because it can say everything or anything—it inaugurates no actual type of analysis."

the sort of empirical matter-of-fact explanations that scientists and historians are accustomed to look for, but rather as providing the overall metaphysical framework within which these sorts of explanations can take place. But this, it must be borne in mind, is not an explanation of anything. This is not a "science" but a kind of meta-science, or to call it by its proper name, meta-physics.

Whatever may be the difficulties with the concept of structural causality, Althusser's intention can be seen to be in keeping with that of Spinoza as well as many of the great metaphysical thinkers of the past who have tried to provide a complete and comprehensive account of the whole, of everything that is. This attempt to explain the whole, or at least all forms of historical existence, in terms of one overriding cause, whether it be God or the mode of production, is the link that unites traditional metaphysics with Althusser's brand of structural Marxism. At some point within this account of the whole, however, it becomes necessary to explain the existence of man and where he stands in relation to it. This brings us to question the moral intention of Althusserian structuralism summed up in the statement that Marxism is a "theoretical anti-humanism."

Theoretical Anti-Humanism

The most controversial and in some respects the most telling feature of Althusser's structural Marxism is its claim to be a "theoretical anti-humanism." Althusser announces this anti-humanism in the boldest possible language:

> Strictly in respect to theory, therefore, one can and must speak openly of Marx's *theoretical anti-humanism,* and see in this *theoretical anti-humanism* the absolute (negative) precondition of the (positive) knowledge of the human world itself, and of its practical transformation. It is impossible to *know* anything about men except on the absolute precondition that the philosophical (theoretical) myth of man is reduced to ashes. So any thought that

appeals to Marx for any kind of restoration of a theoretical anthropology or humanism is no more than ashes, *theoretically* [*FM*, 229–30].

Theoretical anti-humanism becomes for Althusser the Marxist pendant to the structuralist motto that "man is dead" or, as he puts it, that any philosophy of the "subject" must be henceforth repudiated as an intrusion of ideology. "For the corollary of theoretical Marxist anti-humanism is the recognition and knowledge of humanism itself: as an *ideology* . . . Marx's theoretical *anti-humanism* . . . recognizes a necessity for humanism as an *ideology*" (*FM*, 230–31).

This theoretical anti-humanism or the "decentering" of the subject is not something that structuralism alone has initiated but has been central to every modern discipline aspiring to scientific status. In his *Introductory Lectures on Psychoanalysis*, Freud observed that in the past few centuries the "naive self-love" of man has been progressively humbled by advances in science.[13] The first blow came when Copernicus discovered that the earth was not the center of the universe but a tiny speck within a cosmic system of almost infinite vastness. The second blow fell when Darwin dislodged the human species from its supposedly privileged place within the animal kingdom, showing man to be just one in a long line of evolutionary forms. The third blow came when Freudian psychoanalysis showed that the ego is not even "master in its own house" but subject to deeper unconscious drives and motivations of which the mind may be only dimly aware. Finally, in our own day this process of "decentering" continues with Althusser, Foucault, and Lévi-Strauss, who have tried to eliminate the influence of man altogether from their historical and ethnographic research.

Althusser's claim to decenter the subject is intended as a radical denial of "humanism" in the social sciences. Humanism is understood very generally to be the doctrine according to which man is a being of a special kind endowed with a privileged

[13]Trans. James Strachey (New York: Norton, 1966), pp. 284–85.

position in the world. Humanism is the name for the doctrine which seeks to draw social and political inferences from some purported "essence of man" or "human nature" (*FM*, 227). If the "human" is to be in any sense a term of distinction, it is only intelligible because man is seen as a being possessed of certain capacities which distinguish him from the rest of nature. Chief among these capacities is often considered to be choice, that is, the ability to initiate free and responsible actions to which judgments of praise and blame can be afixed. Beings governed by necessity alone cannot be truly human in the fullest sense of the term, since what is human depends upon the ability to choose one course of action over another. However, what Althusser and the structuralists contend is that man, who was previously considered to be the author of his own actions, can, when submitted to scientific analysis, be shown to be subject to the same causal laws as everything else in nature. This is to deny that man, the human subject, is in any way free in his volitions since his choices are themselves the outcome of this all-embracing network of causes. Man appears merely as a support for certain impersonal forces at work which determine his activity in a variety of ways of which he may be only dimly aware.

Althusser's own brand of anti-humanism begins with a denial that man or even groups of men form the primary unit of Marxian analysis. Marx, he says, was not interested in man as such, but in certain "ever-pre-given" relations of production which mechanically distribute the roles and functions that agents play out in their daily lives. Indeed, he quotes from Marx's last work, the *Randglossen zu Adolph Wagners "Lehrbuch der politischen Ökonomie"* (1882) to show that by the end of his life Marx had left the vestiges of his earlier humanism far behind. "My analytical method," Marx says here, "does not start from man but from the economically given social period" (cited in *FM*, 219). Not our lived subjective experience, what the phenomenologists call "le vécu," but the various structures—economic, political, and ideological—which constitute the social formation are the real "subjects" of history.

Within *Capital*, Althusser finds warrant for his theoretical anti-humanism in Marx's use of the term *Träger*. *Träger* is a fairly commonplace German word which means literally "bearer" or "support." Althusser uses it to show that the true subjects of history are certain relations of production and that men are never anything more than the bearers/supports of them. Before going into this in more detail, however, it should be kept in mind that Althusser does not merely bring this concept with him in order to give his reading of Marx a fashionable structuralist flavor. Rather it is a concept which Marx uses regularly throughout *Capital* to show the way in which men are simply "personifications" of the social relations of production. At one point we read: "In the course of our investigations we shall find, in general, that the characters who appear on the economic stage are but the personifications [*Träger*] of the economic relations that exist between them."[14] And in another passage Marx says:

> As the conscious representative [*Träger*] of this movement the possessor of money becomes a capitalist. His person or rather his pocket is the point from which the money starts and to which it returns. The expansion of the value, which is the objective basis or mainspring of the circulation M-C-M, becomes his subjective aim, and it is only in so far as the appropriation of ever more and more wealth in the abstract becomes the sole motive of his operations, that he functions as a capitalist, that is, as capital personified and endowed with a consciousness and a will.[15]

Althusser uses the *Träger* concept explicitly as a polemical weapon against the humanist thesis that would make man into the unique subject or creator of his own history. For Althusser, it is not man who is at the center of the historical stage, but certain relations of production which distribute the roles and positions which men simply act out. There are only a limited number of places within the system which an individual can occupy and these places are continually reproduced and continually develop what they demand of their occupants. Men cannot, therefore, be

---

[14]*Capital*, 1: 85.
[15]*Ibid.*, 1: 152.

regarded as active agents of this process. They are simply its bearers/supports. "The structure of the relations of production," Althusser says,

> determines the *places* and *functions* occupied and adopted by the agents of production, who are never anything more than the occupants of these places, insofar as they are the "supports" [*Träger*] of these functions. The true "subjects" (in the sense of constitutive subjects of the process) are therefore not these occupants or functionaries, are not, despite all appearance, the "obviousness" of the "given" of naive anthropology, "concrete individuals" "real men"—but *the definition and distribution of these places and functions. The true "subjects" are these definers and distributors: the relations of production* (and political and ideological social relations) [*RC,* 180].

What this passage is polemicizing against is the claim put forward most forcefully by Sartre and other members of the existential-phenomenological school that all important human behavior is the outcome of conscious human choice and deliberation. On the existentialist or "humanist" account we are what we are by virtue of the choices we have made. This is intended to apply not only to those areas of our lives that are manifestly the result of reflective decision, but to those we ordinarily consider to be prereflective or the result of reflex response. Such things as emotions, feelings, and instincts, which we are often thought to suffer, are said to be in some sense the product of choice, a selective response to a situation. To ascribe conduct to social forces, to inalterable laws of nature including human nature, is to misdescribe reality. It is also, so Sartre and his followers would say, ethically repulsive since it is an evasion of personal responsibility. Indeed, such an evasion is for them itself a type of choice although a particularly craven one since our options are always at least two: to do or not to do. In this respect we are always what we make ourselves to be.

One need not go quite so far as Althusser to argue that this position conflicts with some quite undeniable features of human

196

behavior. There are, for example, as Freud is famous for pointing out, some significant areas of human activity where we commonly do not know what we are trying to do or are unaware of the tendencies of our actions, and which cannot be understood by reference to concepts like choice, intention, and decision. A neurotic, as described by Freud, is a man who is not aware of and is consequently not fully responsible for his own actions and who constantly finds his actual accomplishments at odds with his sincerely professed intentions. As he has made clear, we frequently mistake or misdescribe the real import of our actions and thereby deceive ourselves into thinking we are doing one thing when in fact we are really doing something very different. It is because the agent does not know what he is ''really'' doing that he can be said to be governed by causal necessity, which it is the promise of psychotherapy to put under rational human control.

Similarly, Althusser has argued in the passage quoted above that in the most profound sense human behavior is determined by the ''places and functions'' occupied by the agents within the social structure. These places or roles overlap so that there is no unified center, whether spiritual or material, from which our behavior emanates. We are in this sense ''decentered.'' One is, for instance, a professor, a husband, a member of a political organization, a sports enthusiast, and so on without any one of these areas of our lives determining exclusively who or what we are. Each of these areas overlaps to such an extent that the whole can truly be said to be ''overdetermined'' in precisely the way we have seen Althusser (following Freud) use that term. Here Althusser is quite right to point out the multiple sources of the determination of our behavior rather than reducing it to material interests, libidinal drives, or some other central point from which everything can be explained. But Althusser goes too far in suggesting that everything we do is so conditioned by the various roles and positions that we occupy. This cannot account for the work of judgment, appraisal, and argument that goes on both in the mind and between agents effecting and altering our conduct. It may be, of course, that all Althusser really wishes to say is that within the broad set of constraints imposed upon the individual by the mode of production he is still free to do and act as he chooses. This would be a way of capturing a degree of freedom and self-determination within an overall system of structural causality. In this respect, too, Althusser would give a new twist to the Spinozist dictum that freedom is the recognition of necessity. But Althusser does not actually say this and, as the *Träger* concept indicates, goes so far as to imply that we are largely passive beings determined by structural vectors over which we exert no control. In this sense, then, Althusserian determinism is the reverse side of Sartrean decisionism. Neither adequately sets out the way in which choices, reasons, and decisions are constrained by external conditions, on the one hand, but without ceasing to function as choices, reasons, and decisions, on the other.

The aim of the *Träger* concept is a means of denying the phenomenological notion of intentionality or the specifically Marxist version of this that man makes history. Taking his repudiation of intentional behavior to its logical limits, Althusser maintains that the production and reproduction of social life is not something carried out by intelligent agents in full awareness of what it is they are doing, but takes place, so to speak, behind the backs of men who are never anything more than *Träger* or supports of the system within which they find themselves. There is no action within the Althusserian universe understood as behavior consciously directed toward the pursuit of some freely chosen end or purpose. There is only a set of reactive responses determined ''in the last instance'' by the needs of the production process. The stage, Althusser says, is set and players merely perform according to scripts already written out for them in advance:

> Now we can recall that highly symptomatic term *''Darstellung,''* compare it with this ''machinery'' and take it literally, as the very existence of this machinery in its effects: the mode of existence of the stage direction (*mise en scène*) of the theatre which is simul-

taneously its own stage, its own script, its own actors, the theatre whose spectators can on occasion, be spectators only because they are first of all forced to be its actors, caught by the constraints of a script and parts whose authors they cannot be, since it is in essence *an authorless theatre* [*RC,* 193].

One point needs to be re-emphasized here. No matter how much like a theatre, a machine, or an artificial construction a society may appear, we must not lose sight of the fact that this is still an analogy which on inspection does not hold. This analogy assumes rather than proves that societies are like self-compensating mechanisms in which the individual parts are adjudged by their contribution to the overall working or efficiency of the whole. But to insist that what human beings do (or refrain from doing), they do because of their place within the social whole is to fall into the same objectivism criticized above. Althusser is so concerned to deny the individualist or voluntarist theory of action that he overlooks the fact that the production and reproduction of social life is above all a skilled performace, sustained and made to happen by intelligent social actors. All the world may indeed be a stage, as Althusser's theatrical metaphor suggests, in which we are all merely actors playing a part, but even given this constraint we still feel it necessary to draw a distinction between the performance of an Olivier and that of an untrained novice. Seen in this light, individuals are never simply "representatives" of a set of prescribed social roles—no matter what Althusserian or Goffmanesque sociology claims. Nor can human action be explained solely in causal or functional terms, that is, in terms of how it keeps the system going. Social actors must be understood at least in part as intentional subjects acting in response to an understood situation and whose actions must also be seen in terms of its symbolic or meaningful character for them. It is the meaningful side of human behavior that in the last instance Althusserian structuralism cannot understand.

To sum up: Althusser's "objectifying" conception of production relations as distinct from the social agents who constitute them is the basis for his claim that Marxism is a "theoretical anti-humanism." This anti-humanism amounts to a denial of the role of individual will or agency in history. Since to be an agent means to be capable of framing intentional aims and projects by the light of an independent intelligence, to eliminate agency is to eliminate man and any teleological conception of human nature. The elimination of any substantive ground for free action constitutes the core of the doctrine of scientific structuralism. This brings us, at long last, to the final teaching of the Althusserian project: nihilism.

Nihilism: The Moral Intention of Structuralism

Nihilism, as Nietzsche defines it, is the situation which obtains when "everything is permitted." Everything is permitted when the distinction between reason and unreason, or, put another way, between speech and silence, is taken to be arbitrary or indifferent. Such indifference to reason or speech is only possible when the very concept of man, traditionally understood as the rational animal *par excellence,* has lost its meaning as a term of distinction and consequently where the thesis of a human nature with an objective hierarchy of needs has been reduced to the status of "myth." The conviction that "man is dead" defines the nihilism of Althusser's Marxism and provides the basis for his positive thesis that history is a "process without a subject."

According to Althusser, in *Capital,* Marx "exploded" the myth of a subject-centered history, that is, a conception of history as the progressive realization of human capacities for freedom, equality, rationality, or whatever. In its place Marx found it necessary to adopt the conception of history as a "process without a subject" in which "the dialectic at work in history is not the work of any subject whatsoever, whether absolute (God) or merely human, but that the origin of history is always already thrust back before history, and therefore that there is neither a philosophical origin nor a philosophical subject to history" (*LP,*

117–18). The conclusion we reach is that the teleological historicism of the last century, whether that of Comte, Hegel, or the young Marx, must be replaced by the "scientific" conception of history as a "process" without origin or end, without meaning or purpose. What this means is explained by reference to a footnote in *Capital* to be found, moreover, only in the French edition:

> The word "procès" . . . which expresses *a development considered in the totality of its real conditions* has long been part of scientific language throughout Europe. In France it was first introduced slightly shamefacedly in its Latin form—*processus.* Then, stripped of this pedantic disguise, it slipped into books on chemistry, physics, physiology, etc., and into works of metaphysics. In the end it will obtain a certificate of complete naturalization [*PH,* 185].

The positive legacy of Marx is this idea of history as a process, but a process evacuated of all notions of rationality or intelligibility. In place of the idea of a rational history leading men progressively toward some final end state, Althusser has suggested that history is opaque in its essence, unilluminated by any intelligible necessity or some transcendent absolute. History is instead a "process without a subject."

> Once one is prepared to consider just for a moment that the whole Hegelian teleology is contained in the expressions . . . of alienation, or in what constitutes the master structure of the category of the dialectic (the negation of the negation), and once one accepts, if that is possible, to *abstract* from what represents the teleology in these expressions, then there remains the formulation: history is *a process without a subject.* I think I can affirm: this category of *a process without a subject,* which must of course be torn from the grip of the Hegelian teleology, undoubtedly represents the greatest theoretical debt linking Marx to Hegel [*PH,* 182–83].

It is the teleological structure of the Hegelian dialectic to which Althusser finally objects and which renders it unfit for appropriation by Marxism:

201

Of course we can now begin to say, what irremediably disfigures the Hegelian conception of History as a dialectical process is its *teleological* concept of the dialectic, inscribed in the very *structures* of the Hegelian dialectic at an extremely precise point: the *Aufhebung* (transcendence-preserving-the-transcended-as-the-internalized-transcended), directly expressed in the Hegelian category of the *negation of the negation* (or negativity) [*PH,* 181].

What are we to make of this? First, these passages express a darker, more pessimistic side of Althusserian Marxism than we have seen up to now. His attempt to expel the subject from history (and from knowledge) is part of a broader counter movement now under way in the humanities and the social sciences whose outcome has been declared under the slogan "the death of man."[16] This opposition, which encompasses not only structuralism but various forms of systems theory, literary criticism, and even religious historiography, has registered discontent with the pervasive humanistic conception of man as a self-centered and self-directing agent. The "anti-humanist" leanings of these schools have also been part of a widespread discontent with the politics of liberal individualism and the conception of man as a "possessive individualist" on which it rests.

The spiritual essence of this movement may be characterized by a sort of moral billiousness in the face of the destruction of even historical reason. If history as a process with meaning or purpose is found to be insupportable, then the confident optimism that bolstered the belief in progress must also be rejected as groundless. But then we must face the question: how do we live in the face of this groundlessness or this perception of the transient worthlessness of all values? Nietzsche thought that he had an answer to this horrible truth in his special interpretation of human creativity or his doctrine of the will to power, the will to "overcome" everything including history itself. If an overabun-

---

[16]For a useful account of this movement see Fred J. Dallmayr, *The Twilight of Subjectivity: Contributions to a Post-Individualist Theory of Politics* (Amherst: University of Massachusetts Press, 1981), esp. ch. 1.

dance or "hypertrophy" of history is the source of our malaise, only by turning away from history to nature or to the will to power can the problem of history be solved. The will to power is often understood as a call to radical freedom or radical subjectivity. It is a call to create *ex nihilo* or to destroy everything that stands in the way of the creative urge. The will to destroy is the first step toward the will to create.

Althusser takes this creative call to creativity one step further. If literally everything can be overcome, then man himself, "the beast with red cheeks," can be overcome also. Man himself is to be "decentered" or deprived of any position of privilege if Marxism is to become a fully objective or "scientific" doctrine. This objective or scientific doctrine, which teaches that history itself is limited by a finite number of forms or structures, must put severe restraints upon the creative power of the will. History comes more to embody the fatalism inherent in Nietzsche's "eternal recurrence" than the activism implicit in his theory of the will. In any case, the moral intention of structuralism must now be clear. It is an attempt not to replace man by superman, as Nietzsche had hoped, but to dissolve man altogether, to eliminate even the human as merely another prejudice or myth of Western ideology. The dissolution of history becomes the first step in the direction of the dissolution of man.[17]

The most prominent spokesman for this tendency has been Althusser's contemporary Michel Foucault, who has become famous for his attempt to trace the dissolution of the subject in the disciplines of psychology, sociology, and philology. Throughout his researches into the history and philosophy of these disciplines, Foucault's aim has been to elicit "the fundamental codes of a culture" which delineate the way the world is defined and perceived. What Foucault believed himself to have discovered is that underlying the thought of any period was a certain "epis-

[17]For the structuralist appropriation of Nietzsche see Gilles Deleuze, *Nietzsche et la philosophie* (Paris: Presses Universitaires de France, 1962); Pierre Klossowski, *Nietzsche et le cercle vicieux* (Paris: Mercure de France, 1969); Descombes, *Modern French Philosophy*, pp. 180–86.

teme" or "archive" which like the Althusserian problematic is unconscious and yet defines the system of signs and regularities for what is to be included and excluded from the domain of knowledge. His starting point, as he states it in the Preface to *Les mots et les choses,* is a text from Borges which deserves to be quoted in full not only for itself but for what it reveals about the structuralist enterprise. This passage quotes "a 'certain Chinese encyclopedia' in which it is written that 'animals are divided into: (a) belonging to the Emperor, (b) embalmed, (c) tame, (d) sucking pigs, (e) sirens, (f) fabulous, (g) stray dogs, (h) included in the present classification, (i) frenzied, (j) innumerable, (k) drawn with a very fine camelhair brush, (l) *et cetra,* (m) having just broken the water pitcher, (n) that from a long way off look like flies."[18] It is, he says, from the sense of wonderment that we feel when we confront seriously this classification—"the stark impossibility of thinking *that*"—that Foucault has called into question the possible arbitrariness underlying all knowledge.

Foucault's point is to study the system of rules that governs the cycle of knowledge. Since these norms are deeply sedimented, constituting as they do the limits of the intellectual world, they are not easy to disclose. In the Renaissance, for instance, the basic conception of knowledge was founded upon the notion of resemblance. Relations of similitude and analogy were believed to link together the microcosm and the macrocosm, the book of nature and the book of the world. All this changed, however, during the Classical period, when the idea of representation replaced that of resemblance and the world was seen not in terms of qualitative symbolic correspondences (the Great Chain of Being), but in quantifiable identities and differences. It was only, Foucault maintains, at the end of this period or in the age of Enlightenment, with its attempt to mathematize and idealize nature, that the concept of man came into common currency. Prior to that time, the "subject" simply did not exist.

[18]Foucault, *The Order of Things,* p. xv.

Foucault associates the appearance of man, the human subject, with the demise of ancient metaphysics, with its belief in a transcendent absolute that sustained it. Once the classical metaphysics fell into disrepute, a new humanist and historicist perspective arose to take its place. "Before the end of the eighteenth century," Foucault asserts, "man did not exist—any more than the potency of life, the fecundity of labour, or the historical density of language; he is quite a recent creature, which the demiurge of knowledge fabricated with its own hands less than two hundred years ago." And he goes on to say: "As the archaeology of our thought easily shows, man is an invention of recent date. And one perhaps nearing its end."[19]

In direct opposition, then, to the "human sciences," a counter movement growing out of the new disciplines of psychoanalysis, ethnology, and linguistics has developed placing relatively greater emphasis not on the subject but on the structural conditions which lie outside the reach of human intentionality and design. These structural sciences, like Freudian analysis and Saussurean linguistics, sought to disclose not the products of human doing but the principles presupposed in all human doings. To reverse the order of Hegelian priorities, structuralism sought to reveal substance not as subject but as structure. Foucault declares that Nietzsche gave the lead to this movement by declaring the death of God, which one hundred years later has been followed by the pronouncement on the death of man. "In our own day and once again," Foucault writes, "Nietzsche indicated the turning point from a long way off, it is not so much the absence or the death of God that is affirmed as the end of man." This is not, of course, to suggest the absurd hypothesis that human beings as a species, *homo sapiens,* are bound to disappear. It is only to remind us that without some transcendental basis upon which to ground humanism, man himself begins to appear increasingly problematic. "Rather than the death of God or rather, in the wake of that death and in a profound correlation with it—

[19]Pages 308, 387.

what Nietzsche's thought heralds is the end of his murderer; it is the explosion of man's face in laughter, and the return of masks; it is the scattering of the profound stream of time by which he felt himself carried along and whose pressure he suspected in the very being of things; it is the identity of the Return of the Same with the absolute dispersion of man."[20]

This dissolution of man into these a priori structures of knowledge (Foucault) or production relations (Althusser) is no mere misanthropy or rhetorical exaggeration on the part of this counter movement. It is rather the final aim of their program designed to dethrone the privileged status accorded to the subject by modern philosophers from Descartes to Sartre. Structuralism, as the cases of Althusser and Foucault have indicated, is avowedly anti-humanistic because it refuses to grant man any unique place in the hierarchy of nature but sees him as determined in his outcomes by structural causes of which he may be completely unaware. Anti-humanism does not amount to a denial that there are individual men who observe, think, write, and so on; nor does it deny that there are more or less cohesive cultural groups with their own systems of signs and symbols. What it does deny is the theoretical basis for humanism which seeks to attribute a unique essence such as freedom, volition, or choice to man or to see these attributes as in any sense meaningful. As Foucault maintains:

> We can see that what manifests this peculiar property of the human sciences is not that privileged and singularly blurred object which is man. For the good reason that it is not man who constitutes them and provides them with a specific domain; it is the general arrangement of the *episteme* that provides them with a site, summons them, and establishes them—thus enabling them to constitute man as their object. We shall say, therefore, that a "human science" exists, not wherever man is in question, but wherever there is analysis—within the dimension proper to the unconscious—of norms, rules, and signifying totalities which unveil to consciousness the conditions of its forms and content.[21]

[20]Page 385.
[21]Page 364.

Lévi-Strauss argues essentially the same thesis in a passage from *The Savage Mind*. Here he remarks that the goal of ethnographic research is "not to constitute, but to dissolve man."

> The pre-eminent value of anthropology is that it represents the first step in a procedure which involves others. Ethnographic analysis tries to arrive at invariants beyond the empirical diversity of human societies. . . . However, it would not be enough to reabsorb particular humanities into a general one. The first enterprise opens the way for others . . . which are incumbent on the exact natural sciences: the reintegration of culture in nature and finally of life within the whole of its physico-chemical conditions.[22]

This should, once more, not be understood as a prophecy of doom. The dissolution of man or the "reintegration" of culture into nature does not mean that the species man will disappear. What will disappear is the search for some substantive embodiment of the human subject in terms of qualities or attributes like spirit, soul, or consciousness. Whether this more substantive embodiment of the self takes the form of the Cartesian *cogito,* the Kantian "I think" or the Husserlian transcendental ego makes little difference. It is the search for something more basic and permanent to man that is destined to disappear, as Foucault has poetically put it, "like a face drawn in sand at the edge of the sea."[23]

The same generally gloomy and pessimistic vision pervades Althusser's "anti-humanism" as well. In his attempt to refute the humanist thesis that it is man who makes history or makes himself, Althusser has been led to explain history without men or without reference to their conscious intentions and purposes, which have meaning for them but frequently result in unintended consequences. History becomes a "process without a subject" in which one combination of structures transforms itself into another independently of the individuals who inhabit them. Only by

[22]Page 247.
[23]*The Order of Things*, p. 387.

detaching history from the standpoint or perspective of any "constitutive subject" can we avoid systematic "misrecognition." Yet to aim at this type of impersonality in history, I would suggest, is to produce something which is not history at all. Take away the human perspective and there is nothing intelligible left any more than there would be anything visible if we sought to look at a physical object but from no particular point of view. To attempt to judge man in the light of these unconscious structures is to understand the human in the light of the subhuman and is, therefore, to fail to see what is distinctively human in man.

I can only note in conclusion how far removed Althusser's "theoretical anti-humanism" is from the revolutionary humanism of classical Marxism. Marx's optimism concerning the eventual outcome of history is based ultimately on the belief in a continual expansion of human productive powers and consequently upon man's ever-increasing ability to subjugate nature for his own ends and purposes. Althusser is correct in one respect. Marx did not identify the subject of history with Man or with the realization of some abstractly conceived human essence. This view, he is right to see, is a Feuerbachian conception which Marx abandoned some time during or shortly after the composition of the *German Ideology* and the *Theses on Feuerbach*. In place of Man, however, Marx locates the center of historical gravity with the productive forces of society, whose ability to expand remains the one historical constant over time, giving history a progressive and linear direction. Thus Althusser's description of history as a "process without a subject" founders upon the evidence.

This is not to deny to Althusser whatever merit his intellectual tour de force might have. His is free to reject much of Marx—nay all of Marx—if he sees fit. But why then insist on calling the finished product Marxism? The fact remains that throughout his work Marx retained a fundamentally teleological conception of history whereby the relatively simple forms of social life were seen as containing *in nuce* the more highly developed stages of society. Therefore, it is patently untrue to say that what Marx

208

rejected was the teleological structure of the dialectic and its "master category," the negation of the negation. Two passages, both from his mature work, should suffice to make this clear. The first occurs in the introduction to the *Grundrisse,* in which we read:

> Bourgeois society is the most developed and the most complex historic organization of production. The categories which express its relations, the comprehension of its structure, thereby also allows insights into the structure and the relations of production of all the vanished social formations out of whose ruins and elements it built itself up, whose partly still unconquered remnants are carried along within it, whose mere nuances have developed explicit significance within it, etc. Human anatomy contains a key to the anatomy of the ape. The intimations of higher development among the subordinate animal species, however, can be understood only after the higher development is already known. The bourgeois economy thus supplies the key to the ancient, etc.[24]

The second passage occurs toward the end of *Capital,* volume one, in a discussion of the "historical tendency" of capitalist accumulation. Here Marx comes closest to a dialectical teleology reminiscent of Hegel's *Philosophy of History* in attempting to depict the historical nature of socialism as an illustration of the concept of the negation of the negation:

> The capitalist mode of appropriation, the result of the capitalist mode of production, produces capitalist private property. This is the first negation of individual private property, as founded on the labour of the proprietor. But capitalist production begets, with the inexorability of a law of Nature [*mit der Notwendigkeit eines Naturprocesses*], its own negation. It is the negation of negation. This does not re-establish private property for the producer, but gives him individual property based on the acquisitions of the capitalist era: i.e., on co-operation and the possession in common of the land and of the means of production.[25]

[24]Page 105.
[25]*Capital,* 1: 763.

209

This picture whereby history represents a dialectical progression of stages linking primitive communism, via slavery, feudalism, and capitalism, to the mature communism of the future bears witness to the unshakeable hold of Hegelian teleology on even Marx's most mature reflections.

As we have seen, this optimistic picture of history as leading inexorably toward a secular millennium has come under increasing attack from some of the most advanced thinkers of our age. Expressing the general lack of confidence and faith in the future, the latent pessimism of Althusserian analysis has been ascribed to the very structure of history itself. Even communist society, which for Marx represented the "end" of history in which all the "riddles" which had puzzled human existence would at last be solved, remains for Althusser just one of a number of ways in which the problem of social order and function is achieved. It will remain "in the last instance" forever opaque to those occupying its "places and functions" deceiving them perpetually with an illusion of their own freedom. Knowledge, in the final resort, is not "power," as Enlightenment optimists from Bacon to Marx had assumed. It ends rather in impotence and an awareness of the limitations of the will and on the power of practical activity. In this respect Althusser's structural Marxism corresponds to a type of conservative realism based, no doubt in part, upon the defeat of Marx's original proposals.

By contrast to the Enlightenment belief (that in fact extends back to Protagoras) that "man is the measure of all things," the Althusserian critique of humanism stresses the insurmountable limitations imposed upon man by these nonhuman or extrahuman structures of production. Man is no longer conceived as the active creator of his world, but rather as a supporting agent in a complex web of relationships whose axis revolves around the relations of production. Like Spinoza's Substance or Heidegger's *Dasein*, these relations denote the pre-existing world, which is not the product of either individual or intersubjective design and which cannot be either wished or spirited away in practical deliberations. It is this deepened appreciation of the "realm of necessity,'' which both defines and determines the ''realm of freedom'' within practical life, that may constitute the highest teaching of Althusserian Marxism. To invert the phrase of Descartes', we are no longer ''the masters and possessors of nature'' but its servants. At the deepest level, Althusser's ''theoretical anti-humanism'' teaches the inevitable triumph not of man over history, but of structure over man.

7

Conclusion

A conclusion is scarcely the place to summarize Althusser's relation to the tradition of European Marxism as a whole. Nevertheless, I would like to underscore here two decisive respects in
which he both departs from classical Marxism as well as joins
issue with certain trends in contemporary social theory.

First, one feature that Althusser shares with other currents of
neo-Marxism has been an almost exclusive concern with second-
order problems of scientific method and epistemology. What
distinguishes Althusser and a number of other so-called "Western
Marxists"—Habermas, Colletti, Goldmann, Sartre, and Williams
to mention only a few—has been a preoccupation with the "superstructure" at the expense of more concrete analyses of class
conflict and political power. While no member of this tradition has
as yet declared the fundamental aim of Marxism to be a theory of
knowledge, the common tendency has been to see it as a method of
research the rules of which still remain to be adequately worked
out.[1] One further feature of this new form of methodological
Marxism has been the respectability and esteem accorded to it in

[1]On this theme see in particular Perry Anderson, *Considerations on Western
Marxism* (London: New Left Books, 1976), esp. pp. 52–53.

the universities and intellectual circles of the noncommunist world. And as if to make this new-found respectability secure, Althusser and his contemporaries have proceeded to deck out their theories with an often abstruse and cumbersome vocabulary seemingly designed to make theory the property of a specially trained Marxist professoriat capable of mastering its highly esoteric idiom. Unlike previous generations often forced to conceal their teachings under pain of censorship, Althusser has chosen to express himself in an academic style that one would expect to deter all but the heartiest souls.

The result of this development has had serious ramifications. Perhaps most importantly it has signaled the emergence of two distinct Marxisms. The first is the political Marxism of the workers, activists and party functionaries; the second is the more refined and polished Marxism of the intellectuals and professional theoreticians. While the former has remained, without doubt, a potent political force in the contemporary world, the latter has provided a great deal of stimulation within academic quarters without necessarily bearing on the practical task of the construction of socialism. The result has been that Marxist theory has developed without any real ties to the development of the working class and likewise that the class struggle has been allowed to develop "spontaneously" without the aid of a guiding theoretical orientation. The "absence of any real theoretical culture in the history of the French worker's movement," of which Althusser complained so eloquently in the Introduction to *For Marx* has, ironically, given rise to its antithesis: the creation of an inward-looking, self-sufficient literary cult well beyond the reach of common mortals. And this is surely not what Marx either intended or expected to happen.[2]

The second and perhaps more profound difference between Althusserian Marxism and that of classical Marxism has been its almost total separation of theory from practice. What is meant here by a theory or in Althusser's terms a "theoretical practice?"

[2]R. N. Berki, *Socialism* (New York: Saint Martin's Press, 1975), p. 72.

Unlike empirical theorists, for whom a theory consists of a set of axiomatic principles which can be tested against reality, Althusser maintains that Marxism is a theory or a "science" even if no testable propositions can be deduced from it. A theory, in other words, can be called true not because it fits or corresponds to the world of fact, but because it contains its own "internal criteria" of intelligibility which render it immune from empirical falsification. Like Bachelard, Kuhn, and Feyerabend, Althusser rejects the empiricist or positivist thesis that scientific theories can be judged satisfactory precisely to the extent that they can be proved false by relevant testing. Instead for Althusser the status of historical materialism is more like a conceptual framework or a "problematic" within which it is possible to talk about empirical evidence but for which no evidence can be adduced. Accordingly, Althusser has been led to assert the radical "autonomy" of science as a mode of inquiry which is arguably the central tenet of his doctrine.

This understanding of what constitutes a theory is open to serious reservation. Althusser's rejection of the foundational view of knowledge as too empiricist leads him to adopt a version of the coherence theory of truth. The coherence theory, we have argued, is characteristic of any system of idealist metaphysics that declares that truth contains its own procedures of self-verification, or, in Spinoza's terms, *veritas norma sui et falsi*. But what these procedures are is never made clear. One possibility we have explored is that of logical compatibility, that there can be no contradictions between the various beliefs we are prepared to accept. Another possibility might be that of comprehensivity, that our ideas must take the form of a system which takes in as much as possible. The trouble with making the justification of a theory depend on coherence, however conceived, is that it cuts justification off from the world. The world of fact, of concrete historical reality, becomes, then, a kind of Kantian "thing in itself" which can never be approached directly. The adequacy or inadequacy of a theory can never be determined through some kind of agreement between theory and the world, but always takes place solely within the sealed chamber of the mind. At one level at any rate, the difference between theory and ideology is that the former recognizes its own ideational character while the latter tries to pass itself off as a true representation of what the world is really like.

The problems with Althusserian "theoretical practice" go deeper still. It may be asked how, if the general principle of coherence is correct, we can distinguish between fact and fiction. Merely to say that a body of knowledge is true because it contains a system of mutually supporting judgments, each of which derives its credence from its place in the system as a whole, tells us little we need to know. If a theory is not at some point tied down to a conception of fact, no matter how complex may be its web of internal relations, the whole thing could still be a delusion. Logical coherence is, to be sure, a necessary but scarcely a sufficient criterion for evaluating our knowledge claims. In fact this position may be accused of confusing truth with internal consistency. Presumably several mutually consistent accounts could be given of the same event. But the principle of coherence helps us very little in determining which of these accounts might be the true one or at least the more likely one. It may be of course that there is no one single account of any event, just as it is possible that that there is no one true theology or system of moral norms. But without some more discriminating manner of ranking our accounts, the purely formal criterion of logical consistency runs the risk of falling into a kind of epistemological agnosticism. We are left at best with a criterion for making a plausible explanation, but if we are looking for something more than mere plausibility, Althusser is unable to help us.

The difficulties with Althusserian Marxism stem, I suggest, from its bifurcation between experience, on the one hand, and the claims of science, on the other, Generalities I and III in his language. For Althusser, experience is the medium of illusion, of Spinoza's *experientia vaga,* which produces only error and confusion, "ideology" as he would say. Science alone, based on the conceptual transformation and displacement of experience, yields knowledge. Accordingly, experience appears only as a tissue of myths and illusions from which we must extricate ourselves if we are to obtain the "luminous summits" (Marx) which only science can supply. But how does this occur? How are the raw materials of experience transformed into scientifically valid concepts? With no further account of the process of theory formation, we are left only with recourse to individual genius as an explanation. In the final analysis the problem is settled by Althusser's concept of the epistemological break in which theory is produced by subjects, constituting creators like Marx or Freud, who deliberately produce knowledge. Even structuralist Marxism must at some point be compelled to use the personal pronoun.

The epistemic gulf between the claims of science and the ideology of everyday life is the foundation of Althusserian theoretical practice. Althusser claims, as we have seen, that unlike ideology, science has a set of "interests" purely "internal" to itself alone. Its interest is with knowledge as an end in itself or knowledge for its own sake and not with whatever are the "practico-social" ends of society or of the polity. This attempt to dissociate theory from any kind of ideology or normative discourse follows logically from Althusser's distrust of any knowledge obtained through the senses. In this respect, it might be said that he, not Sartre, is truly the last of the Cartesians. But this understanding of science forgets that theory too has its grounds precisely in that pretheoretical world of experience which it claims to transcend. I cannot possibly hope to demonstrate here whether theory which aspires to this type of apodictic certainty is in any way superior to the language of common sense or practical understanding. I can only assert that it makes no sense, or is conceptually impossible to speak, as Althusser does, of our experience being transformed or displaced by some more adequate or ideal language of scientific explanation, since any such explanation presupposes this experience at its core.

This attempt to insulate theory from practice is not merely an academic accident but is the expression of a real problem within Marxism itself. This problem, as I understand it, has stemmed from and is continually fed by the failure of Marx's predictions to come true. Essentially Marx said that the industrial proletariat of the advanced Western nations would choose to overthrow capitalism by virtue of the very contradictions said to be inherent within it. They have not done so. And this "failure" has led to ever more sophisticated attempts to shore up the theory in the light of the historical record. From Lenin to Althusser, each of the thinkers within the tradition of Western Marxism has had to explain the failure of a revolutionary consciousness to develop. And to do so each of these thinkers has turned increasing attention to the concept of ideology and false consciousness until there is virtually nothing else left. While Marx regarded theory as a means to discipline the revolutionary temperament natural to the proletariat, for Althusser it becomes one more way of explaining not only why this temperament has not, but possibly cannot, develop.

The result of these successive transformations of Marxist theory has been profound. First, it has served to justify the dominance of the intellectuals claiming to be speaking in the name of, or for the true interests of, the proletariat. This goes some way toward explaining, I suspect, why Marxism has become both more attractive to the intelligentsia and less so to the masses. Second, this tendency has served to undercut the original Marxian notion of a unity of theory and practice. The uniqueness of Marxism stems originally from its claim to overcome the traditional bifurcation between theory and practice. The "realization of philosophy" was for Marx more than a slogan, and meant a means of bridging the gap between speculative contemplation and empirical action. By "lowering the sights" of traditional philosophy, Marxism sought both to render theory more practical and practice more theoretical. Interestingly, and for very different reasons, Althusser's claim that theory has its own internal criteria of validation which need not be taken from social or political practice is both a way of reinstating the "autonomy" of theory from practice as well as defending Marxism against empirical or historical refutation. What we are left with is a species of Marxism increasingly disconnected from the realities of political activity and all too ready to find comfort in the consolation of "critique" or "theoretical practice."

One final point needs to be noted. However subversive this dissociation of theory from practice may be from the standpoint of classical Marxism, such an enterprise seems to have some foundation in the current state of the world. After all, if Marx was correct when he argued that the ideas of a thinker must in some sense express the values of his class or social position, then this must be ipso facto true for Althusser, who could not be expected to have escaped the influence of the social reality within which his thought developed. It is a suggestive possibility that a theory in which society is presented as consisting of agentless structures may correspond to a situation dominated by impersonal bureaucratic, if not to say technocratic, methods of control. These methods do indeed reduce human agents to the role of mere functionaries, or *Träger*. That a new technocratic intelligentsia is now in the process of formation is a phenomenon attested to by writers on both sides of what it is no longer fashionable to call the Iron Curtain. It may be that Henri Lefebvre was correct to see in this doctrine a theoretical legitimation of technocracy. If this is true, Althusserian Marxism can perhaps best be seen as the expression of a regime dominated by a kind of bureaucratic, administrative rationality extended to every compartment of human endeavor. It may well be that the doctrine of "theoretical anti-humanism" is the highest expression of the soul of bureaucratic rule, or what Hannah Arendt once called "a kind of no-man rule," the rule of nobody.[3]

[3]Hannah Arendt, *The Human Condition* (Chicago: University of Chicago Press, 1958), p. 40.

Bibliography

Works by Althusser in French

ALTHUSSER, LOUIS. *Montesquieu: La politique et l'histoire.* Paris: Presses Universitaires de France, 1959.
____. *Pour Marx.* Paris: François Maspero, 1965.
____ et al. *Lire le Capital.* 4 vols. Paris: François Maspero, 1965, 1968.
____. *Lénine et la philosophie.* Paris: François Maspero, 1969.
____. *Réponse à John Lewis.* Paris: François Maspero, 1973.
____. *Eléments d'autocritique.* Paris: Hachette, 1974.
____. *Philosophie et philosophie spontanée des savants.* Paris: François Maspero, 1974.

Works by Althusser Translated into English

ALTHUSSER, LOUIS. *For Marx.* Trans. Ben Brewster. London: Allen Lane, Penguin Press, 1969.
____, AND ÉTIENNE BALIBAR. *Reading Capital.* Trans. Ben Brewster. London: New Left Books, 1970.
____. *Lenin and Philosophy and Other Essays.* Trans. Ben Brewster. London: New Left Books, 1971.
____. *Politics and History: Montesquieu, Rousseau, Hegel and Marx.*

219

Trans. Ben Brewster. London: New Left Books, 1972.

———. *Essays in Self-Criticism.* Trans. Grahame Lock. London: New Left Books, 1976.

Works on Althusser

ARON, RAYMOND. *D'une sainte famille à l'autre: Essais sur les marxismes imaginaires.* Paris: Gallimard, 1969.

BADIOU, ALAIN. "Le (re)commencement du matérialisme dialectique." *Critique,* 240 (1967).

BESSE, GUY. "Deux questions sur un article de Louis Althusser." *La Pensée,* 107 (1963).

BOTTIGELLI, EMILE. "En lisant Althusser." *Structuralisme et Marxisme.* Paris: Union Générale d'Edition, 1970.

CALLINICOS, ALEX. *Althusser's Marxism.* London: Pluto Press, 1976.

CONILH, JEAN. "Lecture de Marx." *Esprit,* 360 (1967).

GARAUDY, ROGER. "A propos des Manuscrits de 1844." *Cahiers du communisme,* 3 (1963).

GEORGES, FRANÇOIS. "Lire Althusser." *Les Temps Modernes,* 275 (1969).

GERAS, NORMAN. "Althusser's Marxism: An Account and Assessment." *New Left Review,* 71 (1972).

GLUCKSMANN, ANDRÉ. "Un structuralisme ventriloque." *Les Temps Modernes,* 250 (1967).

GLUCKSMANN, MIRIAM. *Structuralist Analysis in Contemporary Social Thought: A Comparison of the Theories of Claude Lévi-Strauss and Louis Althusser.* London: Routledge & Kegan Paul, 1974.

JAMESON, FREDRIC. "The Re-Invention of Marx." *Times Literary Supplement,* August 22, 1975.

KARSZ, SAUL. *Théorie et politique: Louis Althusser.* Paris: Fayard, 1974.

KOLAKOWSKI, LESZEK. "Althusser's Marx." *Socialist Register* (1971).

LEFEBVRE, HENRI. "Sur une interprétation du marxisme." *L'Homme et la Société,* 4 (1967).

———. "Les paradoxes d'Althusser." *L'Homme et la Société,* 13 (1969).

LEWIS, JOHN. "The Althusser Case." *Marxism Today,* 1–2 (1972).

LIEBICH, ANDRÉ, "Hegel, Marx and Althusser." *Politics and Society,* 9 (1979).

MURY, GILBERT. "Materialisme et hyper-empiricisme." *La Pensée,* 108 (1963).

NANCY, J. L. "Marx et la philosophie." *Esprit,* 349 (1966).

PARIS, ROBERT. "En deçà du marxisme." *Les Temps Modernes,* 240 (1966).

PARKIN, FRANK. "The Academicizing of Marxism." *Dissent,* 2 (1980).

POUILLON, JEAN. "Du côté de chez Marx." *Les Temps Modernes,* 240 (1966).

POULANTZAS, NICOS. "Vers une théorie marxiste." *Les Temps Modernes,* 240 (1966).

RANCIÈRE, JACQUES. "Sur la théorie de l'idéologie: La politique d'Althusser." *L'Homme et la Société,* 27 (1972).

――――. *La leçon d'Althusser.* Paris: Gallimard, 1974.

SCHAFF, ADAM. *Structuralism and Marxism.* New York: Pergamon Press, 1978

SCHMIDT, ALFRED. "Der strukturalistische Angriff auf die Geschichte." *Beiträge zur marxistischen Erkenntnistheorie.* Alfred Schmidt, ed. Frankfurt: Suhrkamp, 1969.

SÉVE, LUCIEN. "Méthode structurale et méthode dialectique." *La Pensée,* 135 (1967).

THOMPSON, EDWARD P. *The Poverty of Theory and Other Essays.* New York: Monthly Review Press, 1978.

VELTMEYER, HENRY. "Towards an Assessment of the Structuralist Interrogation of Marx: Claude Lévi-Strauss and Louis Althusser." *Science and Society,* 4 (1974–75).

VILAR, PIERRE. "Marxist History, a History in the Making: Towards a Dialogue with Althusser." *New Left Review,* 80 (1973).

VINCENT, J. M., ed. *Contre Althusser.* Paris: Union Générale d'Edition, 1974.

WALDECK ROCHET. "Le marxisme et les chemins de l'avenir." *Cahiers du communisme,* 5–6 (1966).

Other Useful Works

ANDERSON, PERRY. *Considerations on Western Marxism.* London: New Left Books, 1976.

――――. *Arguments within English Marxism.* London: New Left Books, 1980.

ARENDT, HANNAH. *The Human Condition*. Chicago: University of Chicago Press, 1958.

ARON, RAYMOND. *The Opium of the Intellectuals*. Trans. Terence Kilmartin. Garden City, N.J.: Doubleday, 1957.

——. *Marxism and the Existentialists*. New York: Harper & Row, 1969.

BACHELARD, GASTON. *La formation de l'esprit scientifique*. Paris: Librairie Philosophique J. Vrin, 1972.

——. *Le nouvel esprit scientifique*. Paris: Presses Universitaires de France, 1972.

BALIBAR, ETIENNE. *Cinq études du matérialisme dialectique*. Paris: François Maspero, 1974.

BERKI, R. N. *Socialism*. New York: Saint Martin's Press, 1975.

BIGO, PIERRE. *Marxisme et humanisme: Introduction à l'oeuvre économique de Karl Marx*. Paris: Presses Universitaires de France, 1961.

CALVEZ, JEAN-YVES. *La pensée de Karl Marx*. Paris: Editions du Seuil, 1956.

COHEN, G. A. *Karl Marx's Theory of History: A Defence*. Oxford: Oxford University Press, 1979.

COLLETTI, LUCIO. *From Rousseau to Lenin: Studies in Ideology and Society*. Trans. John Merrington and Judith N. White. London: New Left Books, 1972.

DESCOMBES, VINCENT. *Modern French Philosophy*. Trans. L. Scott-Fox and J. M. Harding. Cambridge: Cambridge University Press, 1980.

FOUCAULT, MICHEL. *The Order of Things*. Trans. A. M. Sheridan Smith. London: Tavistock Publications, 1970.

——. *Power/Knowledge: Selected Interviews and Other Writings, 1972–1977*. Trans. Colin Gordon. New York: Pantheon Books, 1980.

FREUD, SIGMUND. *The Interpretation of Dreams*. Trans. James Strachey. New York: Avon Books, 1965.

——. *Introductory Lectures on Psychoanalysis*. Trans. by James Strachey. New York: W. W. Norton, 1966.

GADAMER, HANS-GEORG. *Truth and Method*. New York: Seabury Press, 1975.

GARAUDY, ROGER. *Peut-on être communiste aujourd'hui?* Paris: B. Grasset, 1968.

——. *Perspectives de l'homme: Existentialisme, pensée catholique, structuralisme, marxisme*. Paris: Presses Universitaires de France, 1969.

GEUSS, RAYMOND. *The Idea of a Critical Theory.* Cambridge: Cambridge University Press, 1981.

GIDDENS, ANTHONY. *New Rules of Sociological Method: A Positive Critique of Interpretive Sociologies.* New York: Basic Books, 1976.

———. *Central Problems in Social Theory: Action, Structure and Contradiction in Social Analysis.* Berkeley: University of California Press, 1979.

GOLDMANN, LUCIEN. *Recherches dialectiques.* Paris: Gallimard, 1959.

———. *Kant.* Trans. Robert Black. London: New Left Books, 1971.

HABERMAS, JÜRGEN. *Knowledge and Human Interests.* Trans. Jeremy J. Shapiro. Boston: Beacon Press, 1971.

———. *Theory and Practice.* Trans. John Viertel. Boston: Beacon Press, 1974.

HEGEL, G. W. F. *Lectures on the History of Philosophy.* Trans. E. S. Haldane and Frances H. Simpson. London: Routledge & Kegan Paul, 1955.

———. *The Phenomenology of Mind.* Trans. J. B. Baille. London: George Allen & Unwin, 1971.

HORKHEIMER, MAX, AND THEODOR ADORNO. *Dialectic of Enlightenment.* Trans. John Cumming. New York: Seabury Press, 1972.

HYPPOLITE, JEAN. *Studies in Marx and Hegel.* Trans. John O'Neill. London: Heinemann, 1969.

KOJÈVE, ALEXANDRE. *Introduction to the Reading of Hegel.* Allan Bloom, ed. Trans. James H. Nichols, Jr. New York: Basic Books, 1969.

KOLAKOWSKI, LESZEK. *Toward a Marxist Humanism: Essays on the Left Today.* Trans. Jane Z. Peel. New York: Grove Press, 1968.

KUHN, THOMAS S. *The Structure of Scientific Revolutions.* Chicago: University of Chicago Press, 1971.

LAKATOS, IMRE, AND ALAN MUSGRAVE, eds. *Criticism and the Growth of Knowledge.* Cambridge: Cambridge University Press, 1970.

LANE, MICHAEL, ed. *Structuralism: A Reader.* New York: Basic Books, 1970.

LÉVI-STRAUSS, CLAUDE. *The Savage Mind.* Chicago: University of Chicago Press, 1966.

LICHTHEIM, GEORGE. *Marxism in Modern France.* New York: Columbia University Press, 1966.

———. *The Concept of Ideology and Other Essays.* New York: Vintage Books, 1967.

———. *From Marx to Hegel.* New York: Seabury Press, 1971.

223

LUKÁCS, GEORG. *History and Class Consciousness: Studies in Marxist Dialectics.* Trans. Rodney Livingstone. Cambridge, Mass.: MIT Press, 1971.

———. *Political Writings, 1919–1929.* Rodney Livingstone, ed. Trans. Michael McColgan. London: New Left Books, 1972.

MACINTYRE, ALASDAIR. "Epistemological Crises, Dramatic Narrative and the Philosophy of Science." *The Monist,* 4 (1977).

———. "Is Understanding a Religion Compatible with Believing?" *Rationality.* Bryan Wilson, ed. Oxford: Basil Blackwell, 1979.

MANNHEIM, KARL. *Ideology and Utopia.* Trans. Louis Wirth and Edward Shils. New York: Harcourt, Brace & World, 1936.

MARX, KARL. *Early Writings.* Trans. T. B. Bottomore. London: C. A. Watts, 1963.

———. *Capital.* 3 vols. London: Lawrence and Wishart, 1970.

———. *Grundrisse. Foundations of the Critique of Political Economy (1857–58).* Trans. Martin Nicolaus. Harmondsworth: Penguin Books, 1973.

MARX, KARL, AND FRIEDRICH ENGELS. *Selected Works.* 2 vols. Moscow: Foreign Language Publishers, 1958.

———. *The German Ideology.* London: Lawrence and Wishart, 1970.

MERLEAU-PONTY, MAURICE. *The Phenomenology of Perception.* Trans. Colin Smith. New York: Humanities Press, 1962.

———. *Sense and Non-Sense.* Trans. H. and P. Dreyfus. Evanston: Northwestern University Press, 1964.

———. *Adventures of the Dialectic.* Trans. Joseph Bien. London: Heinemann, 1974.

NIETZSCHE, FRIEDRICH. *Beyond Good and Evil.* Trans. Walter Kaufmann. New York: Vintage Books, 1966.

OAKESHOTT, MICHAEL. *Experience and Its Modes.* Cambridge: Cambridge University Press, 1933.

POSTER, MARK. *Existential Marxism in Postwar France: From Sartre to Althusser.* Princeton: Princeton University Press, 1975.

POULANTZAS, NICOS. *Fascism and Dictatorship.* Trans. Judith N. White. London: New Left Books, 1974.

ROSEN, STANLEY. *Nihilism: A Philosophical Essay.* New Haven: Yale University Press, 1969.

SARTRE, JEAN-PAUL. *Search for a Method.* Trans. Hazel E. Barnes. New York: Vintage Books, 1973.

———. *Between Existentialism and Marxism.* Trans. John Matthews. London: New Left Books, 1974.

224

SEBAG, LUCIEN. *Marxisme et structuralisme.* Paris: Payot, 1964.

SPINOZA, BENEDICT DE. *Works.* 2 vols. Trans. R. H. M. Elwes. New York: Dover, 1951.

STRAUSS, LEO. *On Tyranny.* Ithaca: Cornell University Press, 1975.

STRAWSON, P. F. *Individuals: An Essay in Descriptive Metaphysics.* London: Methuen, 1959.

WAHL, JEAN, ed. *Qu'est ce que le structuralisme?* Paris: Editions de Seuil, 1968.

WILLIAMS, RAYMOND. *Marxism and Literature.* Oxford: Oxford University Press, 1977.

WINCH, PETER. *The Idea of a Social Science and Its Relation to Philosophy.* London: Routledge & Kegan Paul, 1958.

WITTGENSTEIN, LUDWIG. *Philosophical Investigations.* Trans. G. E. M. Anscombe. New York: Macmillan, 1968.

Index

Acton, H. B., 144
Adorno, Theodor, 17, 39, 154
Agency, 22–23, 175, 193–94, 196–200
Alienation, 24, 35–36, 38, 39–45, 84, 95. *See also* Fetishism of commodities
Althusser, Louis: anti-humanism of, 19–23; and Bachelard, 73–74; elitism of, 22, 139–40; and Freud, 73, 132, 159, 193; and functional explanation, 27, 166, 173, 181–82; hermeneutics of, 75–82; idealism of, 126–28; and metaphysics, 137, 172, 186, 191–92; nihilism of, 200–211; procedure for reading, 25–26; and Spinoza, 72–73, 187–89, 214–15; and Stalinism, 19–23; and structuralism, 179–92; and technocracy, 140, 218
Anderson, Perry, 17, 20n6, 186, 212n1
Anti-humanism, 19, 23, 192–200, 207–11, 218
Aquinas, Saint Thomas, 30, 36, 95
Arendt, Hannah, 218
Aristotle, 30, 50
Aron, Raymond, 15n1, 22, 59n47, 60n49
Austin, J. L., 16

Auzias, Jean-Marie, 174n1
Avineri, Shlomo, 95n17

Bachelard, Gaston, 27, 73–74, 87–88, 97, 103, 214
Bacon, Francis, 140, 154, 210
Badiou, Alain, 15n1
Balibar, Étienne, 179–80
Base and superstructure, 27, 141; Fundamentalist version of, 142–49, 189; Internal Relatedness version of, 149–57. *See also* Overdetermination
Bergson, Henri, 33, 39
Berki, R. N., 213n2
Bigo, Peirre, 36n6
Blanqui, Auguste, 31
Boudon, Raymond, 174n1
Break, epistemological (*coupure épistémologique*), 18, 27, 74, 82, 85–92, 97, 137, 215–16
Bukharin, Nicolai, 143, 148

Callinicos, Alex, 15n1, 138n36
Canguilhem, Georges, 88
Cause, structural, 72, 187–92
Caute, David, 30n1
Choice. *See* Agency
Cohen, G. A., 145–49
Colletti, Lucio, 17, 110, 155n24, 212
Collingwood, R. G., 77

Combination (*Verbindung*), 179–80
Communism. *See* Socialism
Comte, Auguste, 32, 87, 201
Conjuncture, 26, 30
Cooper, Barry, 60n49
Cottier, Georges M-M, 36n6
Coupure épistémologique. See Break, epistemological

Dallmayr, Fred J., 202n16
Death of man, 58–59, 69–70, 200, 202. *See also* Nihilism
Decenter. *See* Overdetermination
Deconstruction, 69, 175, 180
Deleuze, Gilles, 203n17
Della Volpe, Galvano, 17
Democritus, 96
Descartes, René, 21, 63, 68, 97–98, 111, 113, 206, 211
Descombes, Vincent, 82n8, 203n17
Development, law of, 162
Dilthey, Wilhelm, 39
Dodds, E. R., 159
Durkheim, Emile, 32, 132

Easton, David, 104n2
Eco, Umberto, 122n18
Effect, society, 167
Einstein, Albert, 88, 91
Empiricism, 108, 112, 115–16, 214
Engels, Friedrich, 45, 99, 117, 156n26, 157–59
Epicurus, 96
Epistemology, 74, 108–28, 215
Evans-Pritchard, E. E., 159

Fages, J. B., 174n1
Fanon, Franz, 67n55
Fascism, 154, 164–65
Fessard, Gaston, 36n6
Fetishism of commodities, 38, 84, 95, 147. *See also* Alienation
Feuerbach, Ludwig, 18–19, 36, 93, 96, 110
Feyerabend, Paul, 27, 90, 214
Flaubert, Gustave, 64
Foucault, Michel, 28, 69, 81, 88, 193; and interpretation, 90–91; and nihilism, 203–7

Freedom, 51–53, 59–60. *See also* Agency
Freud, Sigmund, 22, 73, 77, 132, 159, 176, 185, 190, 193, 197, 216
Friedman, George, 157n27
Functionalism, 27, 166, 173, 181–82

Gadamer, Hans-Georg, 26, 80
Galilei, Galileo, 88, 102, 153
Garaudy, Roger, 19, 30, 36, 47n30, 73n2, 137n35, 166n36, 185–86
Geras, Norman, 15n1, 139–40
Geuss, Raymond, 129, 132
Giddens, Anthony, 81n7, 104n2, 173n37
Glucksmann, André, 15n1, 108, 191n12
Goldmann, Lucien, 17, 39, 42–45, 212
Gramsci, Antonio, 17, 132, 142, 167–68

Habermas, Jürgen, 17, 28, 39, 110–11, 117n14, 212
Hegel, Georg W. F.: *History of Philosophy*, 112; *Logic*, 99n20; *Phenomenology of Mind*, 26, 37, 48, 51, 111–14; *Philosophy of History*, 160, 209; *Philosophy of Right*, 54
Heidegger, Martin, 18, 26, 30, 45, 119, 210
Heraclitus, 96
Herodotus, 159
Hierarchy. *See* Structure in dominance
Historicism, 109, 116–19, 140, 184
History, end of, 46–59
Hobbes, Thomas, 49, 96, 140
Horkheimer, Max, 17, 39, 117n14, 154
Humanism, Marxist, 18–20, 30–38, 193–94, 196
Hume, David, 88, 112
Husserl, Edmund, 18, 30, 95, 175
Hyppolite, Jean, 37

Ideology, 73, 85–86, 115, 124, 128–40, 217; descriptive use of, 129–32; Marxist use of, 133; pejorative use of, 129, 132–37; positive use of, 129–30, 137–39; and science, 134–37

Jahn, Wolfgang, 37
Jameson, Fredric, 24–25, 71n1, 77

Kanapa, Jean, 60n49.
Kant, Immanuel, 21–22, 46, 63, 72, 111–12, 154, 176, 182–83
Karsz, Saul, 15n1
Kautsky, Karl, 143–44
Kierkegaard, Søren, 30, 36, 63
Klossowski, Pierre, 203n17
Knowledge, problem of. *See* Epistemology
Kojève, Alexandre, 26, 39, 46–59
Kolakowski, Leszek, 15n1, 125n23
Korsch, Karl, 17
Koyré, Alexandre, 46, 88
Kuhn, Thomas, 27, 77, 81, 88, 97, 128, 214

Lacan, Jacques, 69, 73
Lacroix, Jean, 36n6
Landshut, Sigmund, 34, 36
Lecourt, Dominique, 87n9
Lefebvre, Henri, 15n1, 17–18, 35n5, 44, 175, 218
Lenin(ism), 17, 45, 60, 71, 130, 140, 163, 165, 217
Lévi-Strauss, Claude, 22, 28, 68–69, 169, 176, 193, 207
Lichtheim, George, 17, 30n1
Liebich, André, 97
Linguistics, structural, 68–69, 71, 176–78
Locke, John, 109
Lukács, Georg, 17, 26, 28, 47n30, 64, 142, 148, 150; and Heidegger, 45; historicism of, 117–19; and orthodox Marxism, 25; and reification, 39–45; and science, 153–54

McCarney, Joe, 138n36
Mach, Ernst, 88
Machery, Pierre, 103
Machiavelli, Niccolò, 58
MacIntyre, Alasdair, 97, 125
Maine de Biran, 32–33
Malthus, Thomas, 66
Mannheim, Karl, 118, 137
Marcuse, Herbert, 20, 37, 39, 154
Marx, Karl: *Capital*, 17–19, 24, 28,

31–32, 34, 38, 43, 54, 80, 92, 94–96, 101–3, 117, 123, 133, 146, 179–180, 194–95, 200–201, 209; *Communist Manifesto*, 34, 94; *Contribution to the Critique of Political Economy*, 142; *Critique of Hegel's "Philosophy of Right,"* 35, 93; *Doctoral Dissertation*, 34; *Economic and Philosophic Manuscripts of 1844*, 18, 24, 35, 41, 47–48, 93–95, 151; *Eighteenth Brumaire of Louis Napoleon*, 64; *The German Ideology*, 52–53, 93, 126, 208; *Grundrisse*, 35, 92, 94, 146, 150, 181, 209; *The Holy Family*, 34; *On the Jewish Question*, 93; *The Poverty of Philosophy*, 94, 181, 182n6; *Randglossen zu Adolph Wagner*, 94, 194; *Theses on Feuerbach*, 93, 208; *Wages, Price and Profit*, 94
Mayer, Gustave, 34, 36
Mediation, 62, 151–52
Mehring, Franz, 17
Merleau-Ponty, Maurice, 18, 20, 47, 51, 53n38, 60–62, 68, 115n13
Miller, Eugene, 109n4
Montaigne, Michel de, 23
Mounier, Emmanuel, 36n6

Nair, K., 70n60
Negation of the negation. *See* Supersession
New Left, 20. *See also* Humanism, Marxist
New Left Review, 17, 69
Newton, Sir Issac, 88, 91
Nietzsche, Friedrich, 22, 50, 57, 81, 89, 117, 119, 155–56, 202–3, 205
Nihilism, 28, 58–59, 81, 154–57, 200–211. *See also* Death of man

Oakeshott, Michael, 127
Objectification. *See* Reification
Ollman, Bertell, 142, 152
Overdetermination, 27, 73, 142, 157–73, 197, 203. *See also* Base and superstructure.

Pajitnov, Leonid, 37
Paradigm. *See* Problematic

Parkin, Frank, 166n36
Parsons, Talcott, 104
Pascal, Blaise, 23, 30, 43
Plato, 78, 128, 133
Plekhanov, Georgy, 45, 143
Polanyi, Karl, 136n33
Poster, Mark, 30n1
Poulantzas, Nicos, 164–65
Practice, 27, 104–8; and theory, 106–7, 213–16
Problematic (*problématique*), 27, 77, 81, 82–85, 214
Process without a subject, 22, 28, 200–202, 207–8
Production. *See* Practice
Project, 61, 64–65
Proudhon, Joseph-Pierre, 31, 35, 181
Ptolemy, 88

Queneau, Raymond, 47

Racine, Jean Baptiste, 43
Rader, Melvin, 147
Rancière, Jacques, 15n1, 132n29
Reading, symptomatic, 73, 75–82
Reification, 40–42, 147, 149, 185–86, 199–200. *See also* Alienation
Revolution, 96–100; French, 31–32, 48, 53, 66; Russian, 163–64, 168
Ricardo, David, 76
Ricoeur, Paul, 78
Robespierre, Maximilien de, 53
Rosen, Stanley, 60n48
Rousseau, Jean-Jacques, 52

Sartre, Jean-Paul, 22, 26, 33, 45, 47, 59–70, 174–75, 198, 206; Cartesianism of, 61, 65, 67, 69; and freedom, 23, 59–60, 65–66, 196; historicism of, 119; and Marxist humanism, 17–18, 212; structuralist criticism of, 67–70
Saussure, Ferdinand de, 68, 71, 176
Schaff, Adam, 15n1, 94n16
Schmidt, Alfred, 104n2
Science. *See* Theory
Smith, Adam, 76
Socialism, 46, 56, 133–34, 210
Sorel, Georges, 67
Spinoza, Benedict, de, 21, 26, 55,

72–73, 176, 191–92, 210; and causation, 72, 188–89; and Marxism, 72–73, 187–88; and necessity, 22–23, 198; and truth, 121–22, 214–15
Strauss, Leo, 49n33, 56–58
Strawson, P. F., 68–69
Structure in dominance, 169–73
Supersession (*Aufhebung*), 99, 201–2, 208–9
Superstructure. *See* Base and superstructure

Teleology, 85, 95, 201, 209
Terror. *See* Violence
Thales, 102
Theoreticism, 137
Theory: autonomy of, 106–7, 213–16; emergence of, 85–92 (*See also* Break, epistemological); and ideology, 134–37; verification of, 120–25, 214–15
Thompson, Edward P., 15n1, 17, 19–23
Tocqueville, Alexis de, 28
Totality, 149–51, 160–61
Träger, 23, 195–96, 198, 218
Truth, 121–26, 214–15
Tyranny, 20, 56–57, 66, 140, 218

Unconscious, 69–70, 73, 77–78, 84, 86, 128–29, 177–78, 185, 193, 197

Valéry, Paul, 64
Verification Principle, 112, 116. *See also* Empiricism
Vico, Giambattista, 54
Violence, 51–53, 65–67. *See also* Freedom

Waldeck, Rochet, 21n7, 127
Weber, Max, 39, 154
Williams, Raymond, 144n4, 147n11, 151n18, 212
Winch, Peter, 124
Wittgenstein, Ludwig, 81, 120, 125, 178
Wood, Ellen Meiskins, 146n10

Zévaès, Alexandre, 34n4

Library of Congress Cataloging in Publication Data

Smith, Steven B., 1951–
    Reading Althusser.

    Bibliography: p.
    Includes index.
    1. Althusser, Louis.   2. Philosophy, Marxist.
I. Title.
B2430.A474S65   1984   194   83–45943
ISBN 0–8014–1672–8